Futaribeya

A ROOM FOR TWO

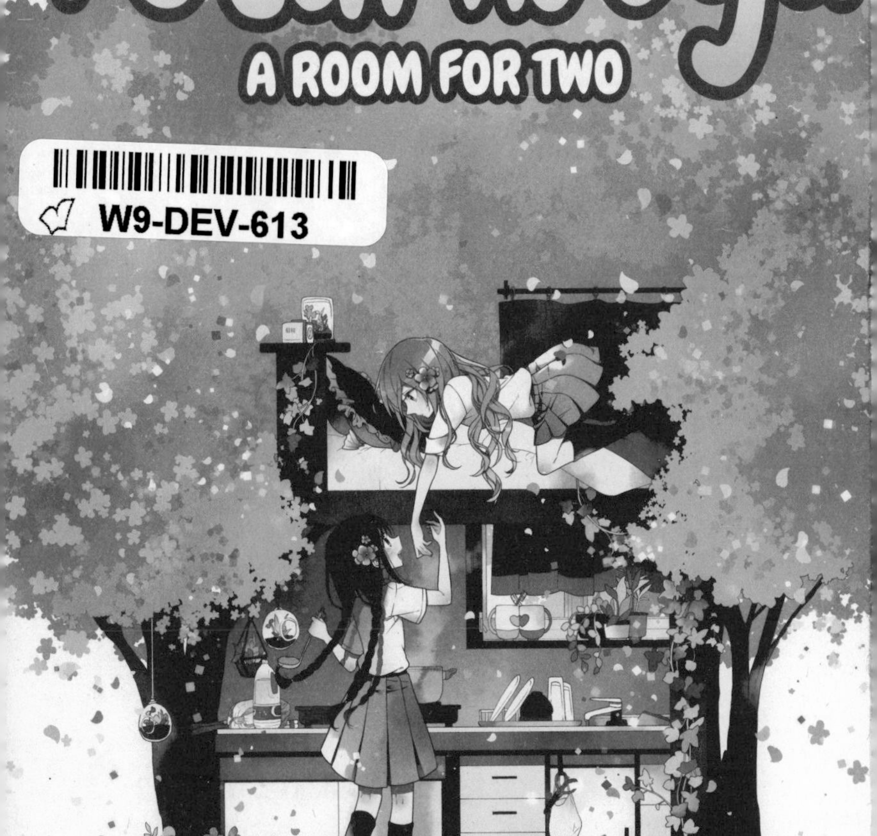

Yukiko

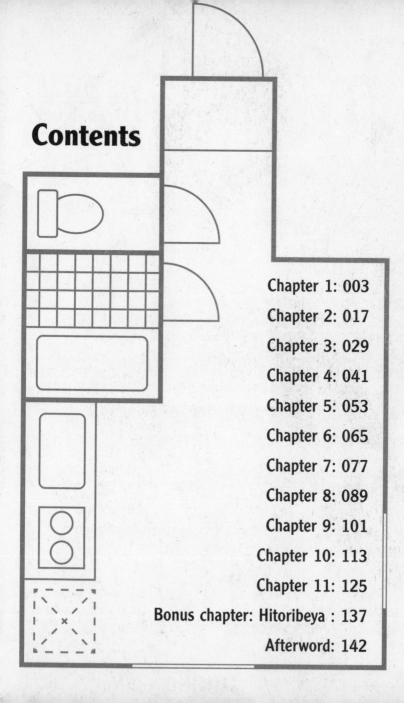

Contents

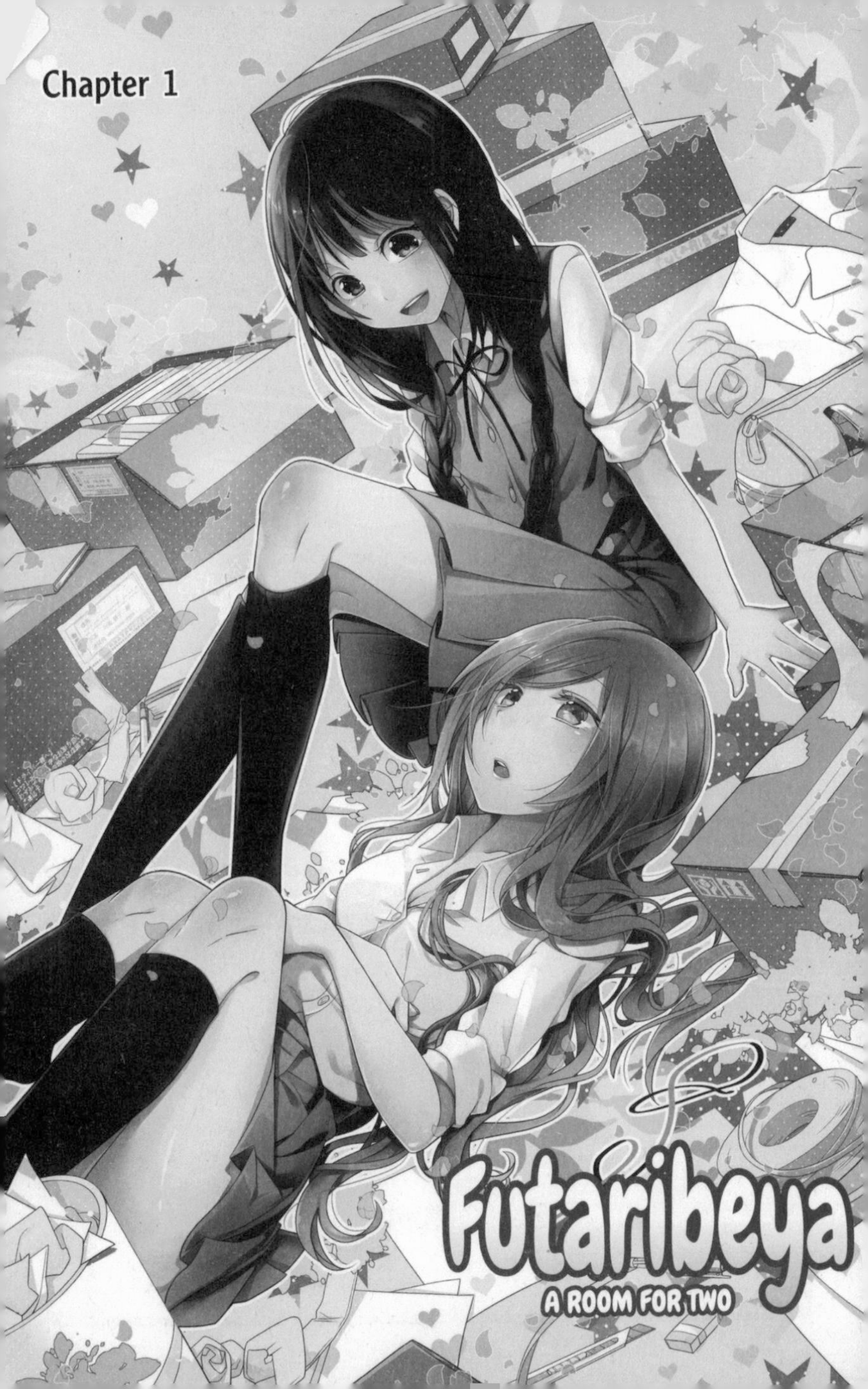
Chapter 1
Futaribeya
A ROOM FOR TWO

Futaribeya
A ROOM FOR TWO

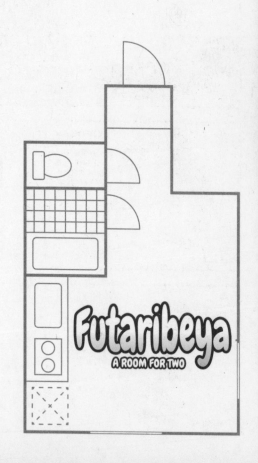

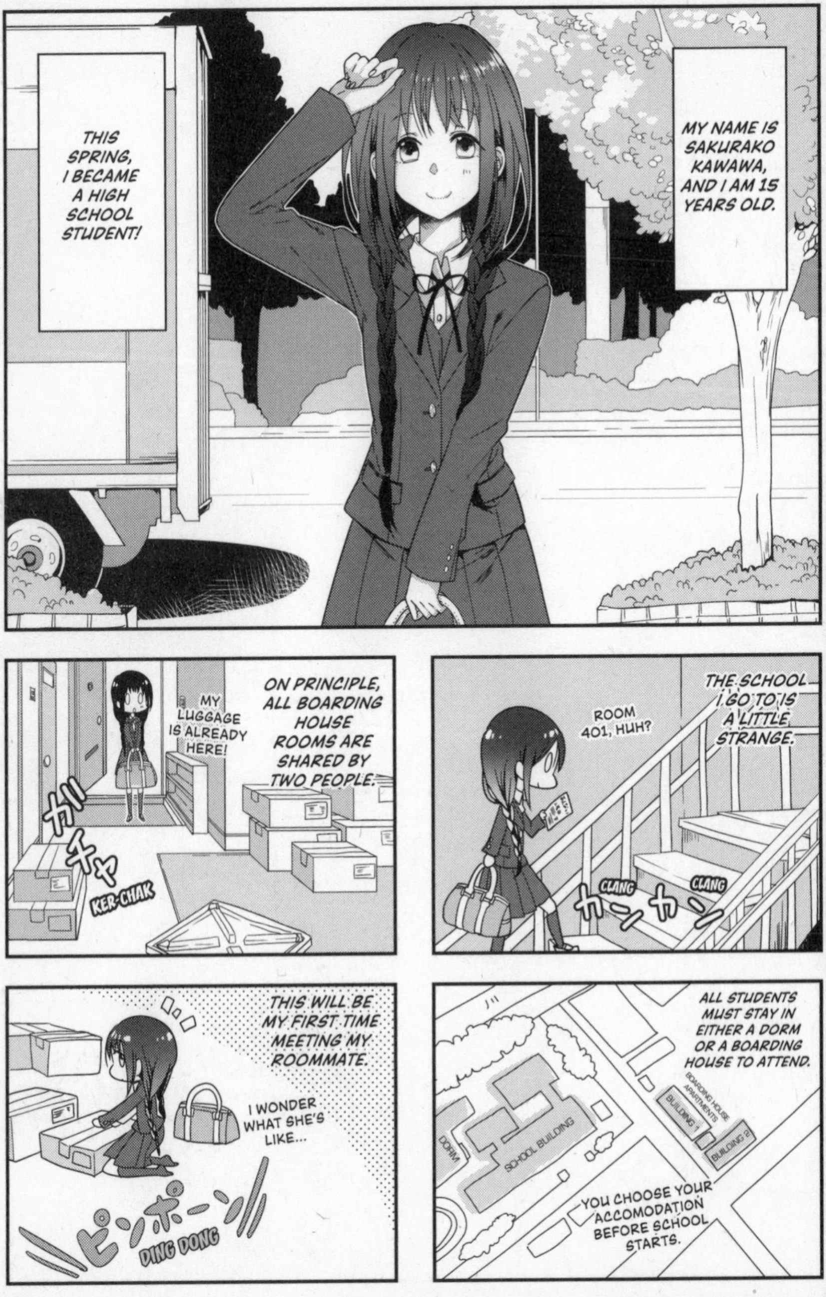
MY NAME IS SAKURAKO KAWAWA, AND I AM 15 YEARS OLD.
THIS SPRING, I BECAME A HIGH SCHOOL STUDENT!
THE SCHOOL I GO TO IS A LITTLE STRANGE.
ROOM 401, HUH?
CLANG
CLANG
ON PRINCIPLE, ALL BOARDING HOUSE ROOMS ARE SHARED BY TWO PEOPLE.
MY LUGGAGE IS ALREADY HERE!
KER-CHAK
ALL STUDENTS MUST STAY IN EITHER A DORM OR A BOARDING HOUSE TO ATTEND.
BOARDING HOUSE APARTMENTS
BUILDING 1
BUILDING 2
DORM
SCHOOL BUILDING
YOU CHOOSE YOUR ACCOMODATION BEFORE SCHOOL STARTS.
THIS WILL BE MY FIRST TIME MEETING MY ROOMMATE.
I WONDER WHAT SHE'S LIKE...
DING DONG

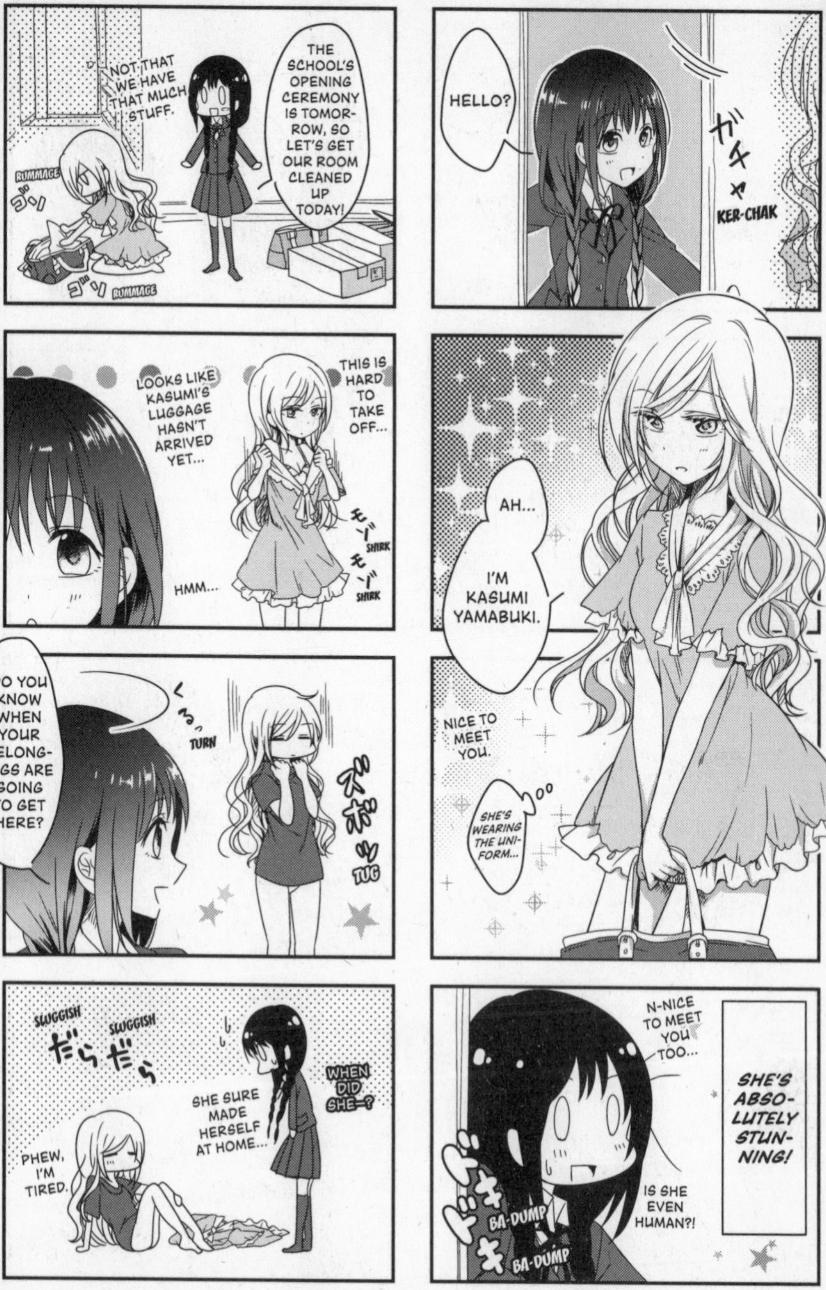
HELLO?
ガチャ
KER-CHAK
AH...
I'M KASUMI YAMABUKI.
NICE TO MEET YOU.
SHE'S WEARING THE UNIFORM...
SHE'S ABSOLUTELY STUNNING!
N-NICE TO MEET YOU TOO...
IS SHE EVEN HUMAN?!
ドキドキ
BA-DUMP
BA-DUMP
THE SCHOOL'S OPENING CEREMONY IS TOMORROW, SO LET'S GET OUR ROOM CLEANED UP TODAY!
NOT THAT WE HAVE THAT MUCH STUFF.
RUMMAGE
ゴソ
ゴソ
RUMMAGE
THIS IS HARD TO TAKE OFF...
LOOKS LIKE KASUMI'S LUGGAGE HASN'T ARRIVED YET...
モゾ
SHIRK
モゾ
SHIRK
HMM...
ズボッ
TUG
くるっ
TURN
DO YOU KNOW WHEN YOUR BELONGINGS ARE GOING TO GET HERE?
WHEN DID SHE—?
SHE SURE MADE HERSELF AT HOME...
SLUGGISH
SLUGGISH
だらだら
PHEW, I'M TIRED.

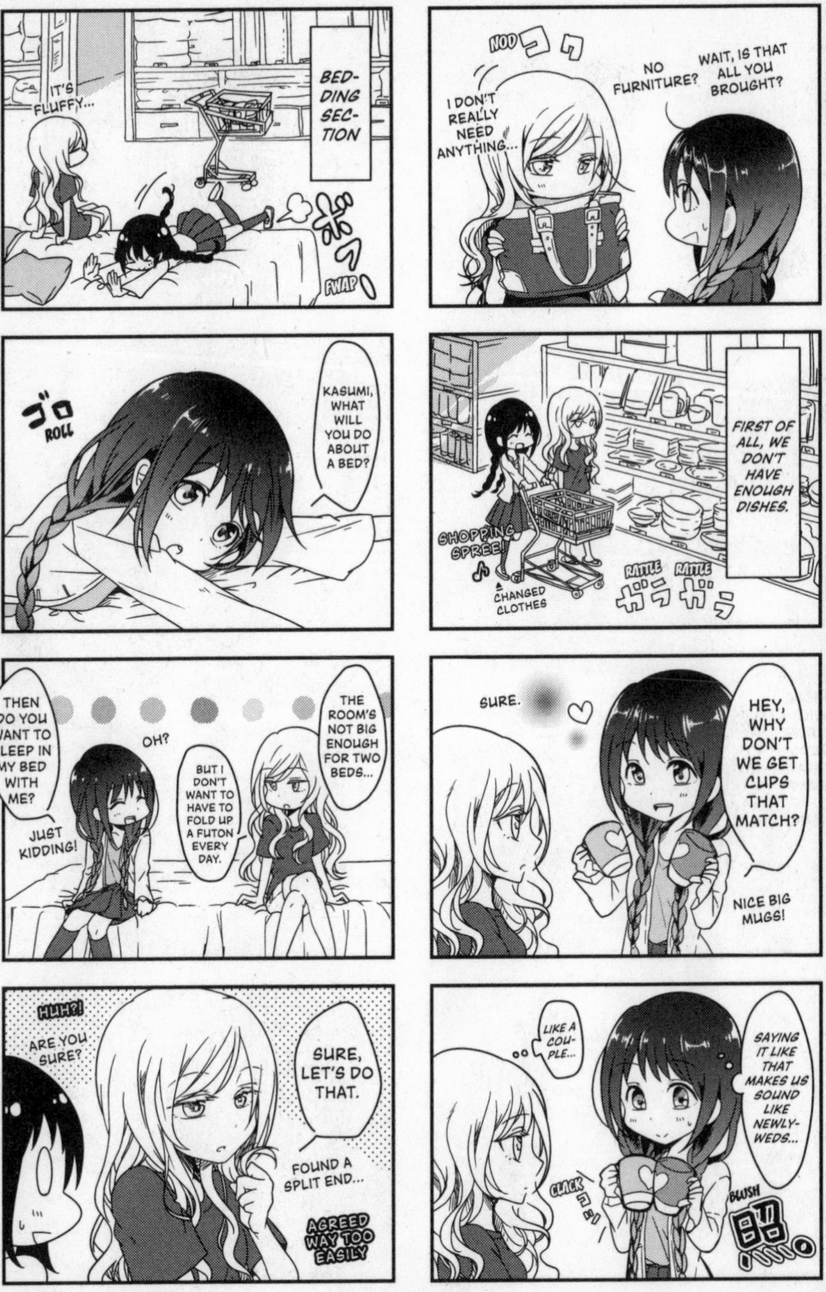
WAIT, IS THAT ALL YOU BROUGHT?
NO FURNITURE?
NOD コク
I DON'T REALLY NEED ANYTHING...
FIRST OF ALL, WE DON'T HAVE ENOUGH DISHES.
RATTLE RATTLE ガラガラ
SHOPPING SPREE! ♪
CHANGED CLOTHES
HEY, WHY DON'T WE GET CUPS THAT MATCH?
NICE BIG MUGS!
SURE.
SAYING IT LIKE THAT MAKES US SOUND LIKE NEWLYWEDS...
BLUSH
LIKE A COUPLE...
CLACK
BEDDING SECTION
FWAP ボフ
IT'S FLUFFY...
KASUMI, WHAT WILL YOU DO ABOUT A BED?
ゴロ ROLL
THE ROOM'S NOT BIG ENOUGH FOR TWO BEDS...
BUT I DON'T WANT TO HAVE TO FOLD UP A FUTON EVERY DAY.
OH?
THEN DO YOU WANT TO SLEEP IN MY BED WITH ME?
JUST KIDDING!
SURE, LET'S DO THAT.
FOUND A SPLIT END...
HUH?!
ARE YOU SURE?
AGREED WAY TOO EASILY

*HOWEVER, IT IS THE STUDENT'S RESPONSIBILITY TO WEAR THE UNIFORM PROPERLY.
AS LONG AS THEY DO NOT SHOW TOO MUCH, PERSONAL CLOTHES ARE ALSO ALLOWED.

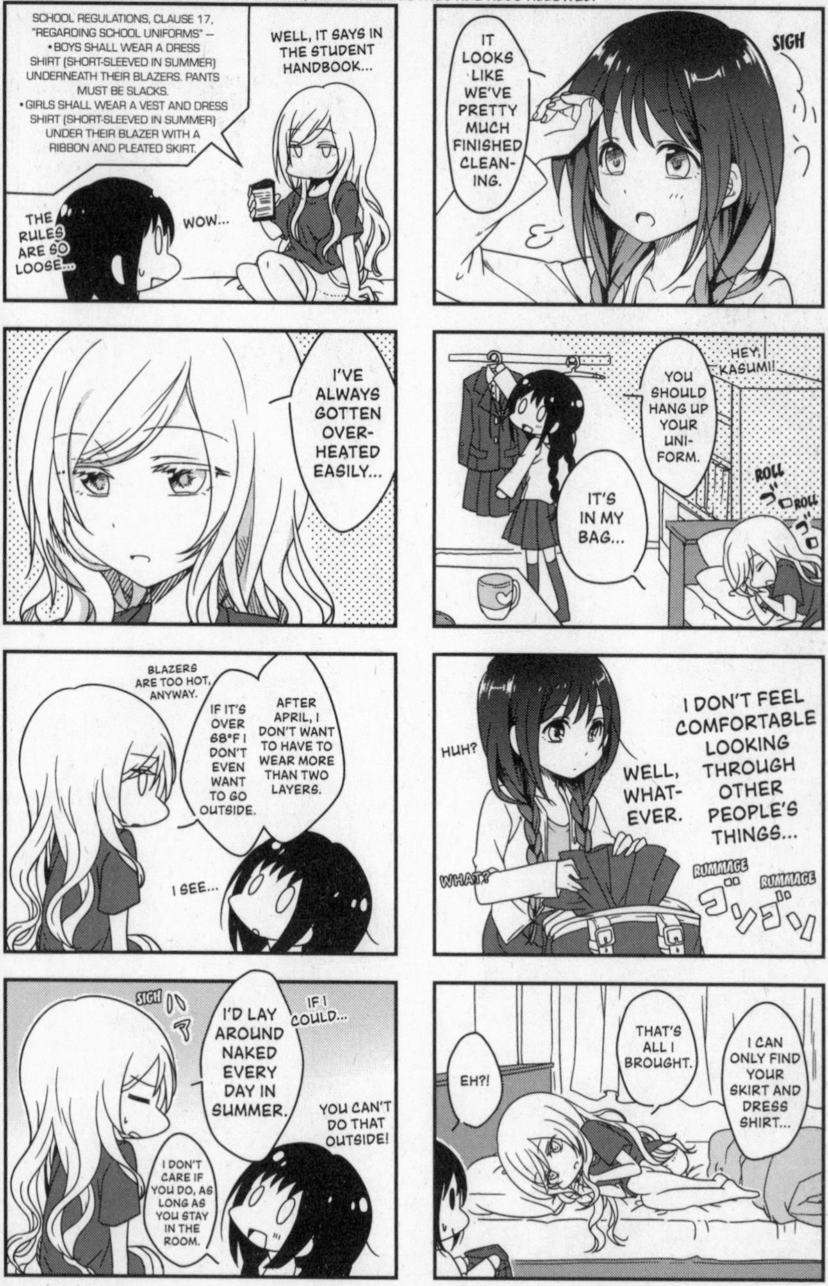
SIGH
IT LOOKS LIKE WE'VE PRETTY MUCH FINISHED CLEAN-ING.
HEY, KASUMI!
YOU SHOULD HANG UP YOUR UNI-FORM.
IT'S IN MY BAG...
ROLL
ROLL
I DON'T FEEL COMFORTABLE LOOKING THROUGH OTHER PEOPLE'S THINGS...
WELL, WHAT-EVER.
HUH?
WHAT?
RUMMAGE
RUMMAGE
I CAN ONLY FIND YOUR SKIRT AND DRESS SHIRT...
THAT'S ALL I BROUGHT.
EH?!
WELL, IT SAYS IN THE STUDENT HANDBOOK...
SCHOOL REGULATIONS, CLAUSE 17, "REGARDING SCHOOL UNIFORMS" — • BOYS SHALL WEAR A DRESS SHIRT (SHORT-SLEEVED IN SUMMER) UNDERNEATH THEIR BLAZERS. PANTS MUST BE SLACKS. • GIRLS SHALL WEAR A VEST AND DRESS SHIRT (SHORT-SLEEVED IN SUMMER) UNDER THEIR BLAZER WITH A RIBBON AND PLEATED SKIRT.
WOW...
THE RULES ARE SO LOOSE...
I'VE ALWAYS GOTTEN OVER-HEATED EASILY...
AFTER APRIL, I DON'T WANT TO HAVE TO WEAR MORE THAN TWO LAYERS.
IF IT'S OVER 68°F I DON'T EVEN WANT TO GO OUTSIDE.
BLAZERS ARE TOO HOT, ANYWAY.
I SEE...
IF I COULD...
I'D LAY AROUND NAKED EVERY DAY IN SUMMER.
SIGH
YOU CAN'T DO THAT OUTSIDE!
I DON'T CARE IF YOU DO, AS LONG AS YOU STAY IN THE ROOM.

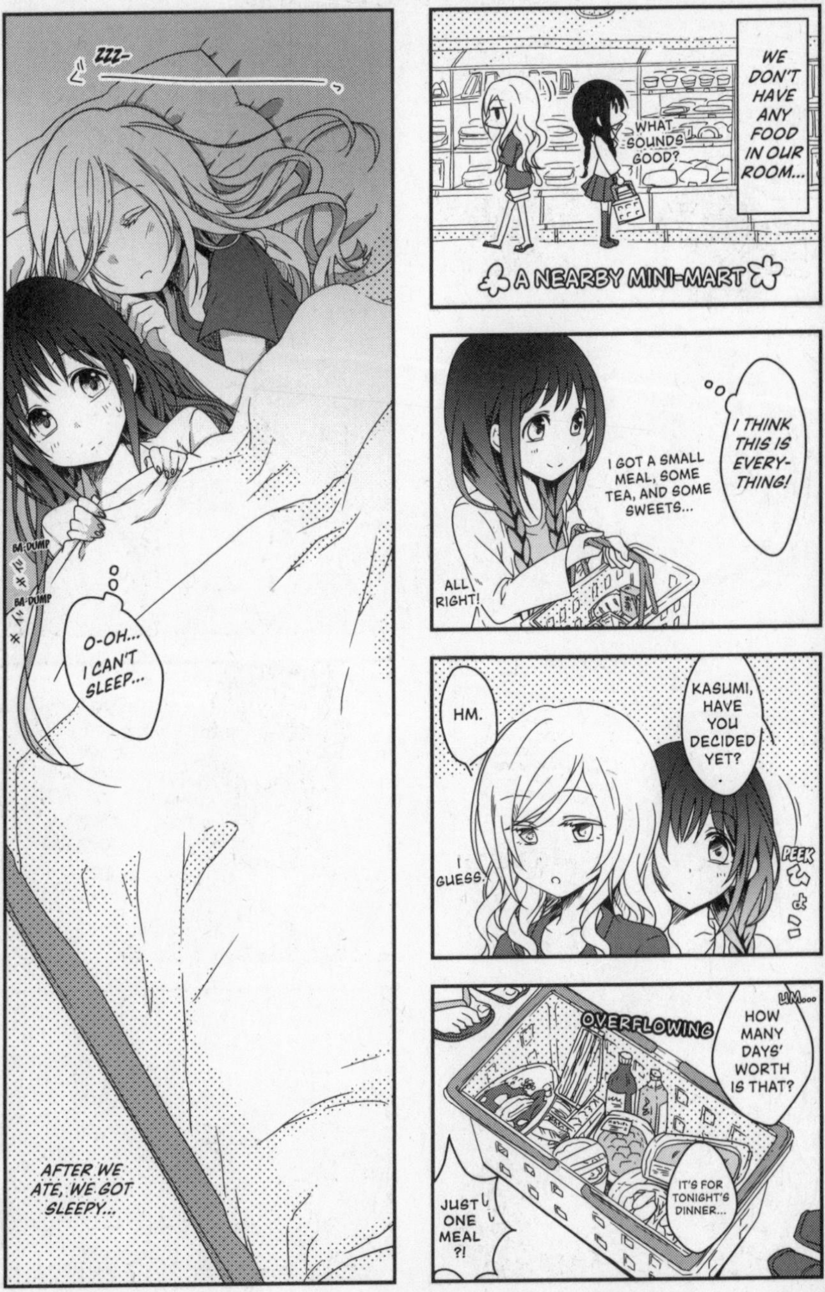
WE DON'T HAVE ANY FOOD IN OUR ROOM...
WHAT SOUNDS GOOD?
A NEARBY MINI-MART
I THINK THIS IS EVERY-THING!
I GOT A SMALL MEAL, SOME TEA, AND SOME SWEETS...
ALL RIGHT!
KASUMI, HAVE YOU DECIDED YET?
PEEK
HM.
I GUESS.
UM...
HOW MANY DAYS' WORTH IS THAT?
OVERFLOWING
IT'S FOR TONIGHT'S DINNER...
JUST ONE MEAL ?!
ZZZ-
BA-DUMP
BA-DUMP
O-OH... I CAN'T SLEEP...
AFTER WE ATE, WE GOT SLEEPY...

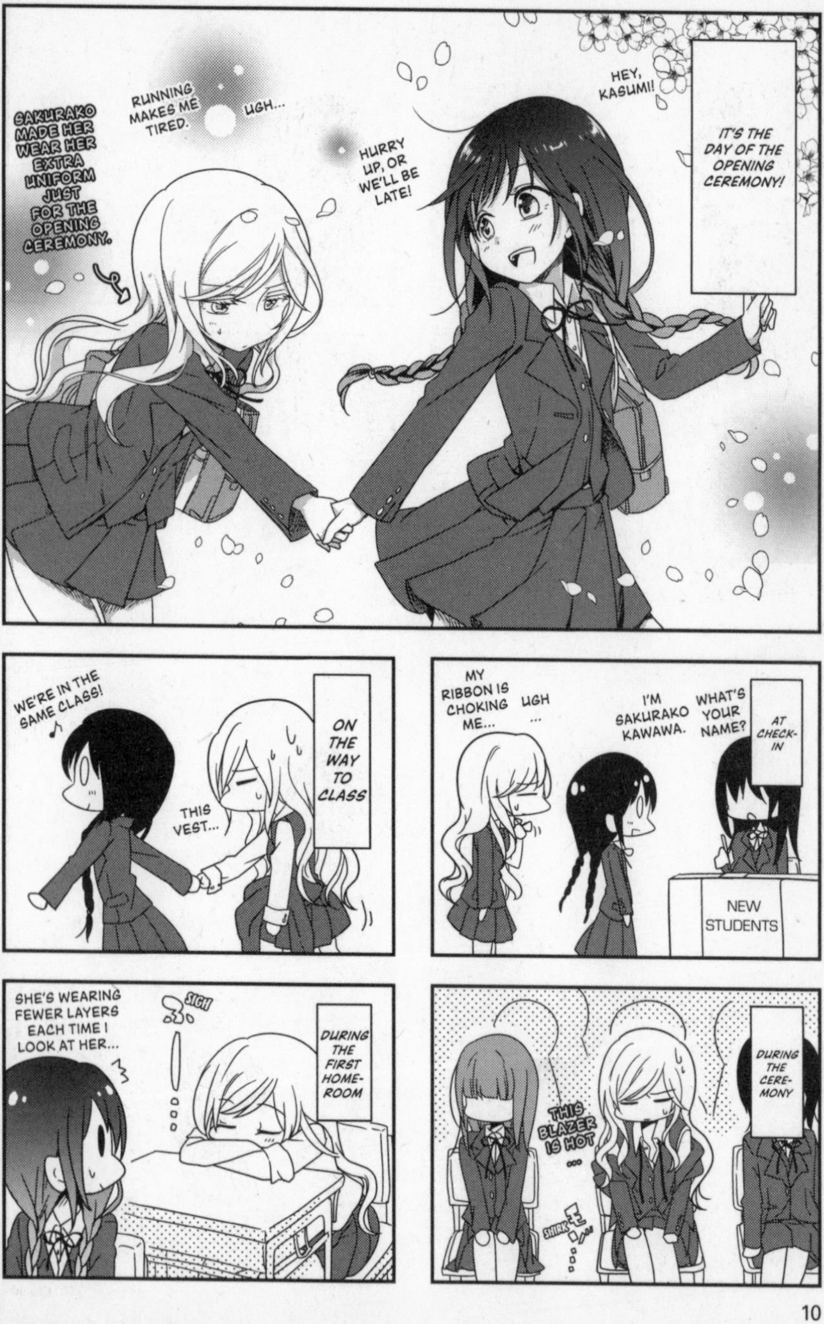
IT'S THE DAY OF THE OPENING CEREMONY!
HEY, KASUMI!
HURRY UP, OR WE'LL BE LATE!
UGH...
RUNNING MAKES ME TIRED.
SAKURAKO MADE HER WEAR HER EXTRA UNIFORM JUST FOR THE OPENING CEREMONY.
AT CHECK-IN
WHAT'S YOUR NAME?
I'M SAKURAKO KAWAWA.
UGH ...
MY RIBBON IS CHOKING ME...
NEW STUDENTS
ON THE WAY TO CLASS
WE'RE IN THE SAME CLASS! ♪
THIS VEST...
DURING THE CEREMONY
THIS BLAZER IS HOT ...
SHIRK
DURING THE FIRST HOME-ROOM
SIGH
SHE'S WEARING FEWER LAYERS EACH TIME I LOOK AT HER...

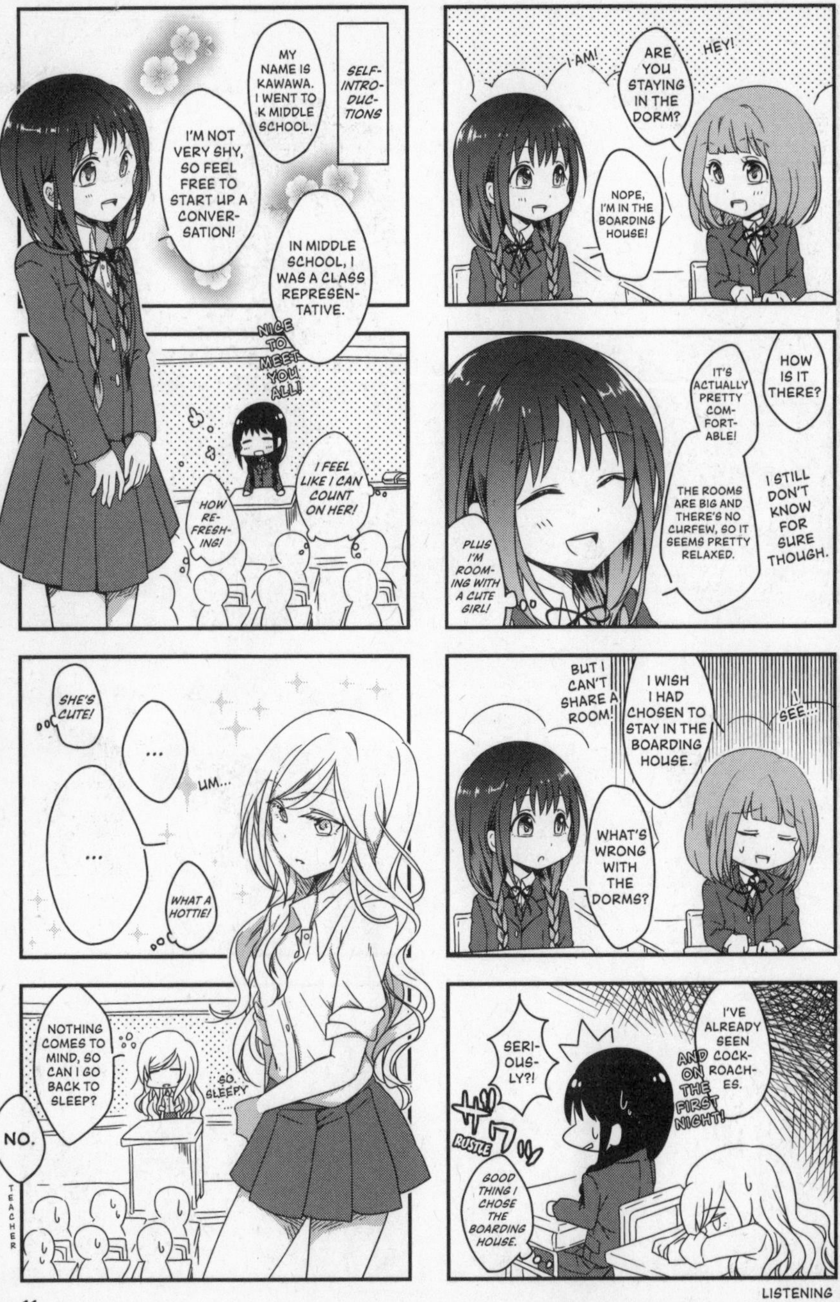
HEY!
ARE YOU STAYING IN THE DORM?
I AM!
NOPE, I'M IN THE BOARDING HOUSE!
HOW IS IT THERE?
IT'S ACTUALLY PRETTY COM-FORT-ABLE!
I STILL DON'T KNOW FOR SURE THOUGH.
THE ROOMS ARE BIG AND THERE'S NO CURFEW, SO IT SEEMS PRETTY RELAXED.
PLUS I'M ROOM-ING WITH A CUTE GIRL!
I SEE...
I WISH I HAD CHOSEN TO STAY IN THE BOARDING HOUSE.
BUT I CAN'T SHARE A ROOM!
WHAT'S WRONG WITH THE DORMS?
I'VE ALREADY SEEN COCK-ROACH-ES.
AND ON THE FIRST NIGHT!
SERI-OUS-LY?!
RUSTLE
GOOD THING I CHOSE THE BOARDING HOUSE.
SELF-INTRO-DUC-TIONS
MY NAME IS KAWAWA. I WENT TO K MIDDLE SCHOOL.
I'M NOT VERY SHY, SO FEEL FREE TO START UP A CONVER-SATION!
IN MIDDLE SCHOOL, I WAS A CLASS REPRESEN-TATIVE.
NICE TO MEET YOU ALL!
I FEEL LIKE I CAN COUNT ON HER!
HOW RE-FRESH-ING!
SHE'S CUTE!
...
UM...
...
WHAT A HOTTIE!
SO SLEEPY
NOTHING COMES TO MIND, SO CAN I GO BACK TO SLEEP?
NO.
TEACHER

LISTENING

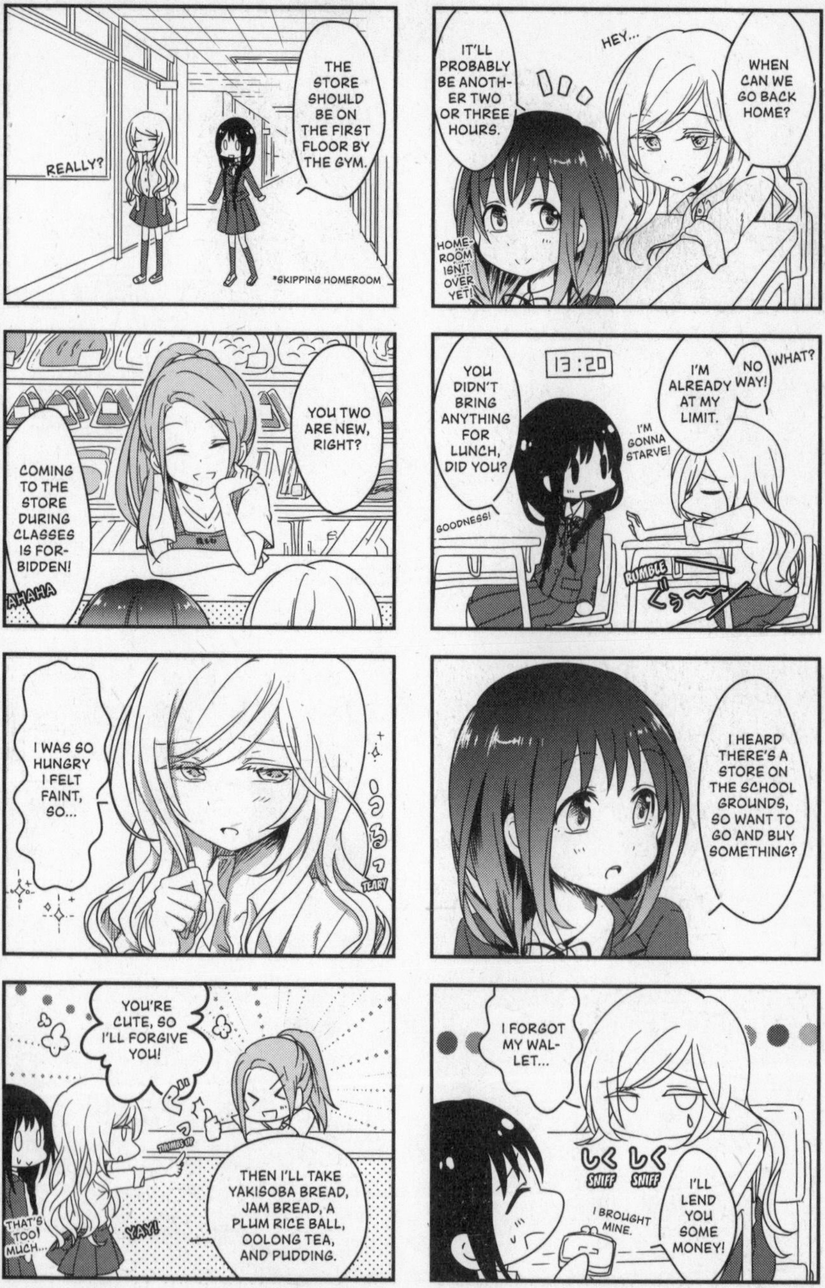
HEY...
WHEN CAN WE GO BACK HOME?
IT'LL PROBABLY BE ANOTHER TWO OR THREE HOURS.
HOMEROOM ISN'T OVER YET!
13:20
WHAT?
NO WAY!
I'M ALREADY AT MY LIMIT.
I'M GONNA STARVE!
YOU DIDN'T BRING ANYTHING FOR LUNCH, DID YOU?
GOODNESS!
RUMBLE
I HEARD THERE'S A STORE ON THE SCHOOL GROUNDS, SO WANT TO GO AND BUY SOMETHING?
I FORGOT MY WALLET...
SNIFF
SNIFF
I'LL LEND YOU SOME MONEY!
I BROUGHT MINE.
THE STORE SHOULD BE ON THE FIRST FLOOR BY THE GYM.
REALLY?
*SKIPPING HOMEROOM
YOU TWO ARE NEW, RIGHT?
COMING TO THE STORE DURING CLASSES IS FORBIDDEN!
AHAHA
I WAS SO HUNGRY I FELT FAINT, SO...
TEARY
YOU'RE CUTE, SO I'LL FORGIVE YOU!
THUMBS UP
THEN I'LL TAKE YAKISOBA BREAD, JAM BREAD, A PLUM RICE BALL, OOLONG TEA, AND PUDDING.
YAY!
THAT'S TOO MUCH...

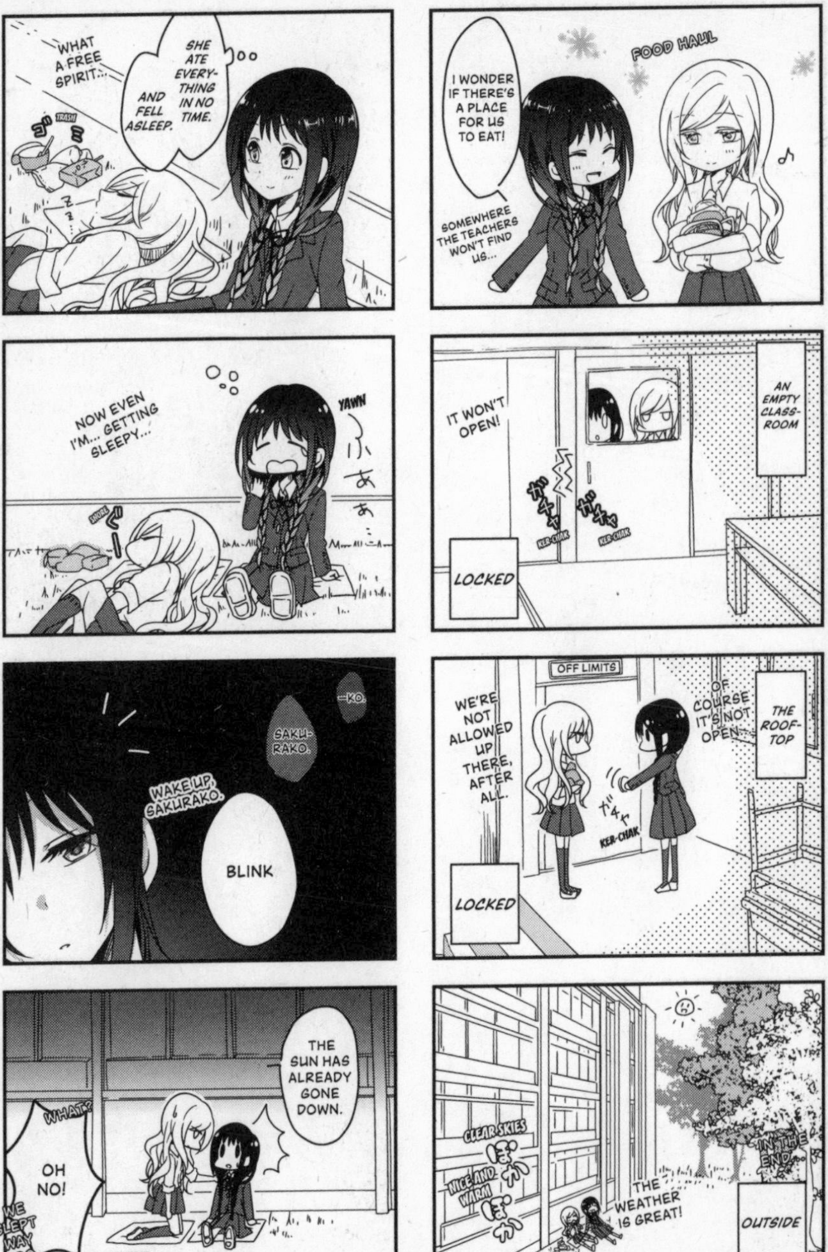
FOOD HALL
I WONDER IF THERE'S A PLACE FOR US TO EAT!
SOMEWHERE THE TEACHERS WON'T FIND US...
AN EMPTY CLASSROOM
IT WON'T OPEN!
ガチャ
KER-CHAK
ガチャ
KER-CHAK
LOCKED
THE ROOFTOP
OF COURSE IT'S NOT OPEN...
OFF LIMITS
WE'RE NOT ALLOWED UP THERE, AFTER ALL.
ガチャ
KER-CHAK
LOCKED
IN THE END...
OUTSIDE
THE WEATHER IS GREAT!
CLEAR SKIES
NICE AND WARM
SHE ATE EVERYTHING IN NO TIME.
AND FELL ASLEEP.
WHAT A FREE SPIRIT...
TRASH!
YAWN
NOW EVEN I'M... GETTING SLEEPY...
SNORE
—KO.
SAKURAKO.
WAKE UP, SAKURAKO.
BLINK
THE SUN HAS ALREADY GONE DOWN.
WHAT?
OH NO!
WE SLEPT WAY TOO MUCH!
19:10

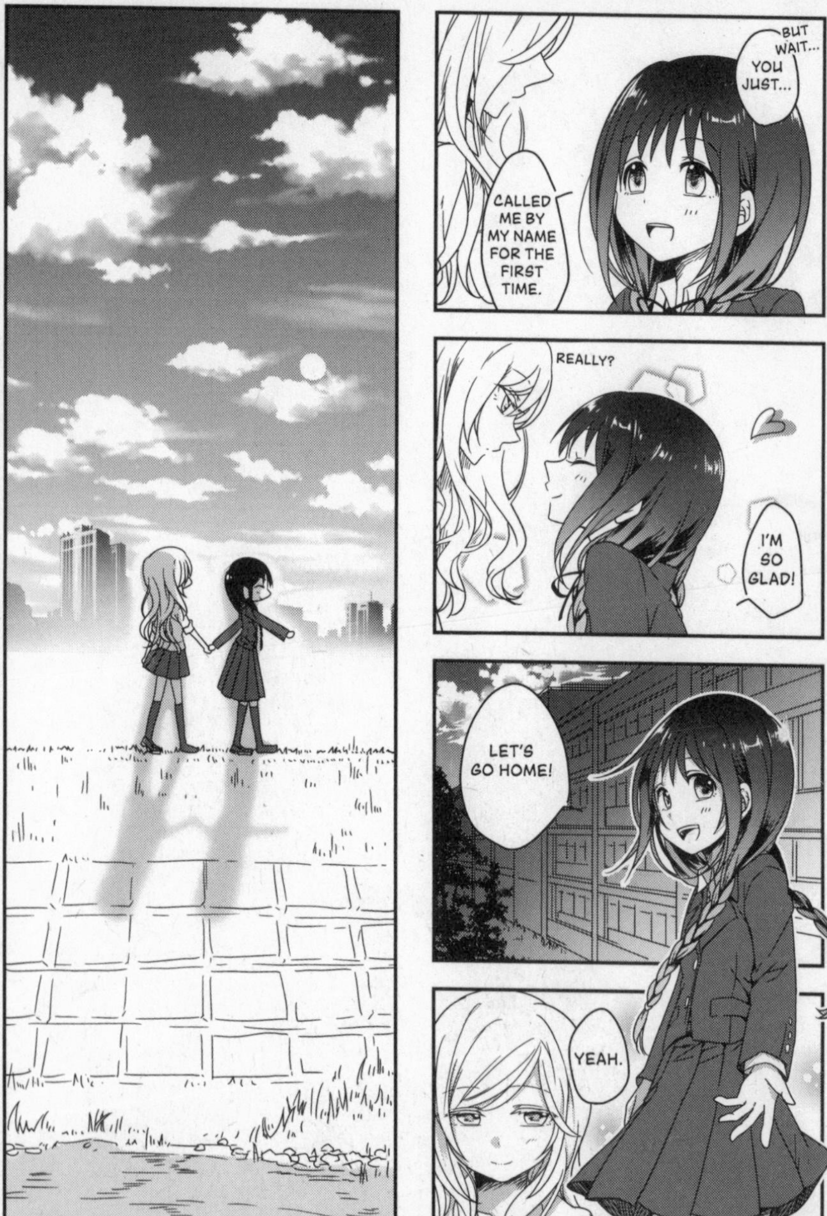
BUT WAIT... YOU JUST...
CALLED ME BY MY NAME FOR THE FIRST TIME.
REALLY?
I'M SO GLAD!
LET'S GO HOME!
YEAH.

Illustration gallery

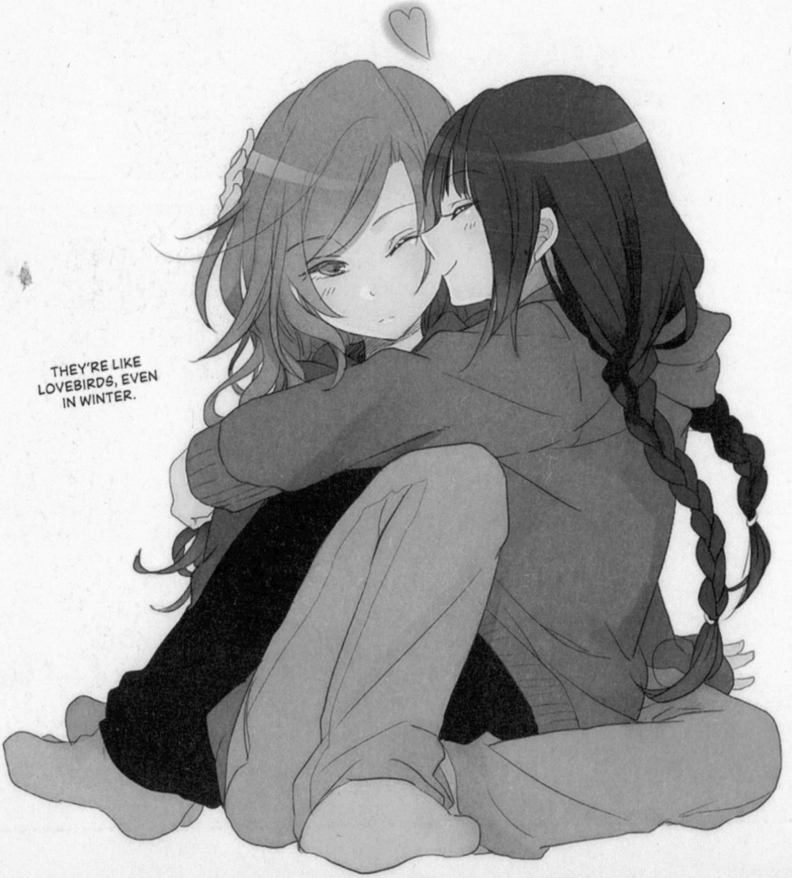
THEY'RE LIKE
LOVEBIRDS, EVEN
IN WINTER.

Futaribeya
A ROOM FOR TWO

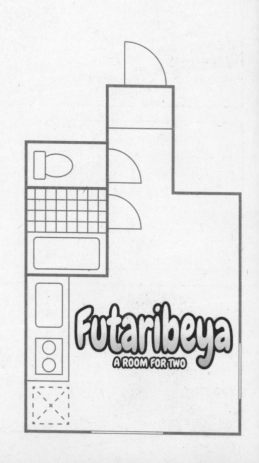

Chapter 2

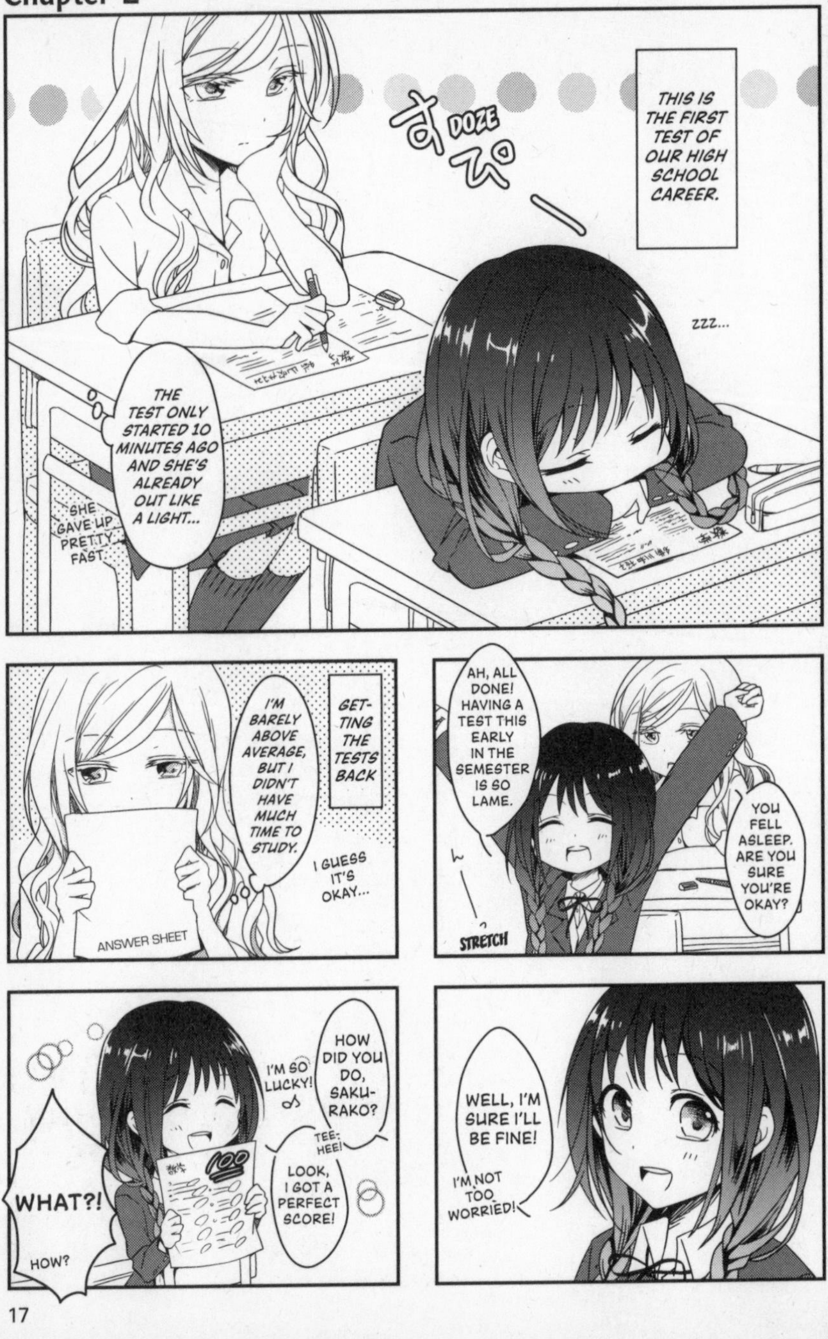

THIS IS THE FIRST TEST OF OUR HIGH SCHOOL CAREER.
すぴー
DOZE
zzz...
THE TEST ONLY STARTED 10 MINUTES AGO AND SHE'S ALREADY OUT LIKE A LIGHT...
SHE GAVE UP PRETTY FAST.
AH, ALL DONE! HAVING A TEST THIS EARLY IN THE SEMESTER IS SO LAME.
YOU FELL ASLEEP. ARE YOU SURE YOU'RE OKAY?
STRETCH
GET-TING THE TESTS BACK
I'M BARELY ABOVE AVERAGE, BUT I DIDN'T HAVE MUCH TIME TO STUDY.
I GUESS IT'S OKAY...
ANSWER SHEET
WELL, I'M SURE I'LL BE FINE!
I'M NOT TOO WORRIED!
HOW DID YOU DO, SAKU-RAKO?
I'M SO LUCKY! ♪
TEE-HEE!
LOOK, I GOT A PERFECT SCORE!
100
WHAT?!
HOW?

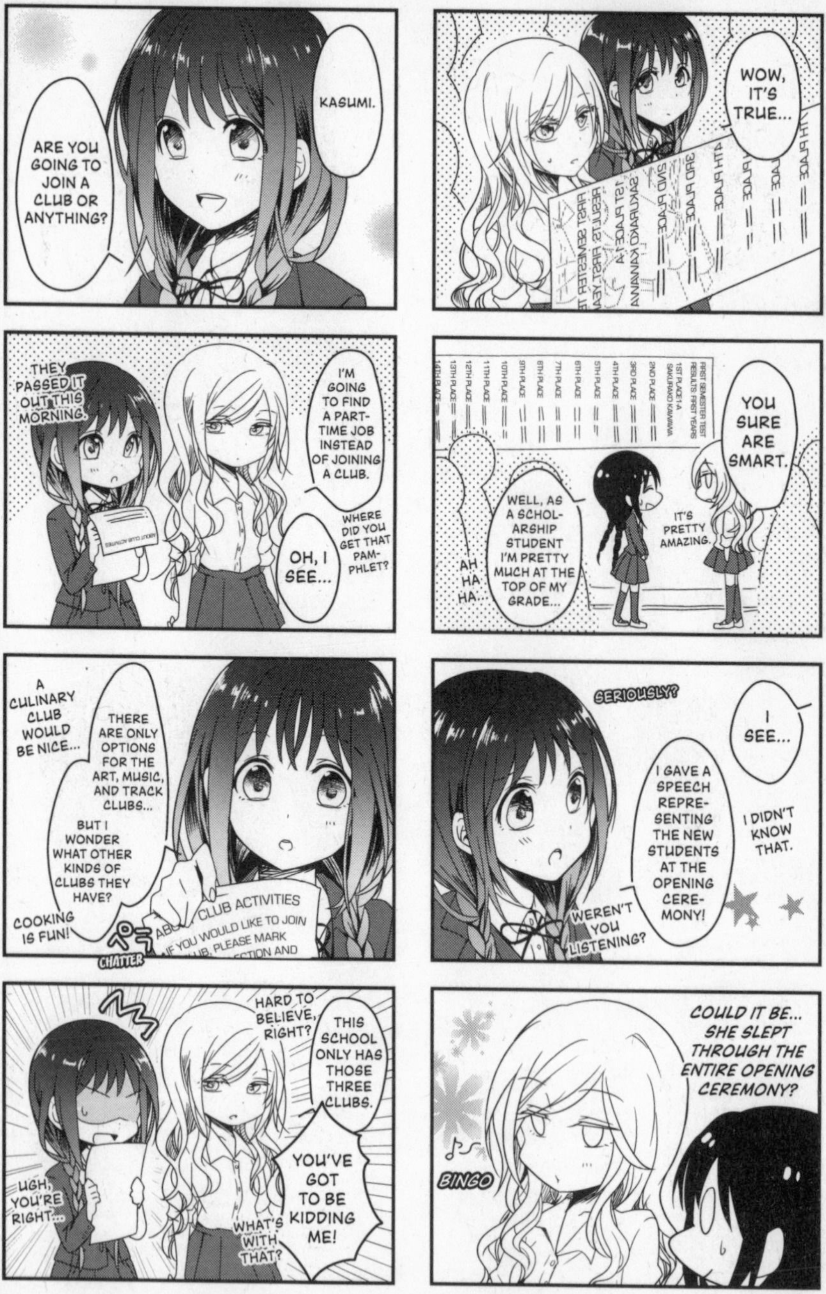
WOW, IT'S TRUE...
FIRST SEMESTER TEST RESULTS FIRST YEARS
YOU SURE ARE SMART.
IT'S PRETTY AMAZING.
WELL, AS A SCHOLARSHIP STUDENT I'M PRETTY MUCH AT THE TOP OF MY GRADE...
AH HA HA...
I SEE...
I DIDN'T KNOW THAT.
SERIOUSLY?
I GAVE A SPEECH REPRESENTING THE NEW STUDENTS AT THE OPENING CEREMONY!
WEREN'T YOU LISTENING?
COULD IT BE... SHE SLEPT THROUGH THE ENTIRE OPENING CEREMONY?
BINGO
KASUMI.
ARE YOU GOING TO JOIN A CLUB OR ANYTHING?
I'M GOING TO FIND A PART-TIME JOB INSTEAD OF JOINING A CLUB.
WHERE DID YOU GET THAT PAMPHLET?
OH, I SEE...
THEY PASSED IT OUT THIS MORNING.
THERE ARE ONLY OPTIONS FOR THE ART, MUSIC, AND TRACK CLUBS...
BUT I WONDER WHAT OTHER KINDS OF CLUBS THEY HAVE?
A CULINARY CLUB WOULD BE NICE...
COOKING IS FUN!
CLUB ACTIVITIES
CHATTER
HARD TO BELIEVE, RIGHT?
THIS SCHOOL ONLY HAS THOSE THREE CLUBS.
YOU'VE GOT TO BE KIDDING ME!
WHAT'S WITH THAT?
UGH, YOU'RE RIGHT...

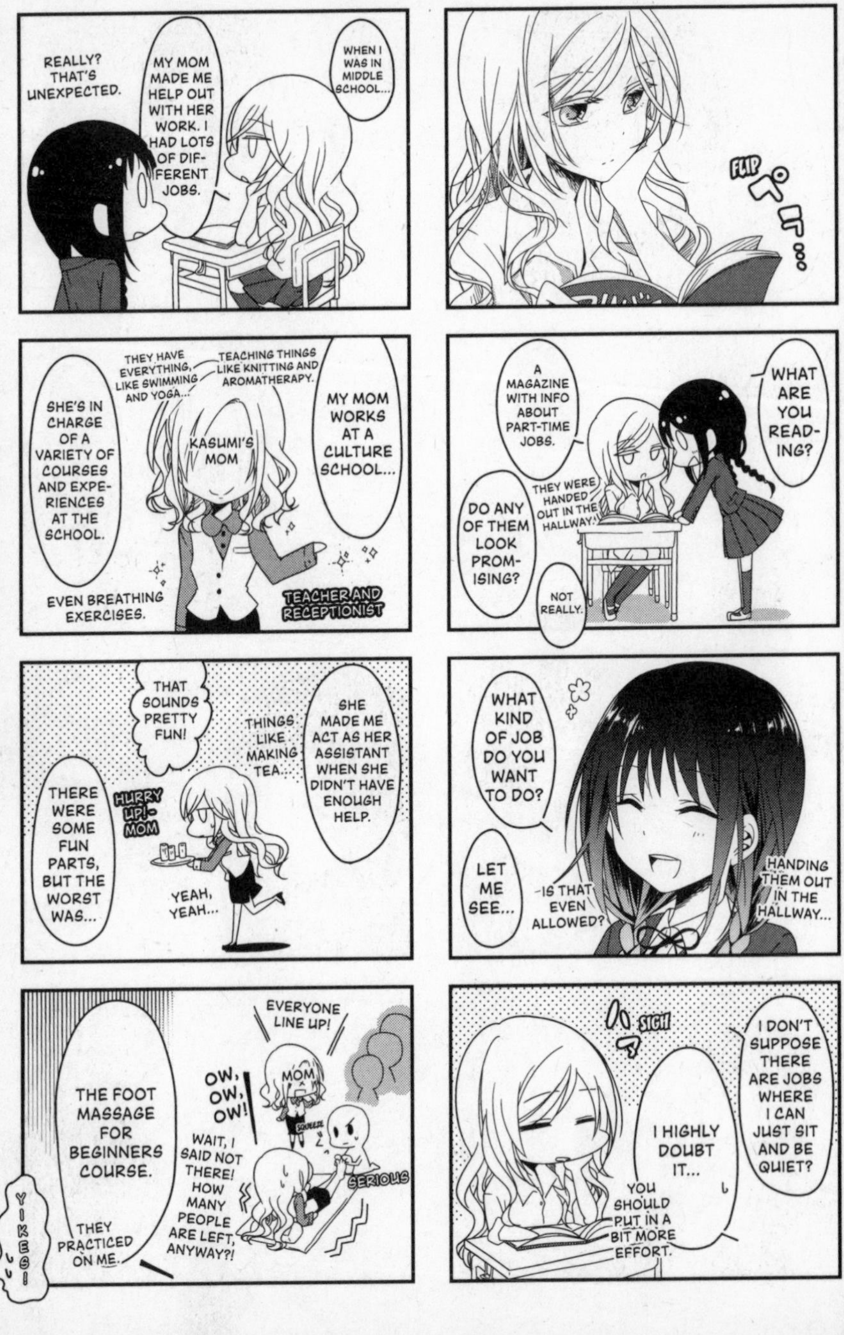
FLIP
WHAT ARE YOU READING?
A MAGAZINE WITH INFO ABOUT PART-TIME JOBS.
THEY WERE HANDED OUT IN THE HALLWAY.
DO ANY OF THEM LOOK PROMISING?
NOT REALLY.
HANDING THEM OUT IN THE HALLWAY...
-IS THAT EVEN ALLOWED?
WHAT KIND OF JOB DO YOU WANT TO DO?
LET ME SEE...
I DON'T SUPPOSE THERE ARE JOBS WHERE I CAN JUST SIT AND BE QUIET?
SIGH
I HIGHLY DOUBT IT...
YOU SHOULD PUT IN A BIT MORE EFFORT.
WHEN I WAS IN MIDDLE SCHOOL...
MY MOM MADE ME HELP OUT WITH HER WORK. I HAD LOTS OF DIF-FERENT JOBS.
REALLY? THAT'S UNEXPECTED.
MY MOM WORKS AT A CULTURE SCHOOL...
TEACHING THINGS LIKE KNITTING AND AROMATHERAPY.
THEY HAVE EVERYTHING, LIKE SWIMMING AND YOGA...
KASUMI'S MOM
SHE'S IN CHARGE OF A VARIETY OF COURSES AND EXPE-RIENCES AT THE SCHOOL.
TEACHER AND RECEPTIONIST
EVEN BREATHING EXERCISES.
SHE MADE ME ACT AS HER ASSISTANT WHEN SHE DIDN'T HAVE ENOUGH HELP.
THINGS LIKE MAKING TEA...
THAT SOUNDS PRETTY FUN!
HURRY UP! -MOM
YEAH, YEAH...
THERE WERE SOME FUN PARTS, BUT THE WORST WAS...
EVERYONE LINE UP!
MOM
OW, OW, OW!
THE FOOT MASSAGE FOR BEGINNERS COURSE.
SERIOUS
WAIT, I SAID NOT THERE! HOW MANY PEOPLE ARE LEFT, ANYWAY?!
THEY PRACTICED ON ME.
YIKES!

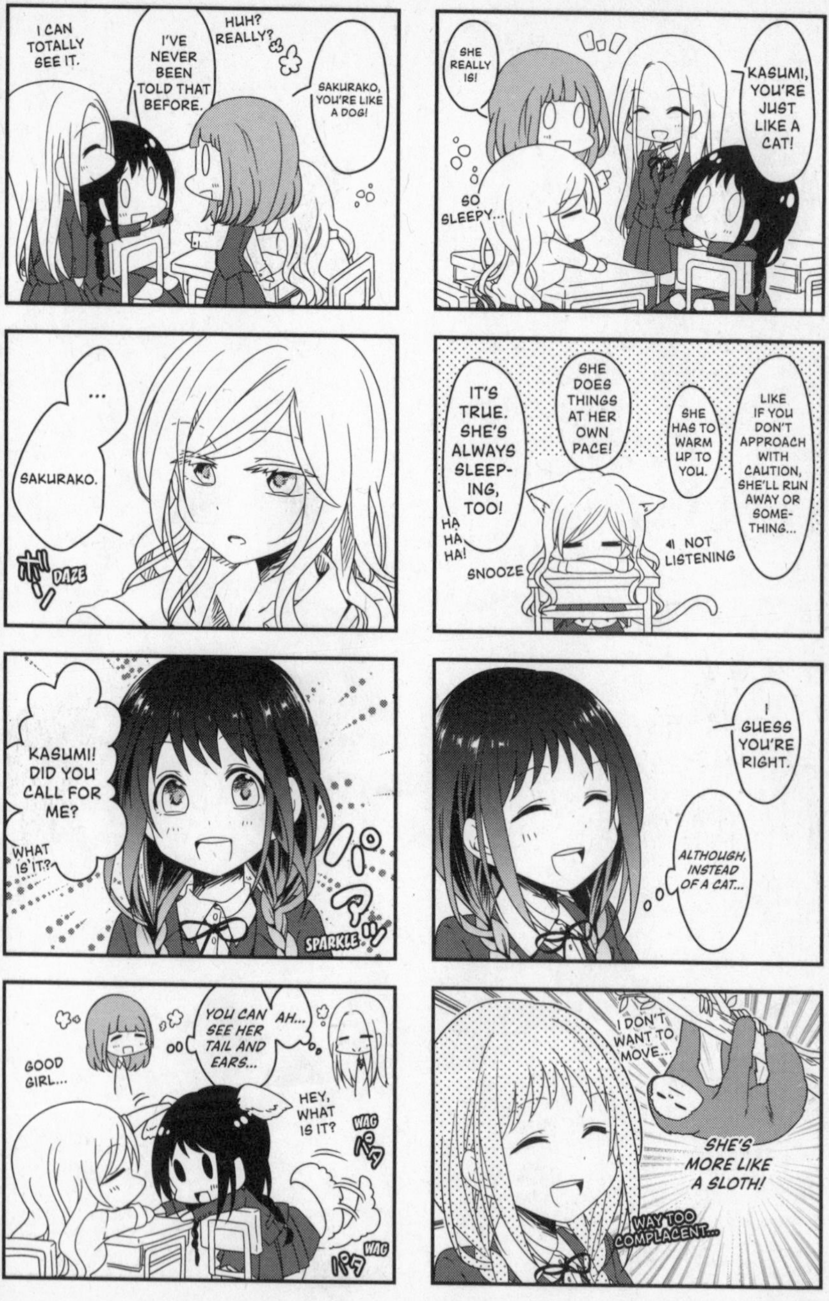
KASUMI, YOU'RE JUST LIKE A CAT!
SHE REALLY IS!
SO SLEEPY...
LIKE IF YOU DON'T APPROACH WITH CAUTION, SHE'LL RUN AWAY OR SOME-THING...
SHE HAS TO WARM UP TO YOU.
SHE DOES THINGS AT HER OWN PACE!
IT'S TRUE. SHE'S ALWAYS SLEEP-ING, TOO!
NOT LISTENING
HA HA HA!
SNOOZE
I GUESS YOU'RE RIGHT.
ALTHOUGH, INSTEAD OF A CAT...
I DON'T WANT TO MOVE...
SHE'S MORE LIKE A SLOTH!
WAY TOO COMPLACENT...
SAKURAKO, YOU'RE LIKE A DOG!
HUH? REALLY?
I'VE NEVER BEEN TOLD THAT BEFORE.
I CAN TOTALLY SEE IT.
...
SAKURAKO.
DAZE
KASUMI! DID YOU CALL FOR ME?
WHAT IS IT?
SPARKLE
AH...
YOU CAN SEE HER TAIL AND EARS...
HEY, WHAT IS IT?
WAG
GOOD GIRL...
WAG

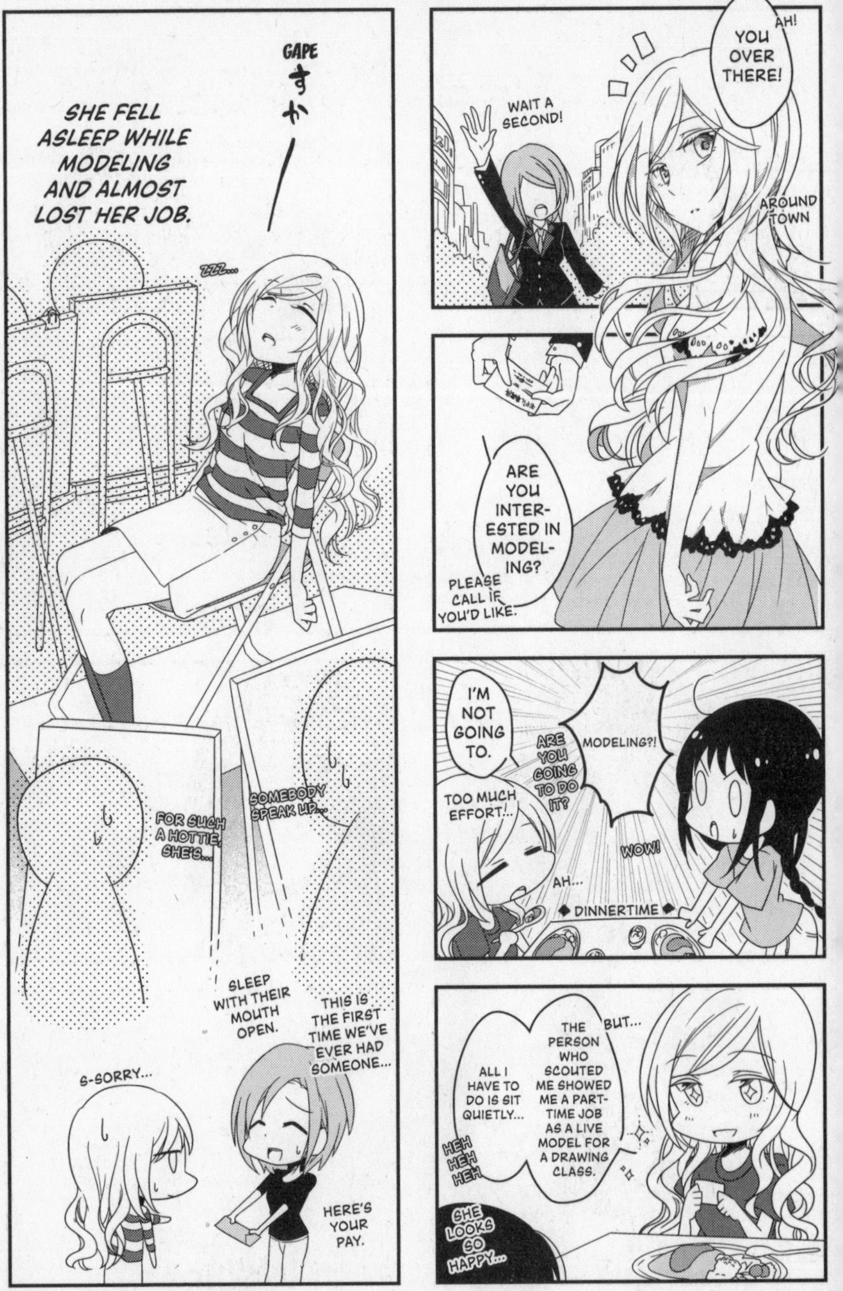
AH!
YOU OVER THERE!
AROUND TOWN
WAIT A SECOND!
ARE YOU INTER-ESTED IN MODEL-ING?
PLEASE CALL IF YOU'D LIKE.
MODELING?!
ARE YOU GOING TO DO IT?
WOW!
I'M NOT GOING TO.
TOO MUCH EFFORT...
AH...
◆ DINNERTIME ◆
BUT...
THE PERSON WHO SCOUTED ME SHOWED ME A PART-TIME JOB AS A LIVE MODEL FOR A DRAWING CLASS.
ALL I HAVE TO DO IS SIT QUIETLY...
HEH HEH HEH
SHE LOOKS SO HAPPY...
GAPE
すか
SHE FELL ASLEEP WHILE MODELING AND ALMOST LOST HER JOB.
ZZZ...
SOMEBODY SPEAK UP...
FOR SUCH A HOTTIE, SHE'S...
THIS IS THE FIRST TIME WE'VE EVER HAD SOMEONE...
SLEEP WITH THEIR MOUTH OPEN.
HERE'S YOUR PAY.
S-SORRY...

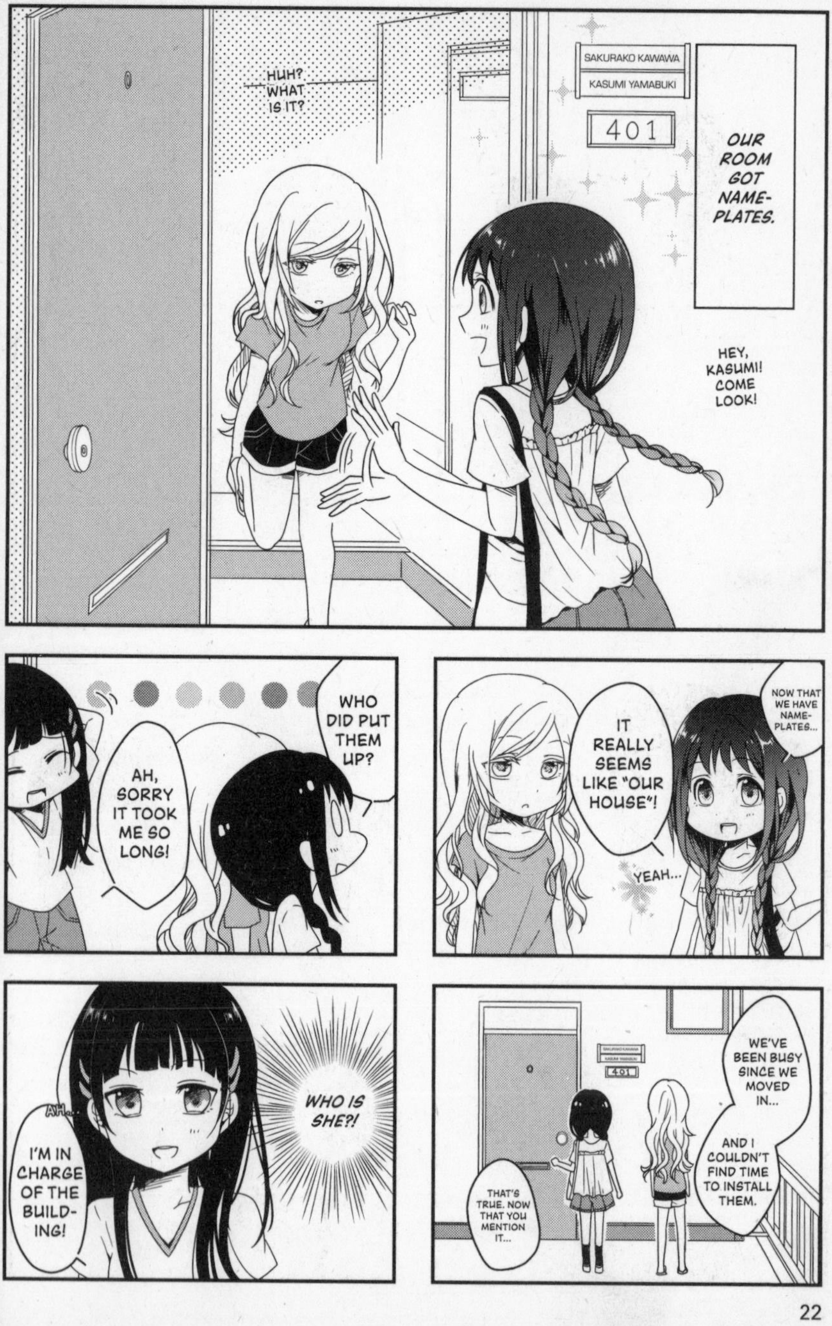
SAKURAKO KAWAWA
KASUMI YAMABUKI
401
OUR ROOM GOT NAME-PLATES.
HEY, KASUMI! COME LOOK!
HUH? WHAT IS IT?
NOW THAT WE HAVE NAME-PLATES...
IT REALLY SEEMS LIKE "OUR HOUSE"!
YEAH...
WHO DID PUT THEM UP?
AH, SORRY IT TOOK ME SO LONG!
WE'VE BEEN BUSY SINCE WE MOVED IN...
AND I COULDN'T FIND TIME TO INSTALL THEM.
THAT'S TRUE. NOW THAT YOU MENTION IT...
WHO IS SHE?!
AH...
I'M IN CHARGE OF THE BUILD-ING!

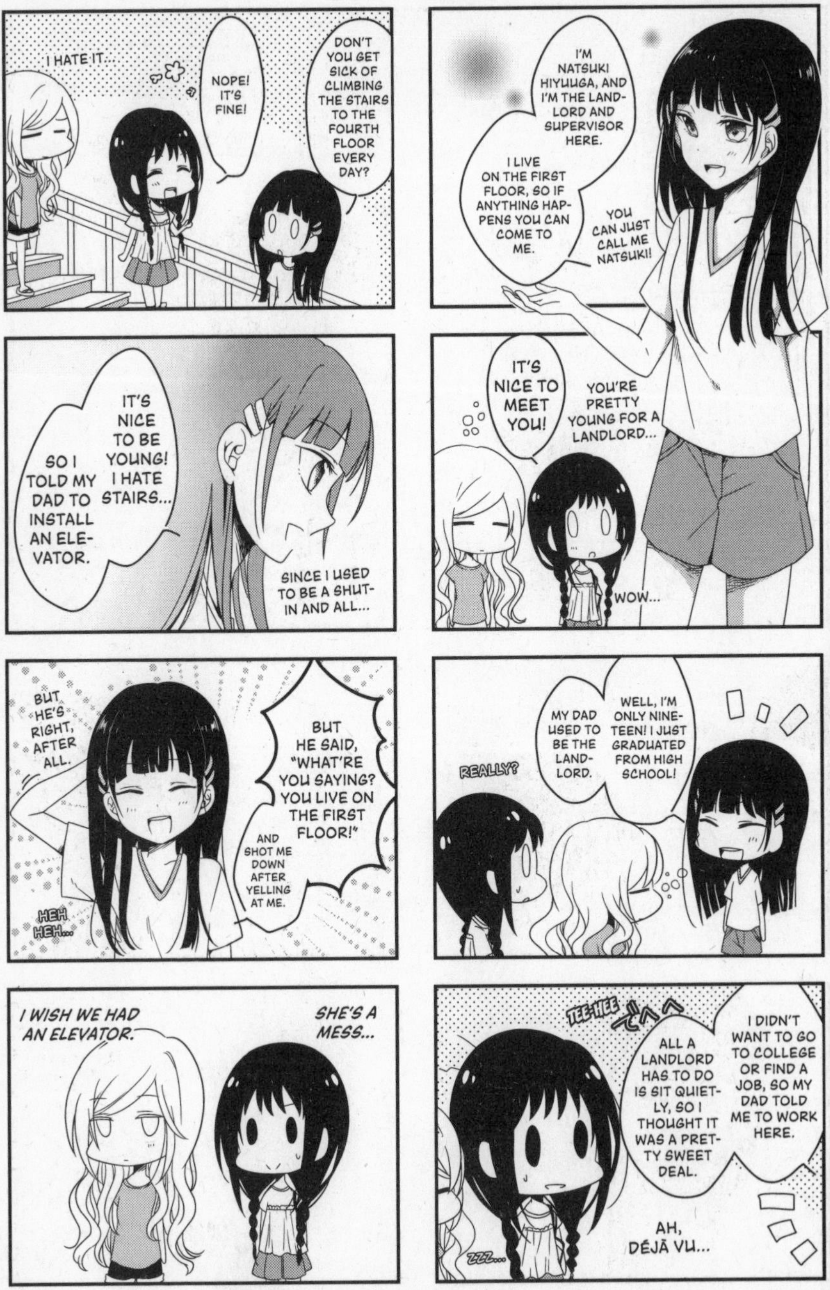
I'M NATSUKI HIYUUGA, AND I'M THE LANDLORD AND SUPERVISOR HERE.
I LIVE ON THE FIRST FLOOR, SO IF ANYTHING HAPPENS YOU CAN COME TO ME.
YOU CAN JUST CALL ME NATSUKI!
IT'S NICE TO MEET YOU!
YOU'RE PRETTY YOUNG FOR A LANDLORD...
WOW...
WELL, I'M ONLY NINETEEN! I JUST GRADUATED FROM HIGH SCHOOL!
MY DAD USED TO BE THE LANDLORD.
REALLY?
TEE-HEE
I DIDN'T WANT TO GO TO COLLEGE OR FIND A JOB, SO MY DAD TOLD ME TO WORK HERE.
ALL A LANDLORD HAS TO DO IS SIT QUIETLY, SO I THOUGHT IT WAS A PRETTY SWEET DEAL.
AH, DÉJÀ VU...
ZZZ...
DON'T YOU GET SICK OF CLIMBING THE STAIRS TO THE FOURTH FLOOR EVERY DAY?
NOPE! IT'S FINE!
I HATE IT...
IT'S NICE TO BE YOUNG! I HATE STAIRS...
SO I TOLD MY DAD TO INSTALL AN ELEVATOR.
SINCE I USED TO BE A SHUT-IN AND ALL...
BUT HE SAID, "WHAT'RE YOU SAYING? YOU LIVE ON THE FIRST FLOOR!"
AND SHOT ME DOWN AFTER YELLING AT ME.
BUT HE'S RIGHT, AFTER ALL.
HEH HEH...
SHE'S A MESS...
I WISH WE HAD AN ELEVATOR.

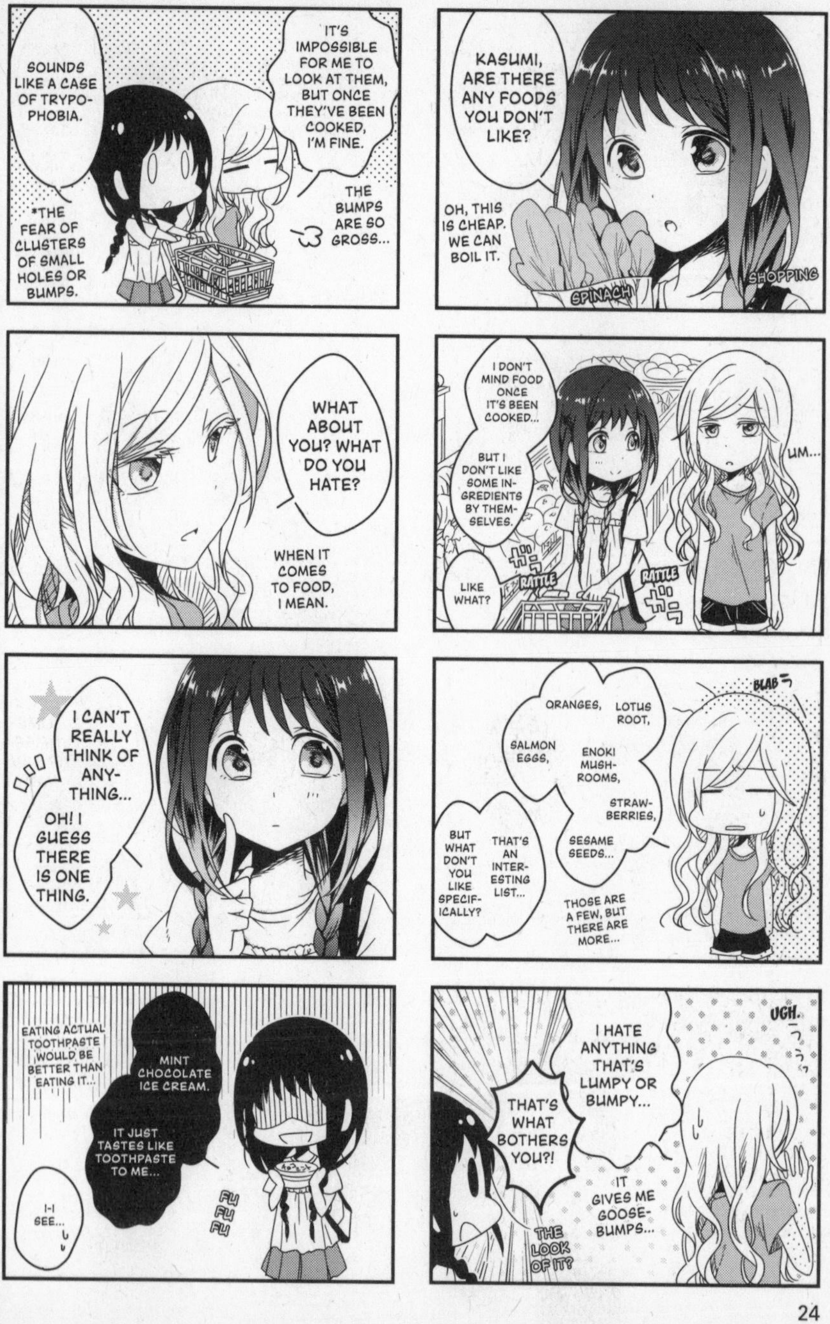
SHOPPING
KASUMI, ARE THERE ANY FOODS YOU DON'T LIKE?
OH, THIS IS CHEAP. WE CAN BOIL IT.
SPINACH
UM...
RATTLE
I DON'T MIND FOOD ONCE IT'S BEEN COOKED...
BUT I DON'T LIKE SOME INGREDIENTS BY THEMSELVES.
RATTLE
LIKE WHAT?
BLAB
ORANGES, LOTUS ROOT, SALMON EGGS, ENOKI MUSHROOMS, STRAWBERRIES, SESAME SEEDS...
THOSE ARE A FEW, BUT THERE ARE MORE...
THAT'S AN INTERESTING LIST...
BUT WHAT DON'T YOU LIKE SPECIFICALLY?
UGH.
I HATE ANYTHING THAT'S LUMPY OR BUMPY...
IT GIVES ME GOOSEBUMPS...
THAT'S WHAT BOTHERS YOU?!
THE LOOK OF IT?
IT'S IMPOSSIBLE FOR ME TO LOOK AT THEM, BUT ONCE THEY'VE BEEN COOKED, I'M FINE.
THE BUMPS ARE SO GROSS...
SOUNDS LIKE A CASE OF TRYPOPHOBIA.
*THE FEAR OF CLUSTERS OF SMALL HOLES OR BUMPS.
WHAT ABOUT YOU? WHAT DO YOU HATE?
WHEN IT COMES TO FOOD, I MEAN.
I CAN'T REALLY THINK OF ANYTHING...
OH! I GUESS THERE IS ONE THING.
MINT CHOCOLATE ICE CREAM.
IT JUST TASTES LIKE TOOTHPASTE TO ME...
EATING ACTUAL TOOTHPASTE WOULD BE BETTER THAN EATING IT...
FU FU FU
I-I SEE...

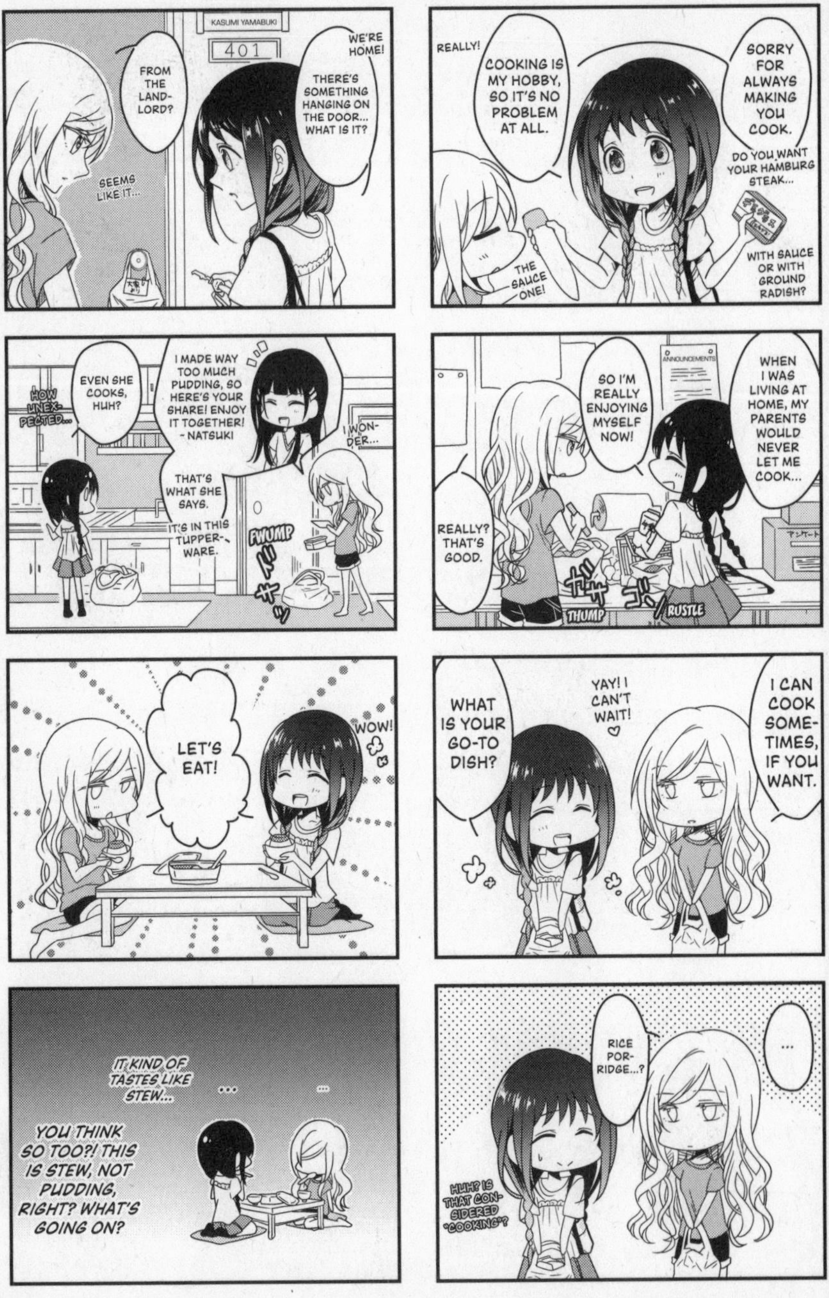
SORRY FOR ALWAYS MAKING YOU COOK.
COOKING IS MY HOBBY, SO IT'S NO PROBLEM AT ALL.
REALLY!
DO YOU WANT YOUR HAMBURG STEAK... WITH SAUCE OR WITH GROUND RADISH?
THE SAUCE ONE!
WHEN I WAS LIVING AT HOME, MY PARENTS WOULD NEVER LET ME COOK...
ANNOUNCEMENTS
SO I'M REALLY ENJOYING MYSELF NOW!
REALLY? THAT'S GOOD.
RUSTLE
THUMP
I CAN COOK SOMETIMES, IF YOU WANT.
YAY! I CAN'T WAIT!
WHAT IS YOUR GO-TO DISH?
...
RICE POR-RIDGE...?
HUH? IS THAT CON-SIDERED "COOKING"?
KASUMI YAMABUKI
401
WE'RE HOME!
THERE'S SOMETHING HANGING ON THE DOOR... WHAT IS IT?
FROM THE LAND-LORD?
SEEMS LIKE IT...
I WON-DER...
I MADE WAY TOO MUCH PUDDING, SO HERE'S YOUR SHARE! ENJOY IT TOGETHER! - NATSUKI
THAT'S WHAT SHE SAYS.
IT'S IN THIS TUPPER-WARE.
FWUMP
EVEN SHE COOKS, HUH?
HOW UNEX-PECTED...
WOW!
LET'S EAT!
...
...
IT KIND OF TASTES LIKE STEW...
YOU THINK SO TOO?! THIS IS STEW, NOT PUDDING, RIGHT? WHAT'S GOING ON?

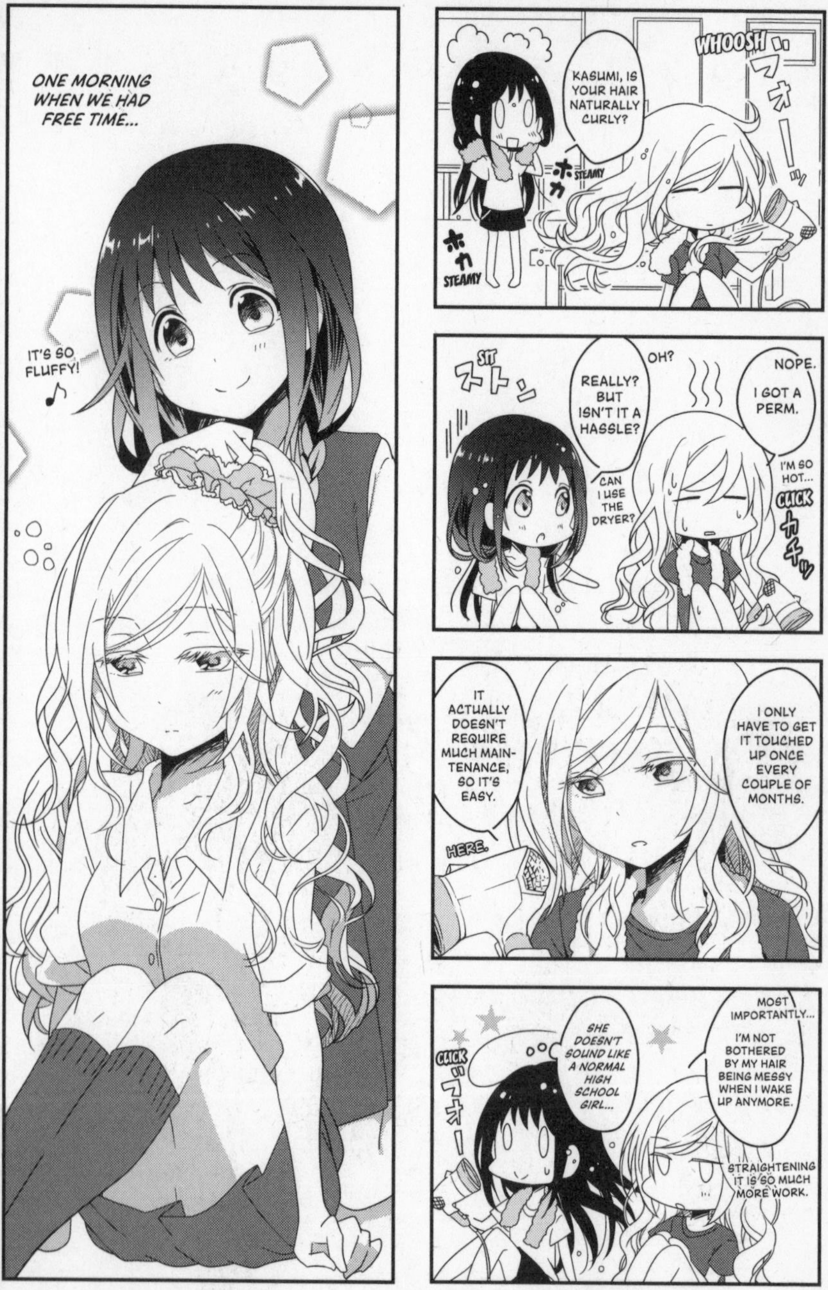
WHOOSH
フォー!!
KASUMI, IS YOUR HAIR NATURALLY CURLY?
ホカ STEAMY
ホカ STEAMY
SIT
ストン
REALLY? BUT ISN'T IT A HASSLE?
OH?
NOPE. I GOT A PERM.
I'M SO HOT...
CAN I USE THE DRYER?
CLICK
カチッ
I ONLY HAVE TO GET IT TOUCHED UP ONCE EVERY COUPLE OF MONTHS.
IT ACTUALLY DOESN'T REQUIRE MUCH MAIN-TENANCE, SO IT'S EASY.
HERE.
MOST IMPORTANTLY... I'M NOT BOTHERED BY MY HAIR BEING MESSY WHEN I WAKE UP ANYMORE.
STRAIGHTENING IT IS SO MUCH MORE WORK.
SHE DOESN'T SOUND LIKE A NORMAL HIGH SCHOOL GIRL...
CLICK
ブォー
ONE MORNING WHEN WE HAD FREE TIME...
IT'S SO FLUFFY! ♪

Illustration gallery

PLAYING THE POCKY GAME* WITH CANDY.

* THE POCKY GAME IS A GAME WHERE TWO PEOPLE PLAY CHICKEN BY
SEEING WHO BREAKS AWAY FIRST WHILE EATING A STICK OF POCKY.

Futaribeya
A ROOM FOR TWO

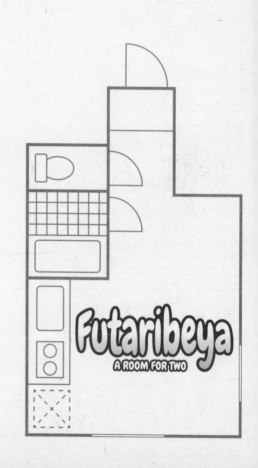

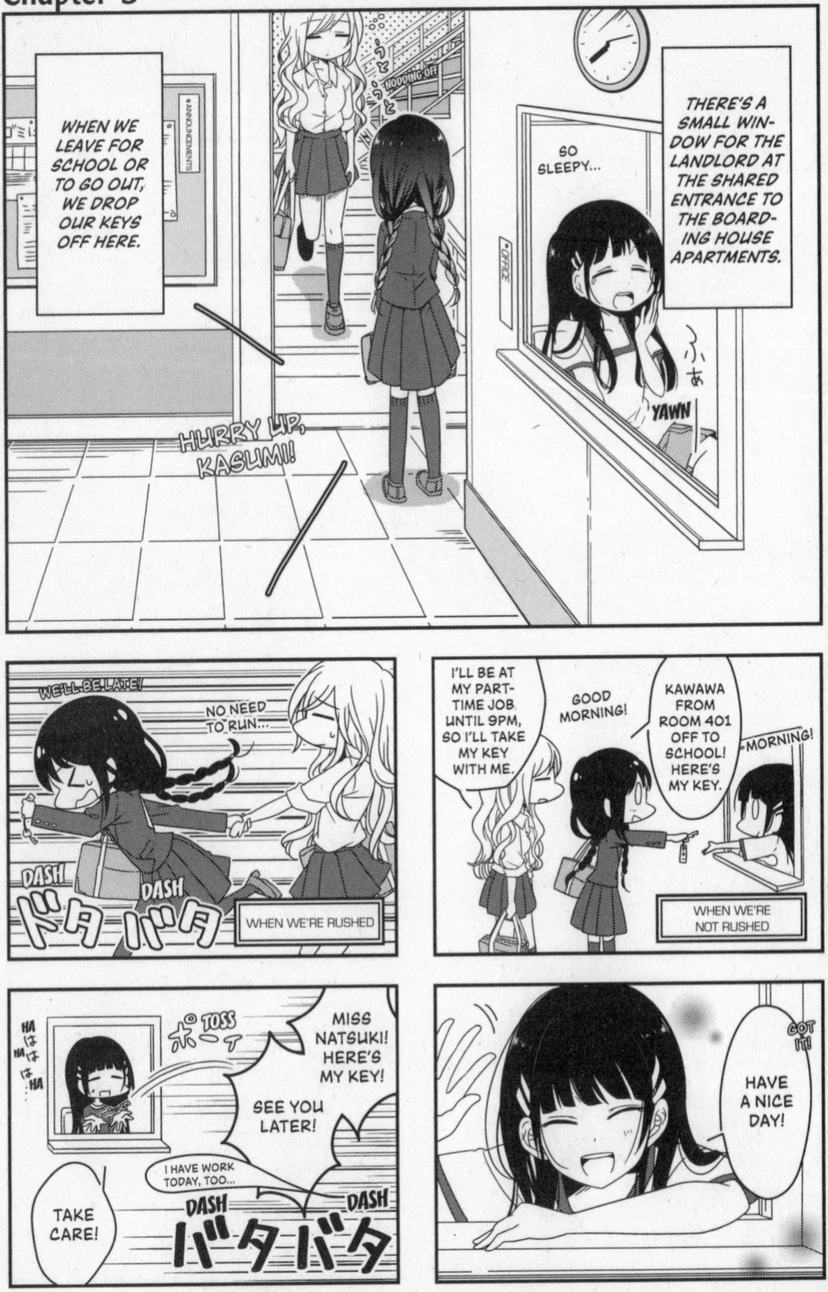
THERE'S A SMALL WINDOW FOR THE LANDLORD AT THE SHARED ENTRANCE TO THE BOARDING HOUSE APARTMENTS.
SO SLEEPY...
YAWN
OFFICE
NODDING OFF
HURRY UP, KASUMI!
ANNOUNCEMENTS
WHEN WE LEAVE FOR SCHOOL OR TO GO OUT, WE DROP OUR KEYS OFF HERE.
KAWAWA FROM ROOM 401 OFF TO SCHOOL! HERE'S MY KEY.
-MORNING!
GOOD MORNING!
I'LL BE AT MY PART-TIME JOB UNTIL 9PM, SO I'LL TAKE MY KEY WITH ME.
WHEN WE'RE NOT RUSHED
WE'LL BE LATE!
NO NEED TO RUN...
DASH
DASH
ドタバタ
WHEN WE'RE RUSHED
GOT IT!
HAVE A NICE DAY!
MISS NATSUKI! HERE'S MY KEY!
TOSS
SEE YOU LATER!
HA HA HA
I HAVE WORK TODAY, TOO...
DASH
DASH
バタバタ
TAKE CARE!

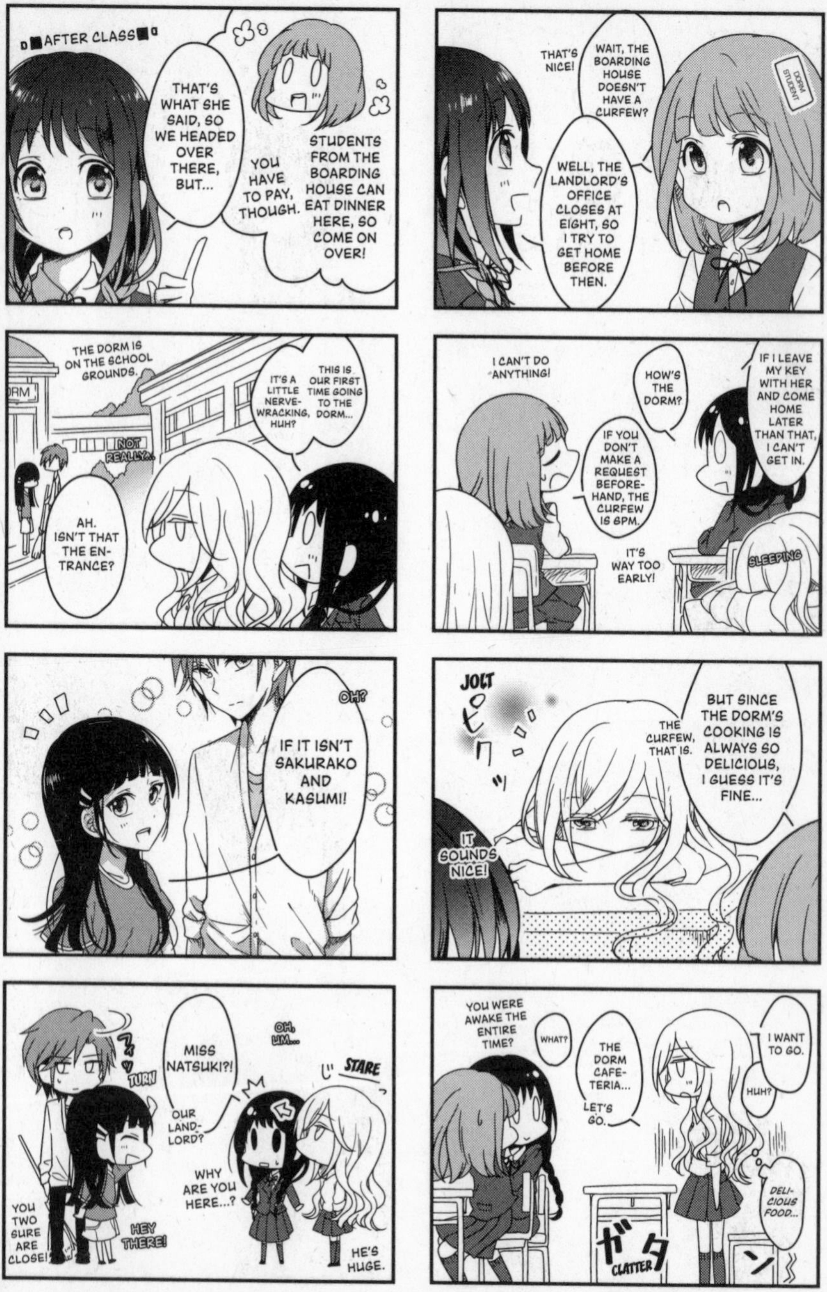
DORM STUDENT
WAIT, THE BOARDING HOUSE DOESN'T HAVE A CURFEW?
THAT'S NICE!
WELL, THE LANDLORD'S OFFICE CLOSES AT EIGHT, SO I TRY TO GET HOME BEFORE THEN.
IF I LEAVE MY KEY WITH HER AND COME HOME LATER THAN THAT, I CAN'T GET IN.
HOW'S THE DORM?
I CAN'T DO ANYTHING!
IF YOU DON'T MAKE A REQUEST BEFORE-HAND, THE CURFEW IS 6PM.
SLEEPING
IT'S WAY TOO EARLY!
BUT SINCE THE DORM'S COOKING IS ALWAYS SO DELICIOUS, I GUESS IT'S FINE...
THE CURFEW, THAT IS.
JOLT
IT SOUNDS NICE!
I WANT TO GO.
HUH?
THE DORM CAFE-TERIA...
WHAT?
YOU WERE AWAKE THE ENTIRE TIME?
LET'S GO.
DELI-CIOUS FOOD...
CLATTER
AFTER CLASS
STUDENTS FROM THE BOARDING HOUSE CAN EAT DINNER HERE, SO COME ON OVER!
YOU HAVE TO PAY, THOUGH.
THAT'S WHAT SHE SAID, SO WE HEADED OVER THERE, BUT...
THIS IS OUR FIRST TIME GOING TO THE DORM...
IT'S A LITTLE NERVE-WRACKING, HUH?
THE DORM IS ON THE SCHOOL GROUNDS.
DORM
NOT REALLY...
AH. ISN'T THAT THE EN-TRANCE?
OH?
IF IT ISN'T SAKURAKO AND KASUMI!
STARE
OH, UM...
MISS NATSUKI?!
OUR LAND-LORD?
TURN
WHY ARE YOU HERE...?
HEY THERE!
HE'S HUGE.
YOU TWO SURE ARE CLOSE!

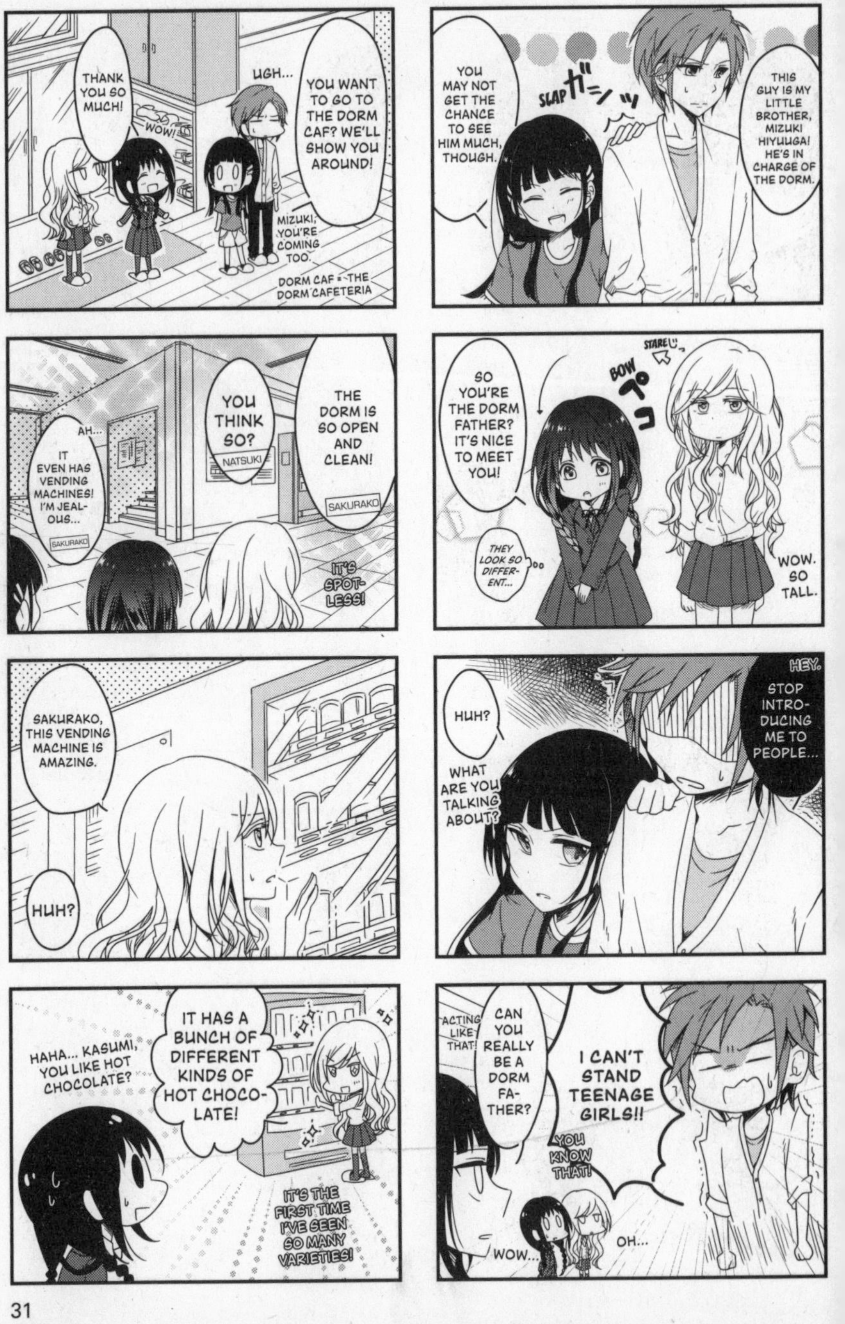
THIS GUY IS MY LITTLE BROTHER, MIZUKI HIYUUGA! HE'S IN CHARGE OF THE DORM.
SLAP ガーンッ
YOU MAY NOT GET THE CHANCE TO SEE HIM MUCH, THOUGH.
STARE じっ
SO YOU'RE THE DORM FATHER? IT'S NICE TO MEET YOU!
BOW ペコ
WOW. SO TALL.
THEY LOOK SO DIFFERENT...
HEY.
STOP INTRODUCING ME TO PEOPLE...
HUH?
WHAT ARE YOU TALKING ABOUT?
I CAN'T STAND TEENAGE GIRLS!!
CAN YOU REALLY BE A DORM FATHER?
ACTING LIKE THAT!
YOU KNOW THAT!
OH...
WOW...
YOU WANT TO GO TO THE DORM CAF? WE'LL SHOW YOU AROUND!
UGH...
THANK YOU SO MUCH!
WOW!
MIZUKI, YOU'RE COMING TOO.
DORM CAF = THE DORM CAFETERIA
THE DORM IS SO OPEN AND CLEAN!
SAKURAKO
YOU THINK SO?
NATSUKI
AH...
IT EVEN HAS VENDING MACHINES! I'M JEALOUS...
SAKURAKO
IT'S SPOTLESS!
SAKURAKO, THIS VENDING MACHINE IS AMAZING.
HUH?
IT HAS A BUNCH OF DIFFERENT KINDS OF HOT CHOCOLATE!
HAHA... KASUMI, YOU LIKE HOT CHOCOLATE?
IT'S THE FIRST TIME I'VE SEEN SO MANY VARIETIES!

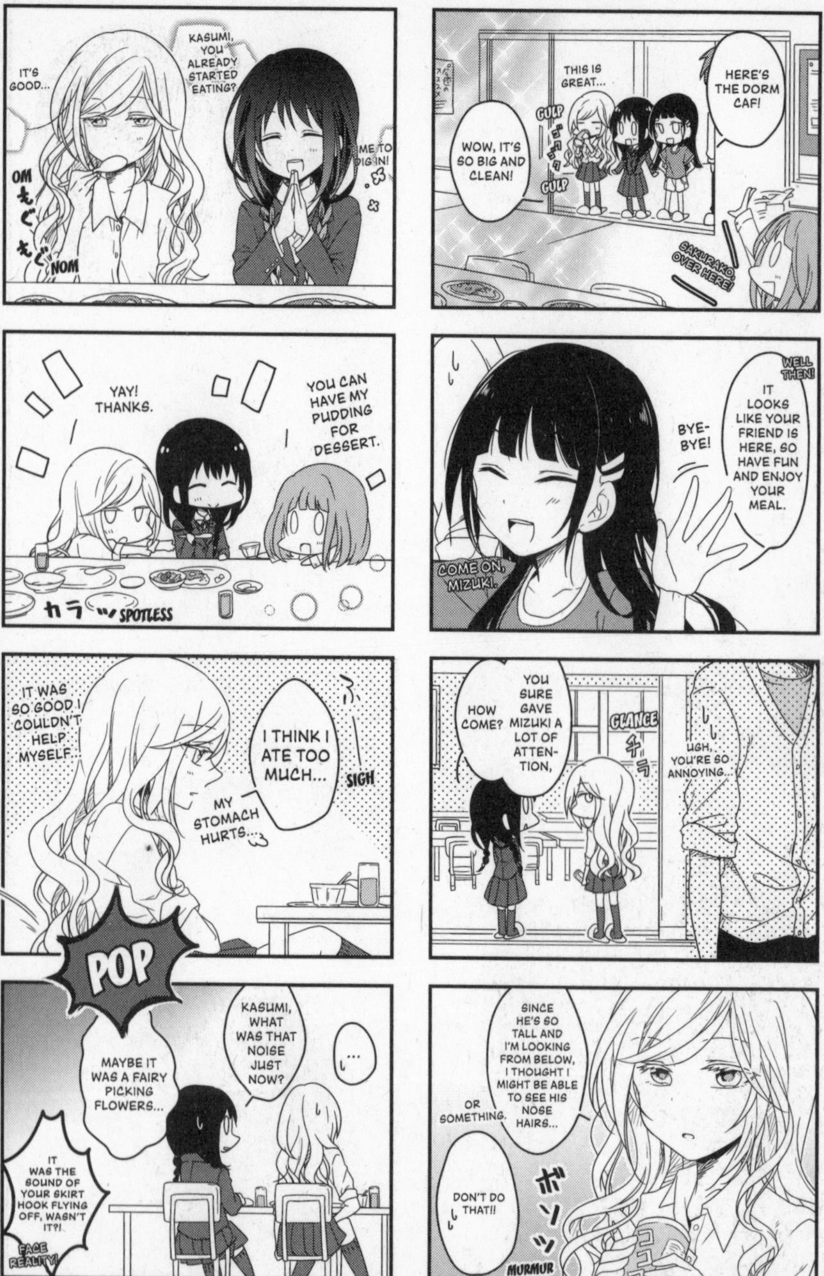
HERE'S THE DORM CAF!
THIS IS GREAT...
GULP ゴクゴク GULP
WOW, IT'S SO BIG AND CLEAN!
SAKURAKO, OVER HERE!
WELL THEN!
IT LOOKS LIKE YOUR FRIEND IS HERE, SO HAVE FUN AND ENJOY YOUR MEAL.
BYE-BYE!
COME ON, MIZUKI.
UGH, YOU'RE SO ANNOYING...
GLANCE チラ
YOU SURE GAVE MIZUKI A LOT OF ATTENTION,
HOW COME?
SINCE HE'S SO TALL AND I'M LOOKING FROM BELOW, I THOUGHT I MIGHT BE ABLE TO SEE HIS NOSE HAIRS...
OR SOMETHING.
DON'T DO THAT!!
ボソッ MURMUR
KASUMI, YOU ALREADY STARTED EATING?
IT'S GOOD...
ME TO DIG IN!
OM もぐもぐ NOM
YOU CAN HAVE MY PUDDING FOR DESSERT.
YAY! THANKS.
カラッ SPOTLESS
ふー SIGH
I THINK I ATE TOO MUCH...
MY STOMACH HURTS...
IT WAS SO GOOD I COULDN'T HELP MYSELF...
POP
...
KASUMI, WHAT WAS THAT NOISE JUST NOW?
MAYBE IT WAS A FAIRY PICKING FLOWERS...
IT WAS THE SOUND OF YOUR SKIRT HOOK FLYING OFF, WASN'T IT?!
FACE REALITY!

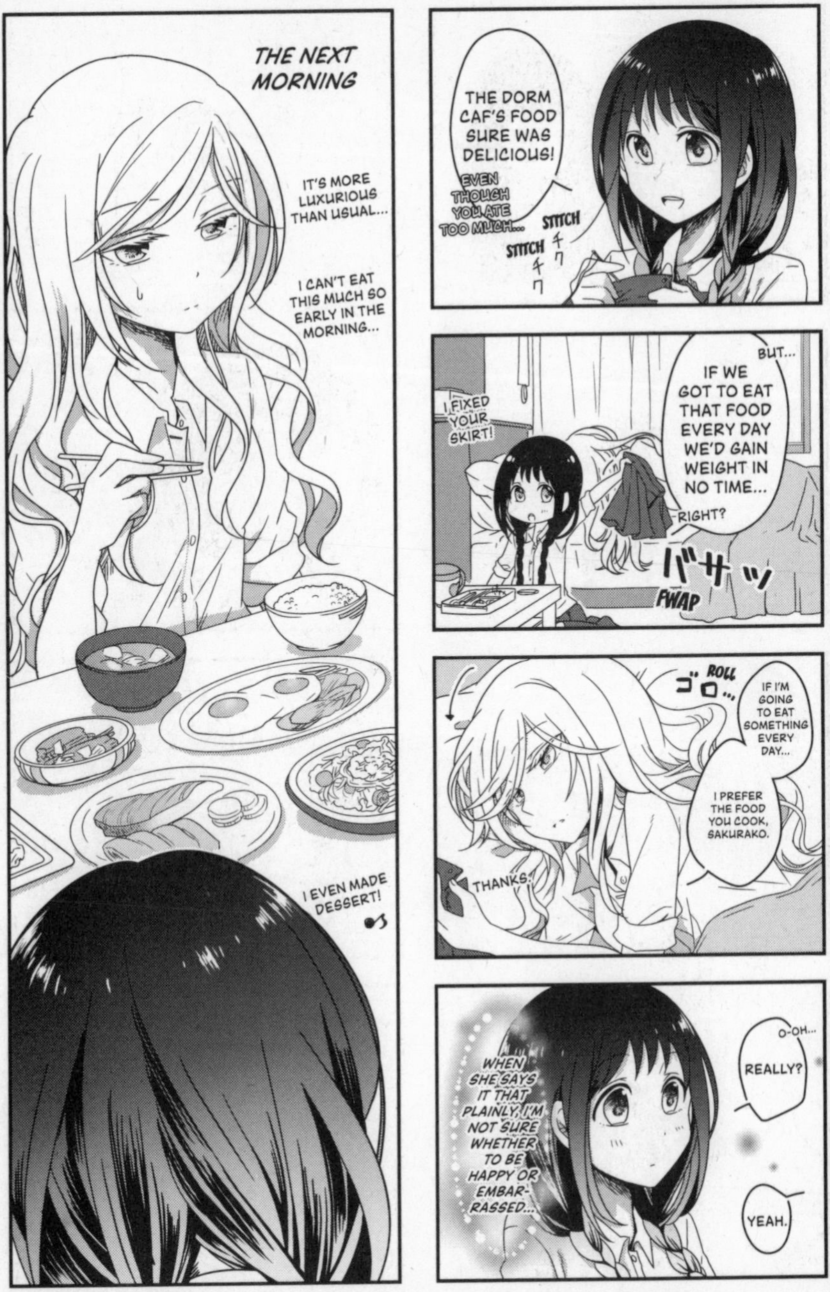
THE DORM CAF'S FOOD SURE WAS DELICIOUS!
EVEN THOUGH YOU ATE TOO MUCH...
STITCH
STITCH
チクチク
BUT...
IF WE GOT TO EAT THAT FOOD EVERY DAY WE'D GAIN WEIGHT IN NO TIME...
-RIGHT?
I FIXED YOUR SKIRT!
バサッ
FWAP
ゴロ...
ROLL
IF I'M GOING TO EAT SOMETHING EVERY DAY...
I PREFER THE FOOD YOU COOK, SAKURAKO.
THANKS.
O-OH...
REALLY?
WHEN SHE SAYS IT THAT PLAINLY, I'M NOT SURE WHETHER TO BE HAPPY OR EMBARRASSED...
YEAH.
THE NEXT MORNING
IT'S MORE LUXURIOUS THAN USUAL...
I CAN'T EAT THIS MUCH SO EARLY IN THE MORNING...
I EVEN MADE DESSERT!

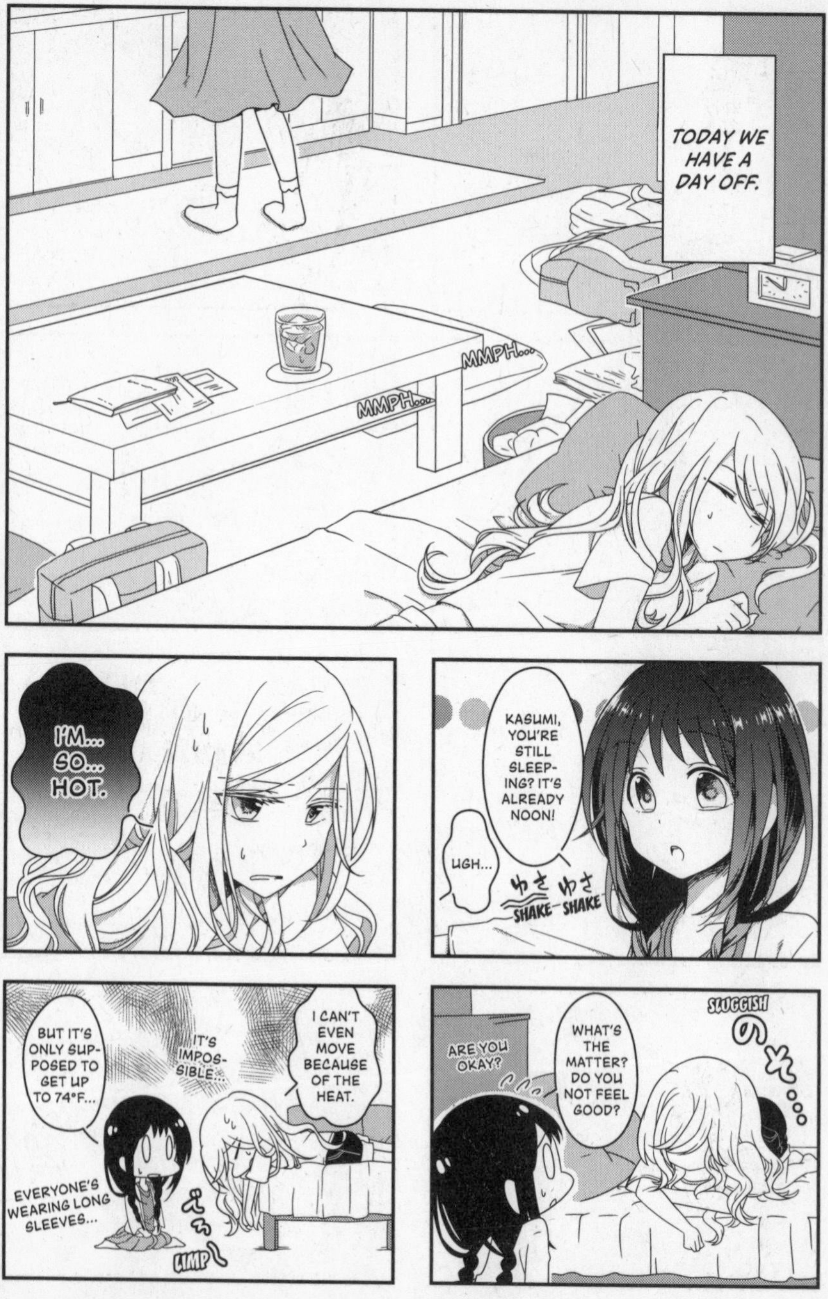
TODAY WE HAVE A DAY OFF.
MMPH...
MMPH...
KASUMI, YOU'RE STILL SLEEPING? IT'S ALREADY NOON!
UGH...
ゆさ ゆさ
SHAKE-SHAKE
I'M... SO... HOT.
SLUGGISH
のそ...
WHAT'S THE MATTER? DO YOU NOT FEEL GOOD?
ARE YOU OKAY?
I CAN'T EVEN MOVE BECAUSE OF THE HEAT.
IT'S IMPOSSIBLE...
BUT IT'S ONLY SUPPOSED TO GET UP TO 74°F...
EVERYONE'S WEARING LONG SLEEVES...
LIMP

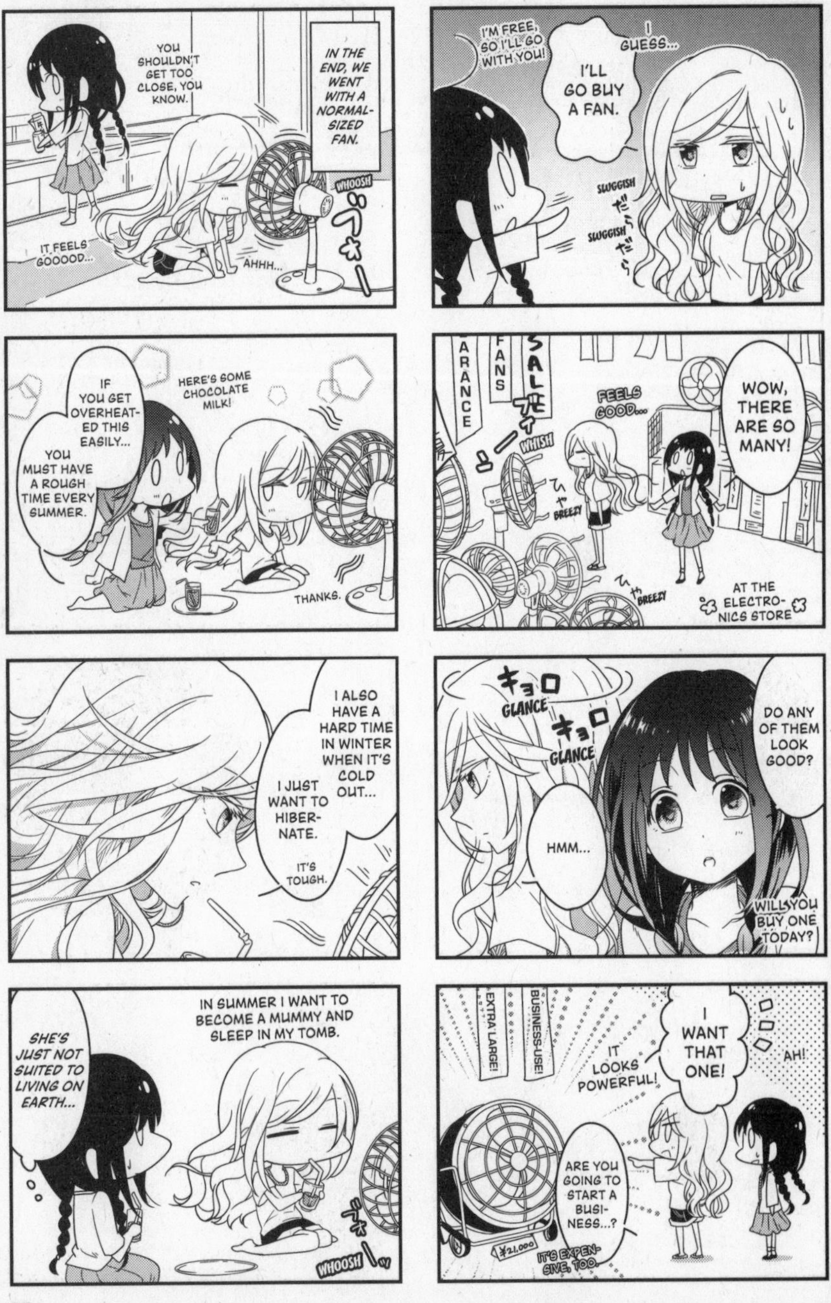
I GUESS...
I'LL GO BUY A FAN.
I'M FREE, SO I'LL GO WITH YOU!
SLUGGISH
SLUGGISH
WOW, THERE ARE SO MANY!
FEELS GOOD...
WHISH
BREEZY
BREEZY
AT THE ELECTRONICS STORE
FANS
CLEARANCE
SALE
GLANCE
GLANCE
DO ANY OF THEM LOOK GOOD?
HMM...
WILL YOU BUY ONE TODAY?
I WANT THAT ONE!
AH!
IT LOOKS POWERFUL!
EXTRA LARGE!
BUSINESS-USE!
ARE YOU GOING TO START A BUSINESS...?
¥21,000
IT'S EXPENSIVE, TOO.
IN THE END, WE WENT WITH A NORMAL-SIZED FAN.
YOU SHOULDN'T GET TOO CLOSE, YOU KNOW.
WHOOSH
IT FEELS GOOOOD...
AHHH...
IF YOU GET OVERHEATED THIS EASILY...
YOU MUST HAVE A ROUGH TIME EVERY SUMMER.
HERE'S SOME CHOCOLATE MILK!
THANKS.
I ALSO HAVE A HARD TIME IN WINTER WHEN IT'S COLD OUT...
I JUST WANT TO HIBERNATE.
IT'S TOUGH.
IN SUMMER I WANT TO BECOME A MUMMY AND SLEEP IN MY TOMB.
SHE'S JUST NOT SUITED TO LIVING ON EARTH...
WHOOSH

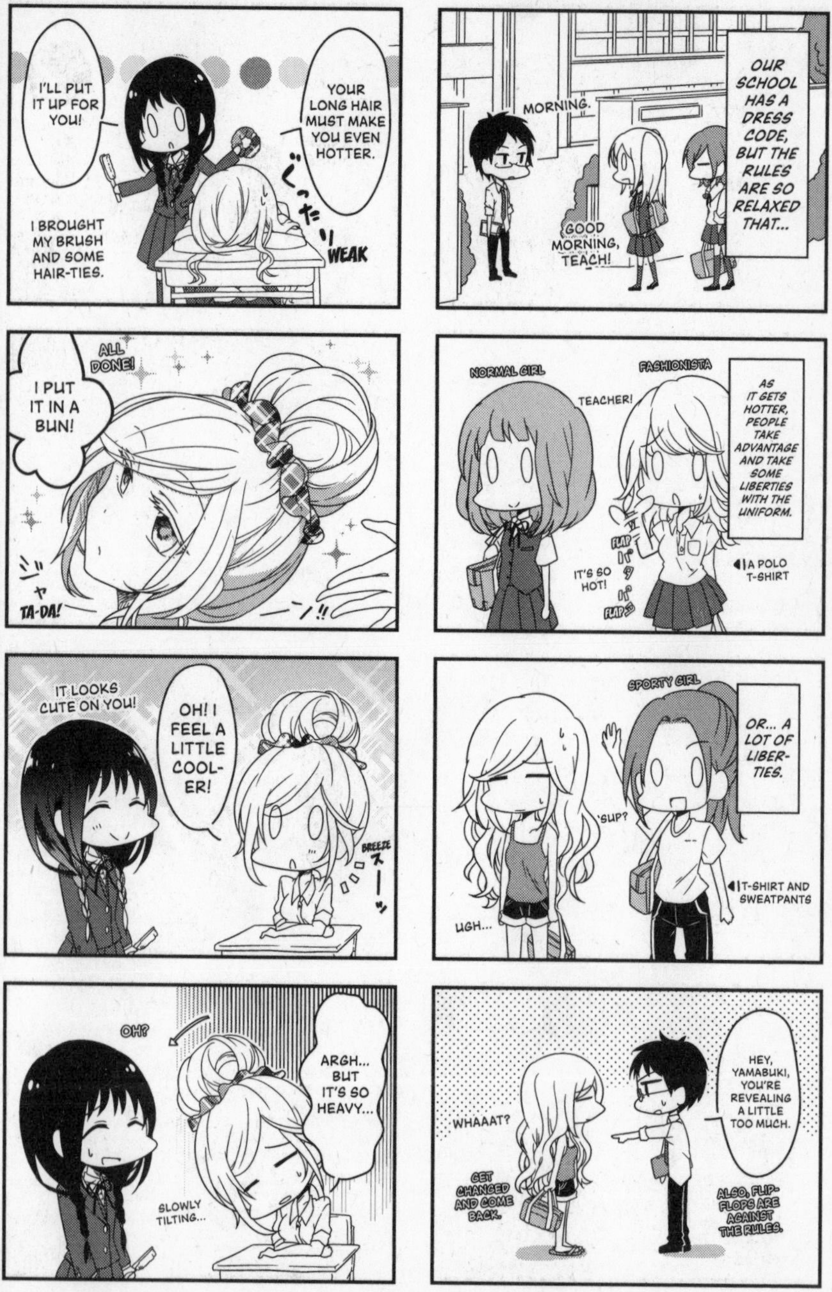
OUR SCHOOL HAS A DRESS CODE, BUT THE RULES ARE SO RELAXED THAT...
MORNING.
GOOD MORNING, TEACH!
AS IT GETS HOTTER, PEOPLE TAKE ADVANTAGE AND TAKE SOME LIBERTIES WITH THE UNIFORM.
FASHIONISTA
TEACHER!
NORMAL GIRL
◀A POLO T-SHIRT
FLAP パタパタ FLAP
IT'S SO HOT!
OR... A LOT OF LIBERTIES.
SPORTY GIRL
'SUP?
◀T-SHIRT AND SWEATPANTS
UGH...
HEY, YAMABUKI, YOU'RE REVEALING A LITTLE TOO MUCH.
ALSO, FLIP-FLOPS ARE AGAINST THE RULES.
WHAAAT?
GET CHANGED AND COME BACK.
YOUR LONG HAIR MUST MAKE YOU EVEN HOTTER.
I'LL PUT IT UP FOR YOU!
ぐったー WEAK
I BROUGHT MY BRUSH AND SOME HAIR-TIES.
ALL DONE!
I PUT IT IN A BUN!
ジャーン!! TA-DA!
OH! I FEEL A LITTLE COOLER!
IT LOOKS CUTE ON YOU!
BREEZE スーーッ
ARGH... BUT IT'S SO HEAVY...
OH?
SLOWLY TILTING...

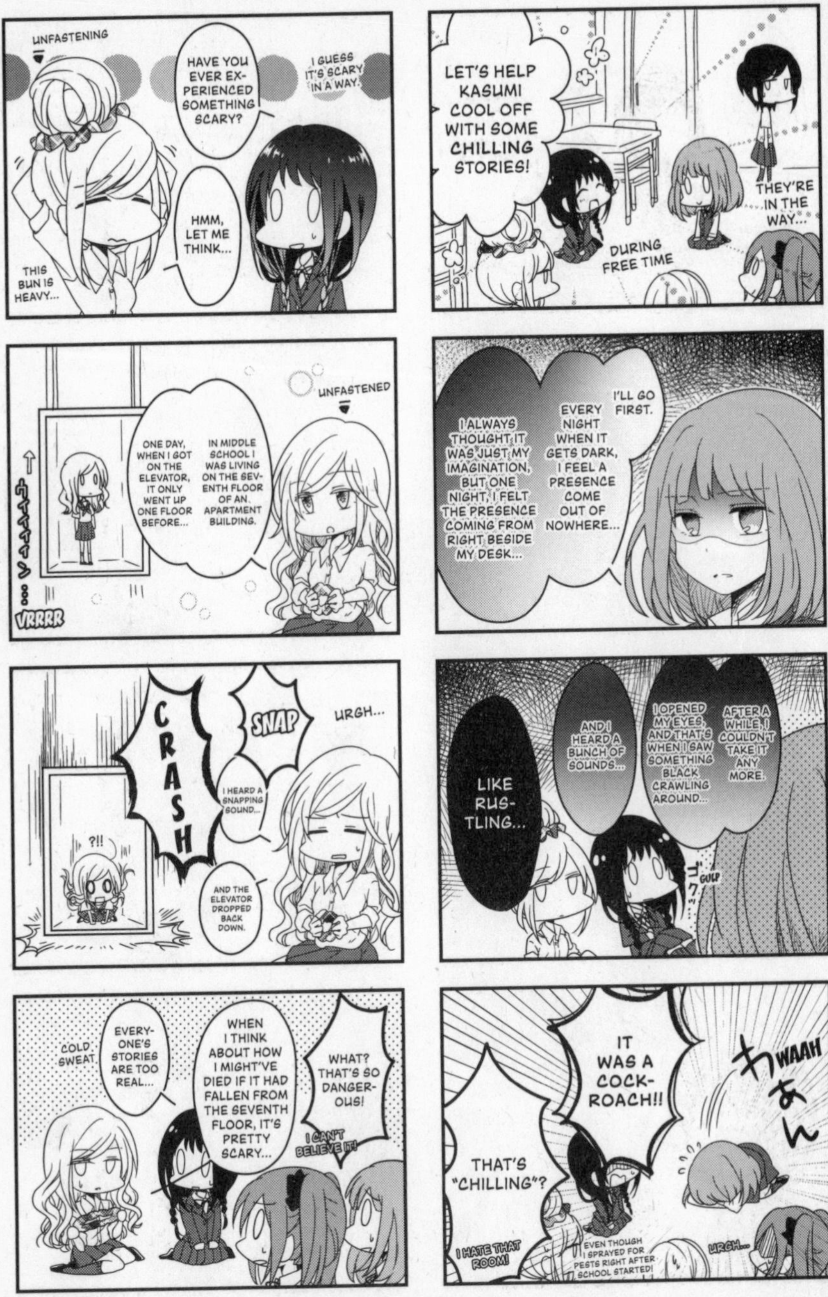
LET'S HELP KASUMI COOL OFF WITH SOME CHILLING STORIES!
THEY'RE IN THE WAY...
DURING FREE TIME
I'LL GO FIRST.
EVERY NIGHT WHEN IT GETS DARK, I FEEL A PRESENCE COME OUT OF NOWHERE...
I ALWAYS THOUGHT IT WAS JUST MY IMAGINATION, BUT ONE NIGHT, I FELT THE PRESENCE COMING FROM RIGHT BESIDE MY DESK...
AFTER A WHILE, I COULDN'T TAKE IT ANY MORE.
I OPENED MY EYES, AND THAT'S WHEN I SAW SOMETHING BLACK CRAWLING AROUND...
AND I HEARD A BUNCH OF SOUNDS...
LIKE RUS-TLING...
GULP
WAAH
IT WAS A COCK-ROACH!!
THAT'S "CHILLING"?
URGH...
EVEN THOUGH I SPRAYED FOR PESTS RIGHT AFTER SCHOOL STARTED!
I HATE THAT ROOM!
I GUESS IT'S SCARY IN A WAY.
HAVE YOU EVER EX-PERIENCED SOMETHING SCARY?
UNFASTENING
HMM, LET ME THINK...
THIS BUN IS HEAVY...
UNFASTENED
IN MIDDLE SCHOOL I WAS LIVING ON THE SEV-ENTH FLOOR OF AN APARTMENT BUILDING.
ONE DAY, WHEN I GOT ON THE ELEVATOR, IT ONLY WENT UP ONE FLOOR BEFORE...
VRRRR
URGH...
SNAP
CRASH
I HEARD A SNAPPING SOUND...
?!!
AND THE ELEVATOR DROPPED BACK DOWN.
WHAT? THAT'S SO DANGER-OUS!
I CAN'T BELIEVE IT!
WHEN I THINK ABOUT HOW I MIGHT'VE DIED IF IT HAD FALLEN FROM THE SEVENTH FLOOR, IT'S PRETTY SCARY...
EVERY-ONE'S STORIES ARE TOO REAL...
COLD SWEAT

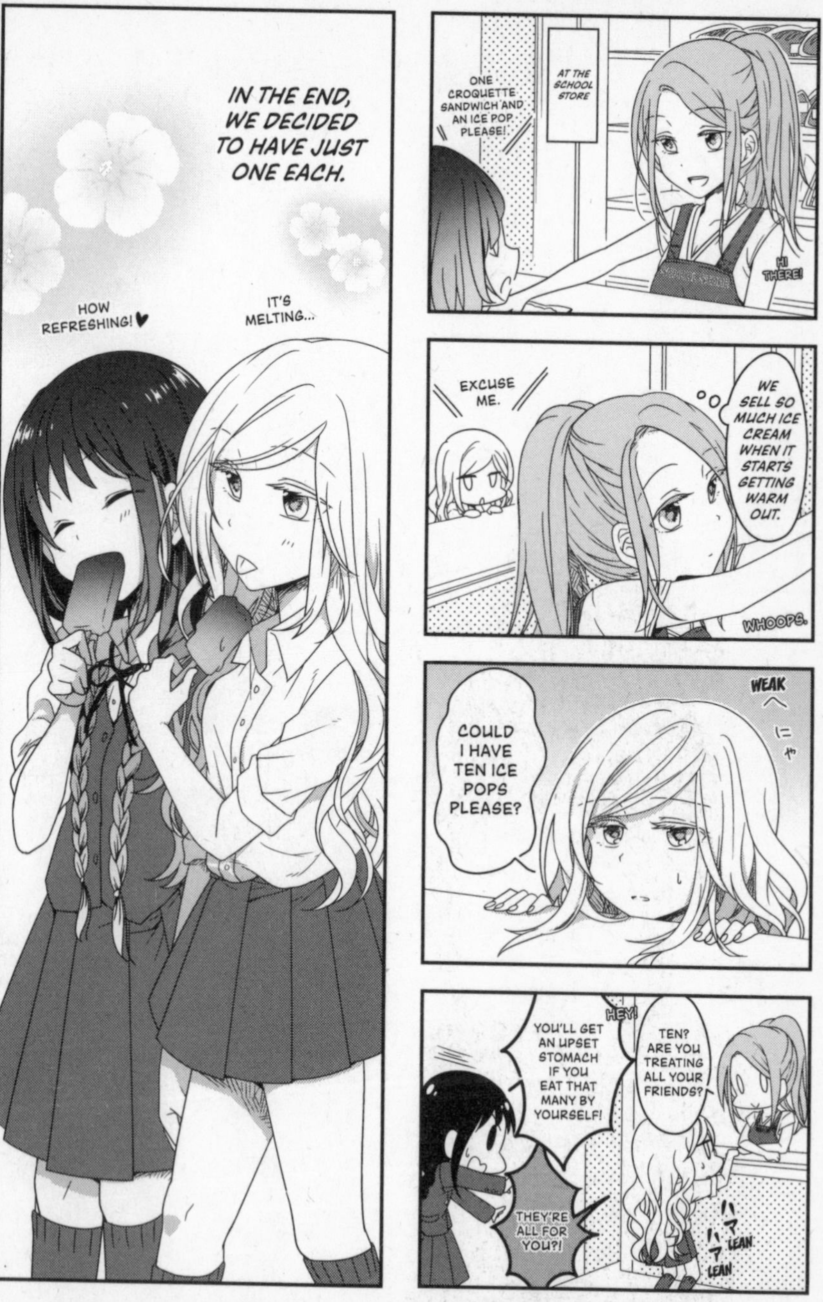
AT THE SCHOOL STORE
ONE CROQUETTE SANDWICH AND AN ICE POP, PLEASE!
HI THERE!
WE SELL SO MUCH ICE CREAM WHEN IT STARTS GETTING WARM OUT.
EXCUSE ME.
WHOOPS.
WEAK
COULD I HAVE TEN ICE POPS PLEASE?
TEN? ARE YOU TREATING ALL YOUR FRIENDS?
HEY!
YOU'LL GET AN UPSET STOMACH IF YOU EAT THAT MANY BY YOURSELF!
THEY'RE ALL FOR YOU?!
LEAN LEAN
IN THE END, WE DECIDED TO HAVE JUST ONE EACH.
IT'S MELTING...
HOW REFRESHING! ♥

Illustration gallery

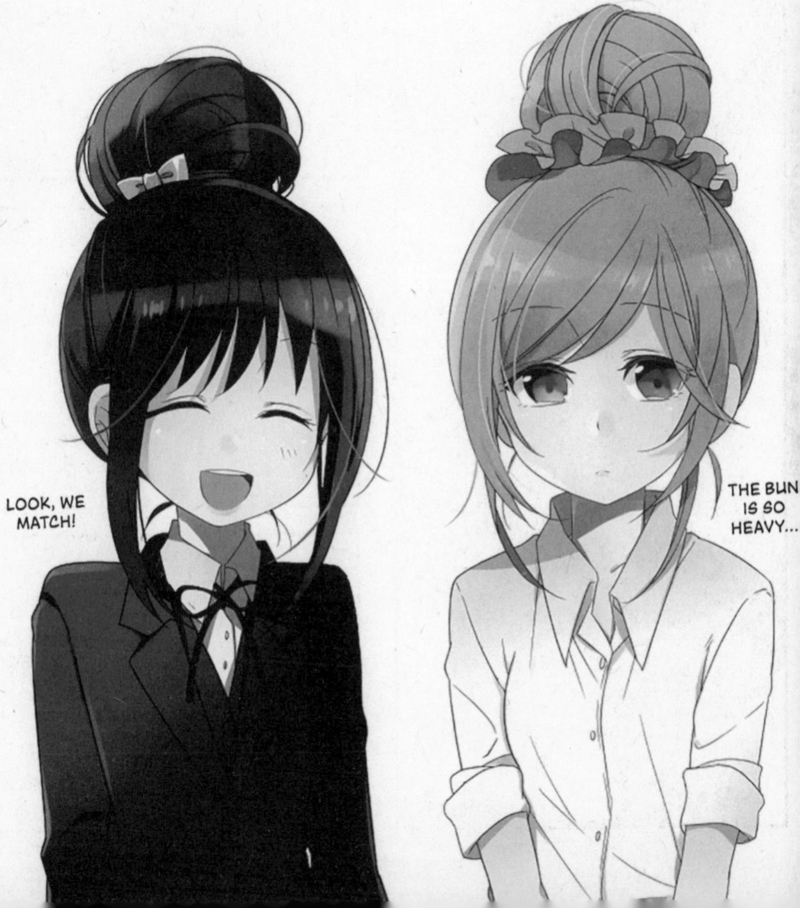
THE BUN IS SO HEAVY...
LOOK, WE MATCH!

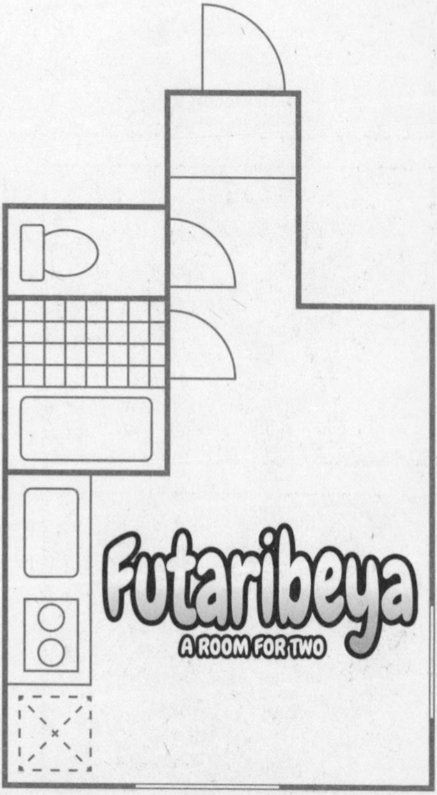
Futaribeya
A ROOM FOR TWO

Chapter 4

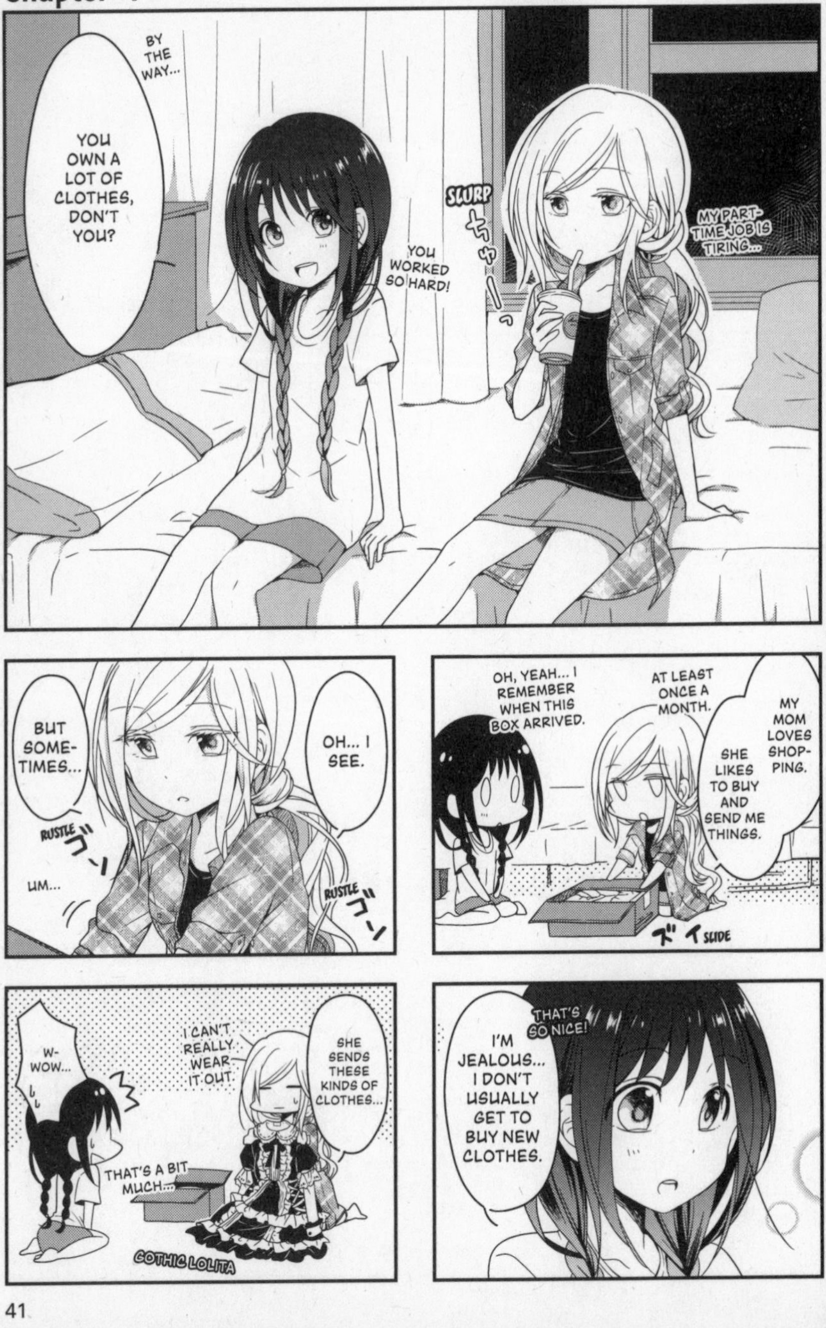
MY PART-TIME JOB IS TIRING...
SLURP
YOU WORKED SO HARD!
BY THE WAY...
YOU OWN A LOT OF CLOTHES, DON'T YOU?
MY MOM LOVES SHOPPING.
SHE LIKES TO BUY AND SEND ME THINGS.
AT LEAST ONCE A MONTH.
OH, YEAH... I REMEMBER WHEN THIS BOX ARRIVED.
SLIDE
OH... I SEE.
BUT SOME-TIMES...
RUSTLE
RUSTLE
UM...
THAT'S SO NICE!
I'M JEALOUS... I DON'T USUALLY GET TO BUY NEW CLOTHES.
SHE SENDS THESE KINDS OF CLOTHES...
I CAN'T REALLY WEAR IT OUT.
W-WOW...
THAT'S A BIT MUCH...
GOTHIC LOLITA

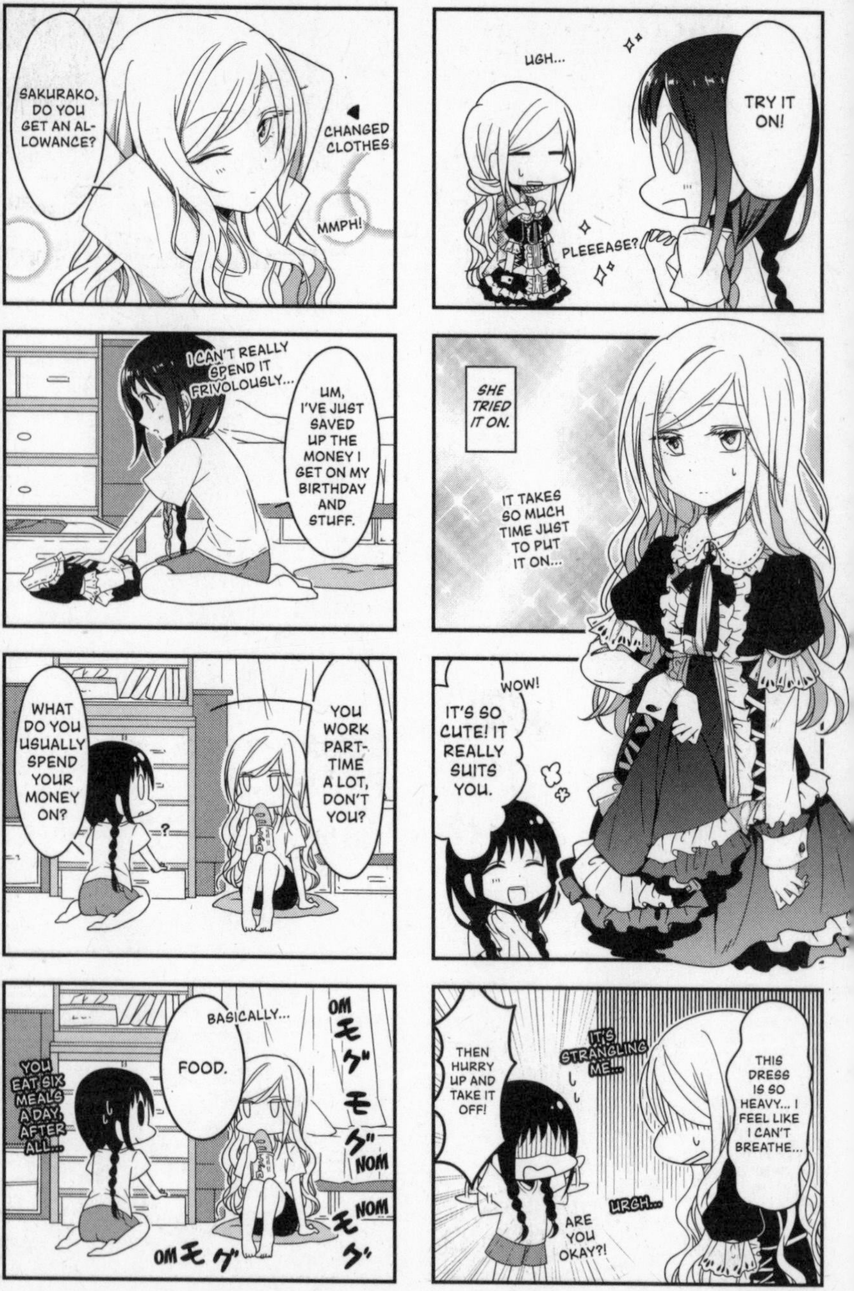
TRY IT ON!
UGH...
PLEEEASE?
SHE TRIED IT ON.
IT TAKES SO MUCH TIME JUST TO PUT IT ON...
WOW!
IT'S SO CUTE! IT REALLY SUITS YOU.
THIS DRESS IS SO HEAVY... I FEEL LIKE I CAN'T BREATHE...
IT'S STRANGLING ME...
THEN HURRY UP AND TAKE IT OFF!
URGH...
ARE YOU OKAY?!
CHANGED CLOTHES
SAKURAKO, DO YOU GET AN AL-LOWANCE?
MMPH!
UM, I'VE JUST SAVED UP THE MONEY I GET ON MY BIRTHDAY AND STUFF.
I CAN'T REALLY SPEND IT FRIVOLOUSLY...
YOU WORK PART-TIME A LOT, DON'T YOU?
WHAT DO YOU USUALLY SPEND YOUR MONEY ON?
OM モグ モグ NOM
BASICALLY...
FOOD.
NOM モグ
OM モグ
YOU EAT SIX MEALS A DAY, AFTER ALL...

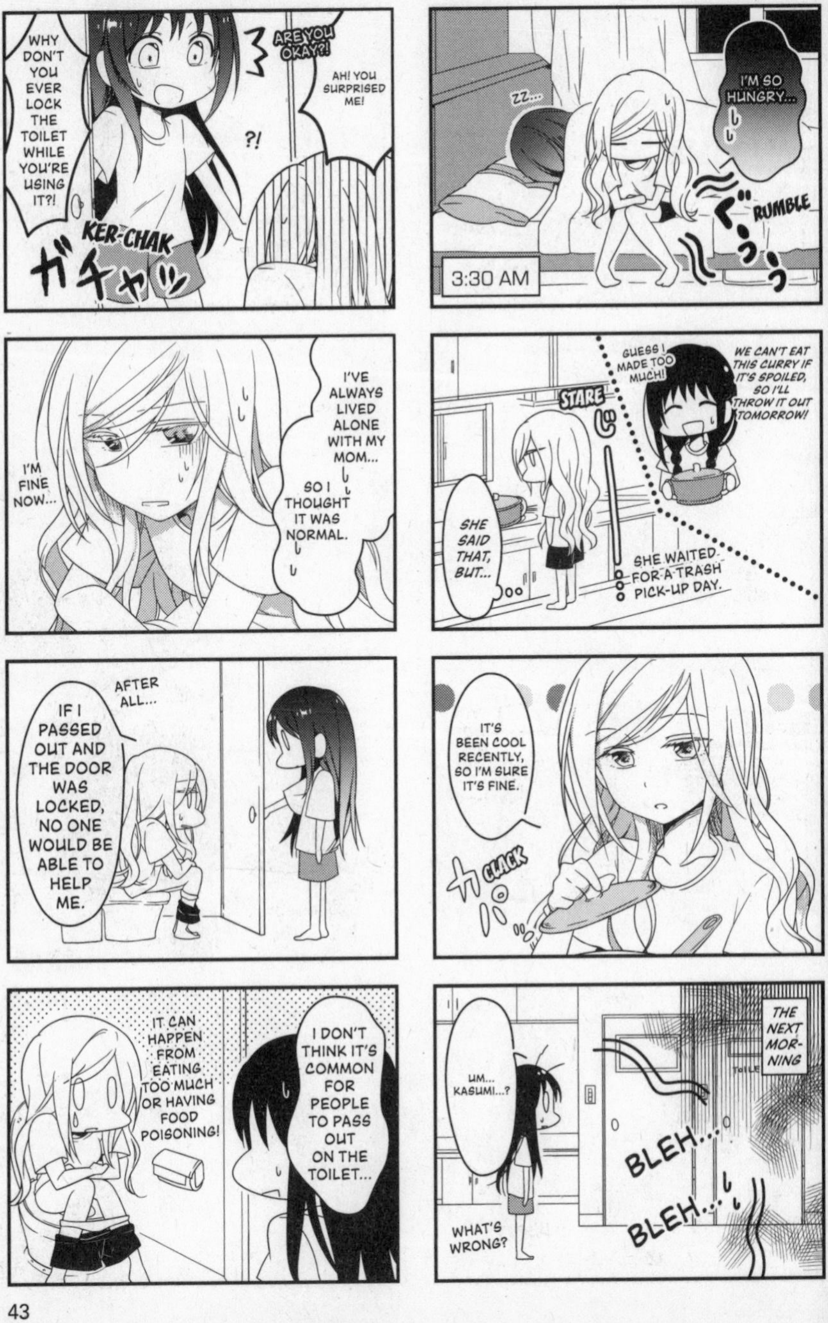
I'M SO HUNGRY...
ZZ...
RUMBLE
3:30 AM
WE CAN'T EAT THIS CURRY IF IT'S SPOILED, SO I'LL THROW IT OUT TOMORROW!
GUESS I MADE TOO MUCH!
STARE
SHE SAID THAT, BUT...
SHE WAITED FOR A TRASH PICK-UP DAY.
IT'S BEEN COOL RECENTLY, SO I'M SURE IT'S FINE.
CLACK
THE NEXT MORNING
BLEH...
BLEH...
UM... KASUMI...?
WHAT'S WRONG?
ARE YOU OKAY?!
AH! YOU SURPRISED ME!
WHY DON'T YOU EVER LOCK THE TOILET WHILE YOU'RE USING IT?!
?!
KER-CHAK
ガチャッ
I'VE ALWAYS LIVED ALONE WITH MY MOM...
SO I THOUGHT IT WAS NORMAL.
I'M FINE NOW...
AFTER ALL...
IF I PASSED OUT AND THE DOOR WAS LOCKED, NO ONE WOULD BE ABLE TO HELP ME.
I DON'T THINK IT'S COMMON FOR PEOPLE TO PASS OUT ON THE TOILET...
IT CAN HAPPEN FROM EATING TOO MUCH OR HAVING FOOD POISONING!

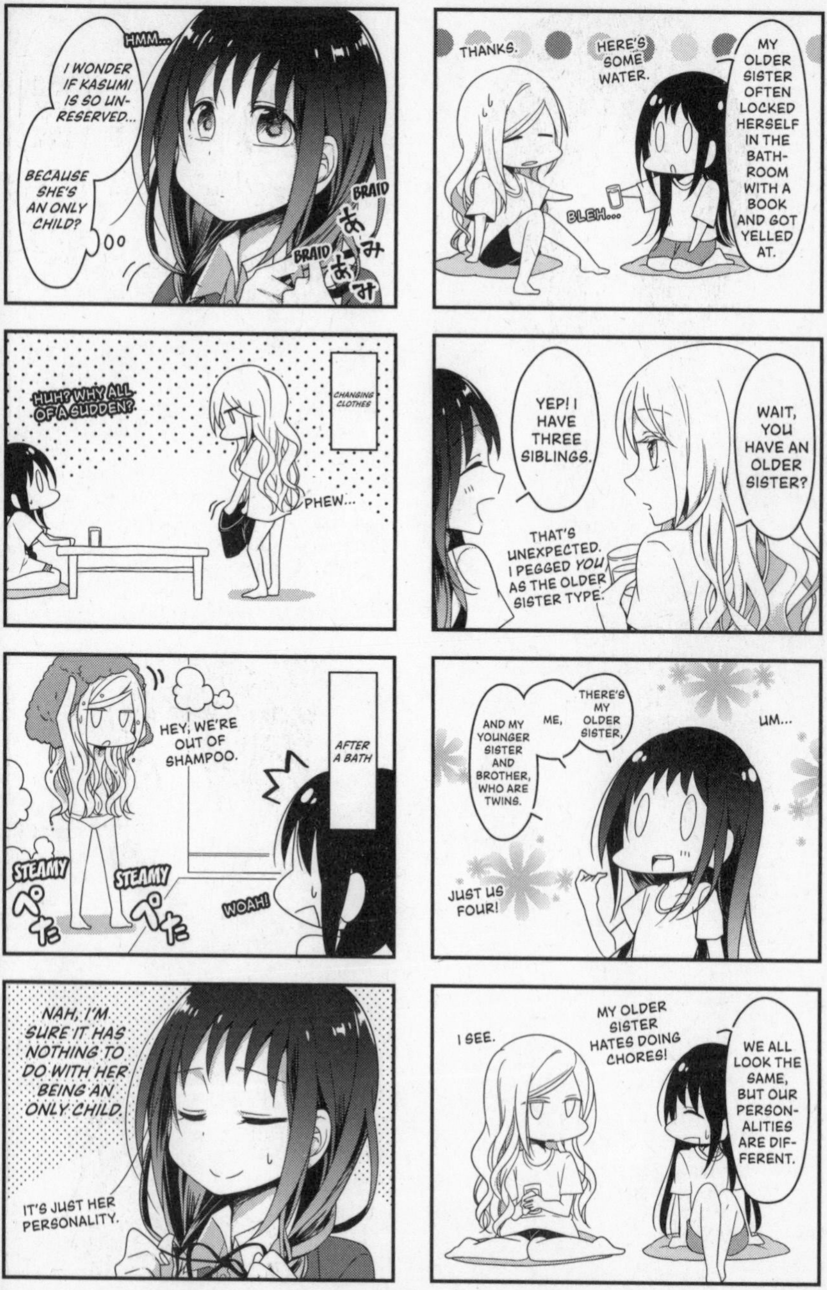

MY OLDER SISTER OFTEN LOCKED HERSELF IN THE BATHROOM WITH A BOOK AND GOT YELLED AT.
HERE'S SOME WATER.
THANKS.
BLEH...
WAIT, YOU HAVE AN OLDER SISTER?
YEP! I HAVE THREE SIBLINGS.
THAT'S UNEXPECTED. I PEGGED YOU AS THE OLDER SISTER TYPE.
UM...
THERE'S MY OLDER SISTER,
ME,
AND MY YOUNGER SISTER AND BROTHER, WHO ARE TWINS.
JUST US FOUR!
WE ALL LOOK THE SAME, BUT OUR PERSONALITIES ARE DIFFERENT.
MY OLDER SISTER HATES DOING CHORES!
I SEE.
HMM...
I WONDER IF KASUMI IS SO UNRESERVED...
BECAUSE SHE'S AN ONLY CHILD?
BRAID
あみ
BRAID
あみ
CHANGING CLOTHES
HUH? WHY ALL OF A SUDDEN?
PHEW...
AFTER A BATH
HEY, WE'RE OUT OF SHAMPOO.
WOAH!
STEAMY
ぺた
STEAMY
ぺた
NAH, I'M SURE IT HAS NOTHING TO DO WITH HER BEING AN ONLY CHILD.
IT'S JUST HER PERSONALITY.

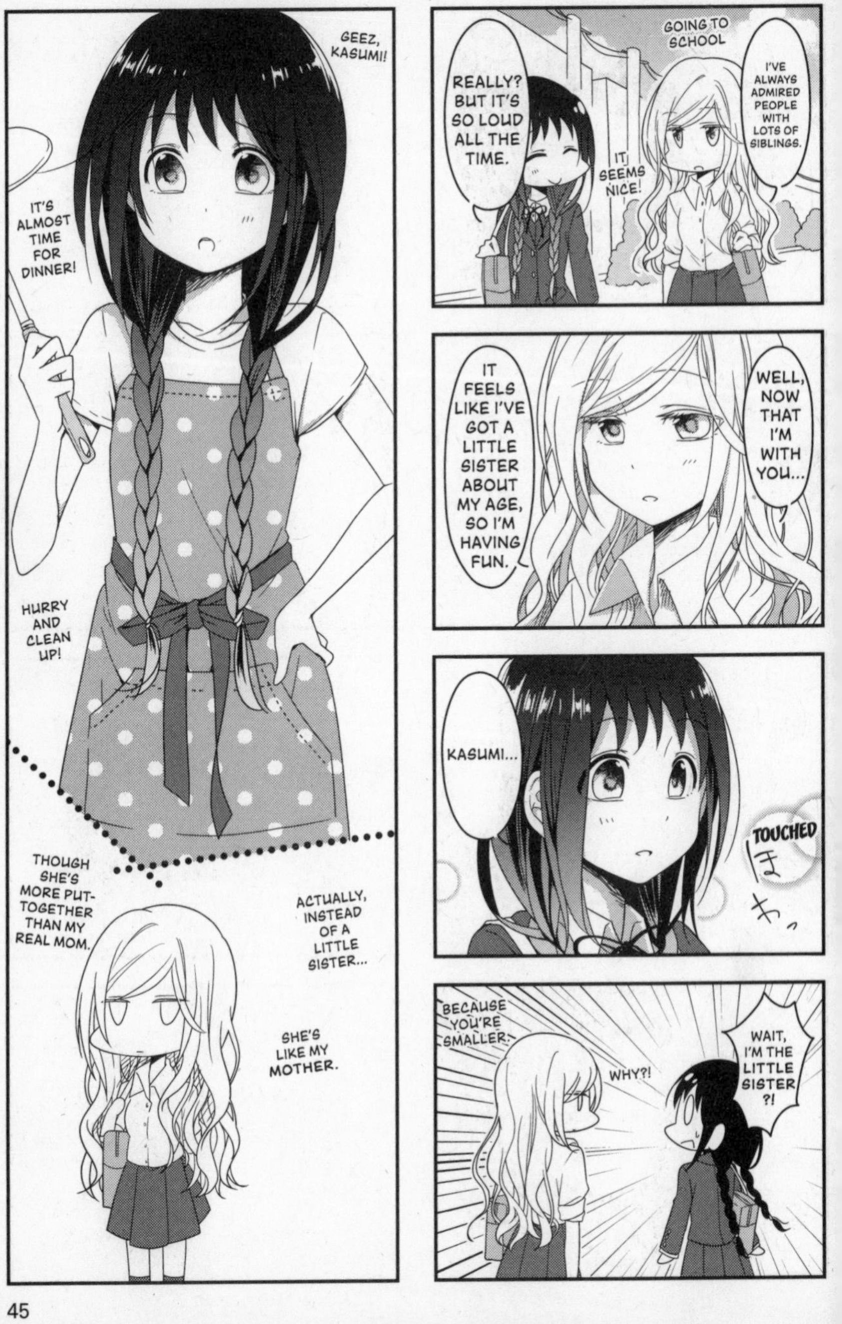
GOING TO SCHOOL
I'VE ALWAYS ADMIRED PEOPLE WITH LOTS OF SIBLINGS.
IT SEEMS NICE!
REALLY? BUT IT'S SO LOUD ALL THE TIME.
WELL, NOW THAT I'M WITH YOU...
IT FEELS LIKE I'VE GOT A LITTLE SISTER ABOUT MY AGE, SO I'M HAVING FUN.
TOUCHED
KASUMI...
WAIT, I'M THE LITTLE SISTER ?!
WHY?!
BECAUSE YOU'RE SMALLER.
GEEZ, KASUMI!
IT'S ALMOST TIME FOR DINNER!
HURRY AND CLEAN UP!
ACTUALLY, INSTEAD OF A LITTLE SISTER...
SHE'S LIKE MY MOTHER.
THOUGH SHE'S MORE PUT-TOGETHER THAN MY REAL MOM.

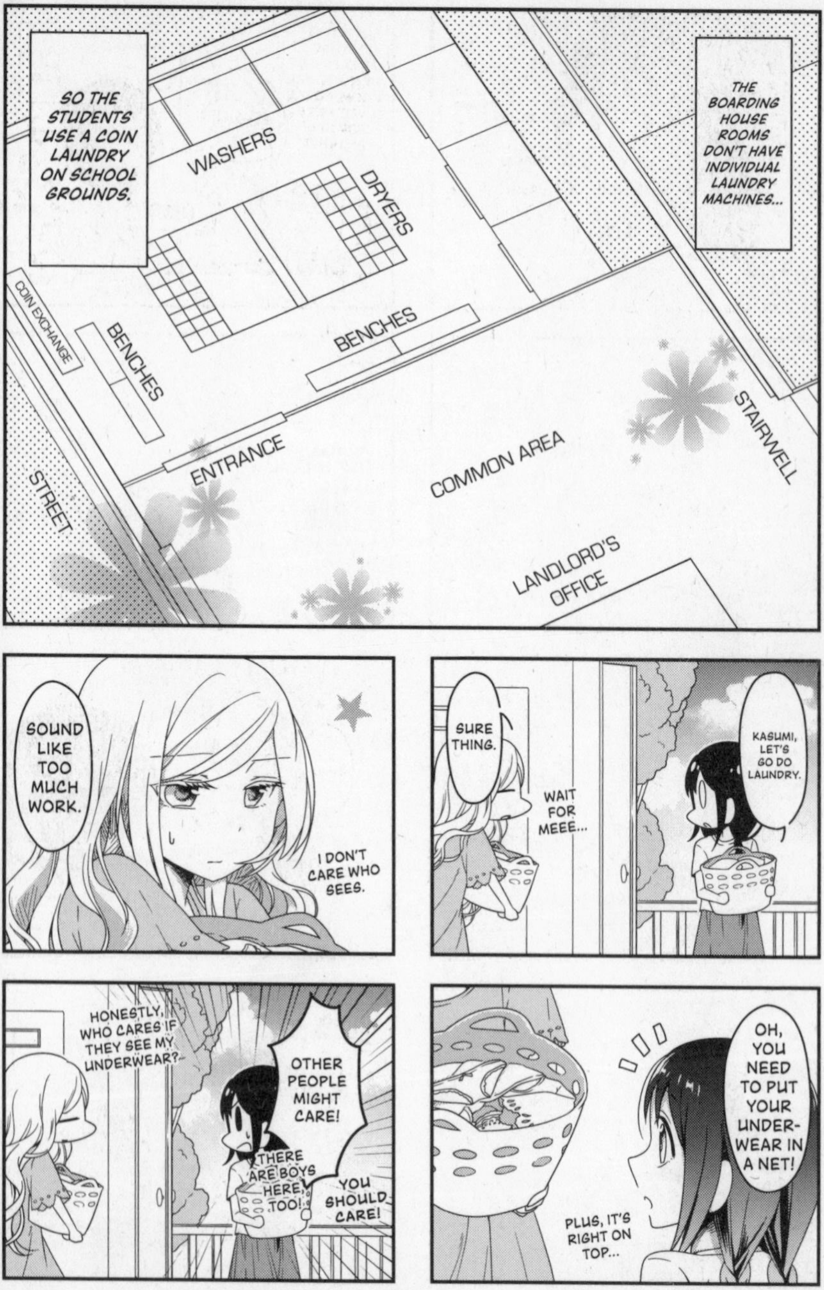
THE BOARDING HOUSE ROOMS DON'T HAVE INDIVIDUAL LAUNDRY MACHINES...
SO THE STUDENTS USE A COIN LAUNDRY ON SCHOOL GROUNDS.
WASHERS
DRYERS
STAIRWELL
BENCHES
COIN EXCHANGE
BENCHES
ENTRANCE
COMMON AREA
STREET
LANDLORD'S OFFICE
KASUMI, LET'S GO DO LAUNDRY.
SURE THING.
WAIT FOR MEEE...
SOUND LIKE TOO MUCH WORK.
I DON'T CARE WHO SEES.
OH, YOU NEED TO PUT YOUR UNDER-WEAR IN A NET!
PLUS, IT'S RIGHT ON TOP...
HONESTLY, WHO CARES IF THEY SEE MY UNDERWEAR?
OTHER PEOPLE MIGHT CARE!
THERE ARE BOYS HERE, TOO!
YOU SHOULD CARE!

*A WORD GAME WHERE THE NEXT WORD MUST START WITH THE LAST LETTER OF THE PREVIOUS WORD

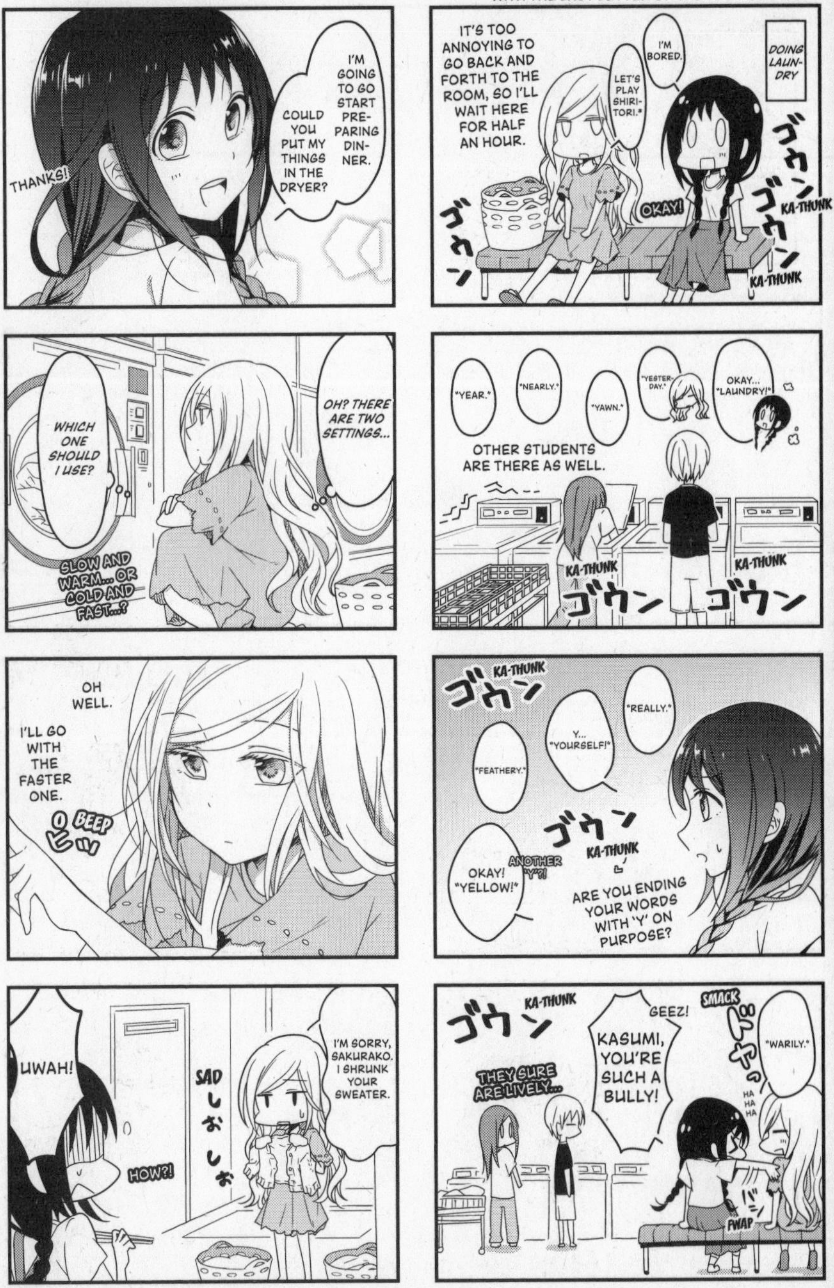
DOING LAUNDRY
I'M BORED.
LET'S PLAY SHIRITORI.*
OKAY!
IT'S TOO ANNOYING TO GO BACK AND FORTH TO THE ROOM, SO I'LL WAIT HERE FOR HALF AN HOUR.
ゴウン ゴウン KA-THUNK
ゴウン KA-THUNK
ゴウン
OKAY... "LAUNDRY!"
"YESTERDAY."
"YAWN."
"NEARLY."
"YEAR."
OTHER STUDENTS ARE THERE AS WELL.
ゴウン KA-THUNK
ゴウン KA-THUNK
ゴウン KA-THUNK
"REALLY."
Y... "YOURSELF!"
"FEATHERY."
ゴウン KA-THUNK
ARE YOU ENDING YOUR WORDS WITH 'Y' ON PURPOSE?
ANOTHER "Y"?!
OKAY! "YELLOW!"
SMACK ドヤッ
"WARILY."
HA HA HA
GEEZ!
KASUMI, YOU'RE SUCH A BULLY!
ゴウン KA-THUNK
THEY SURE ARE LIVELY...
バシッ FWAP
I'M GOING TO GO START PREPARING DINNER.
COULD YOU PUT MY THINGS IN THE DRYER?
THANKS!
OH? THERE ARE TWO SETTINGS...
WHICH ONE SHOULD I USE?
SLOW AND WARM... OR COLD AND FAST...?
OH WELL.
I'LL GO WITH THE FASTER ONE.
ピッ BEEP
I'M SORRY, SAKURAKO. I SHRUNK YOUR SWEATER.
SAD しおしお
UWAH!
HOW?!

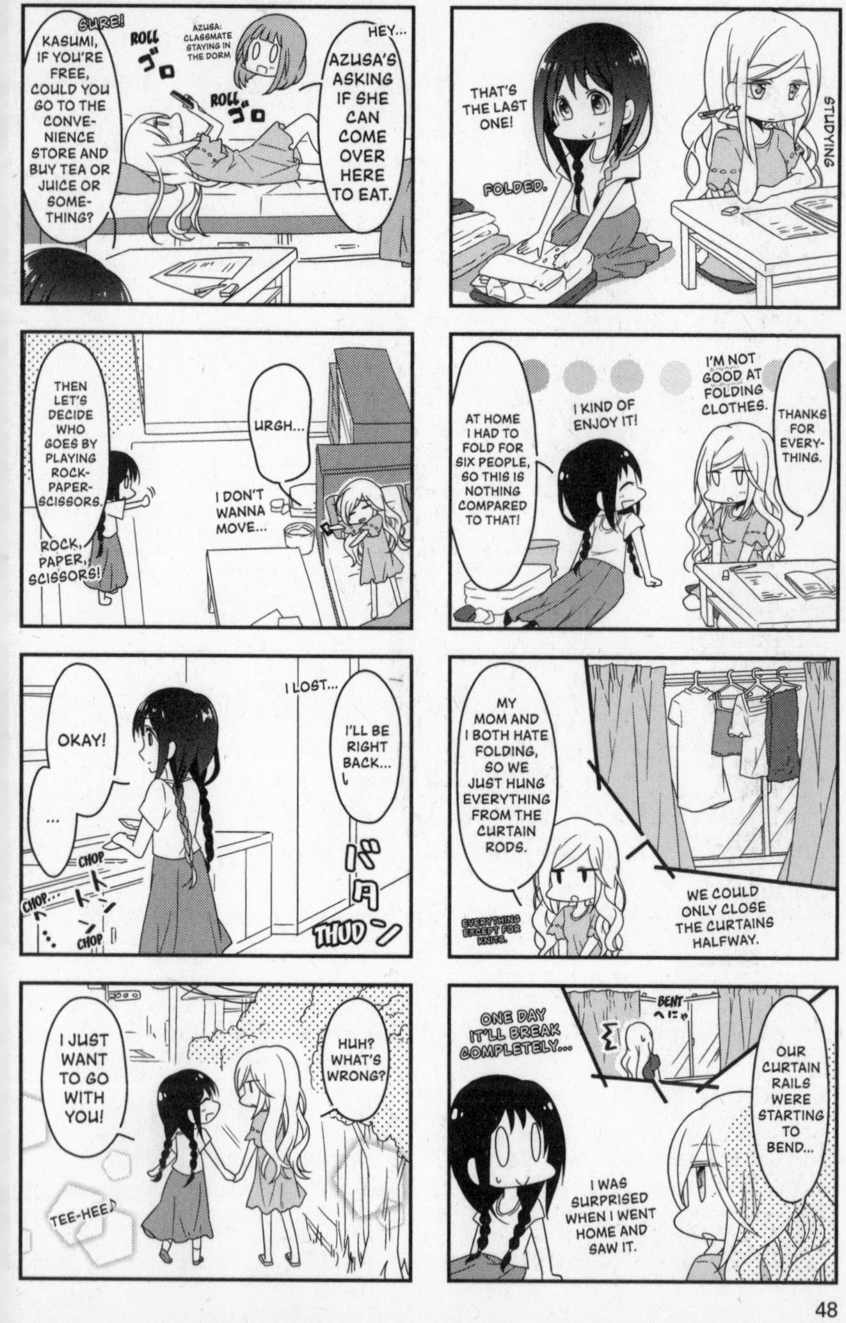

STUDYING
THAT'S THE LAST ONE!
FOLDED.
THANKS FOR EVERYTHING.
I'M NOT GOOD AT FOLDING CLOTHES.
I KIND OF ENJOY IT!
AT HOME I HAD TO FOLD FOR SIX PEOPLE, SO THIS IS NOTHING COMPARED TO THAT!
MY MOM AND I BOTH HATE FOLDING, SO WE JUST HUNG EVERYTHING FROM THE CURTAIN RODS.
WE COULD ONLY CLOSE THE CURTAINS HALFWAY.
EVERYTHING EXCEPT FOR KNITS.
OUR CURTAIN RAILS WERE STARTING TO BEND...
BENT
ONE DAY IT'LL BREAK COMPLETELY...
I WAS SURPRISED WHEN I WENT HOME AND SAW IT.
HEY... AZUSA'S ASKING IF SHE CAN COME OVER HERE TO EAT.
AZUSA: CLASSMATE STAYING IN THE DORM
ROLL
ROLL
SURE!
KASUMI, IF YOU'RE FREE, COULD YOU GO TO THE CONVENIENCE STORE AND BUY TEA OR JUICE OR SOMETHING?
URGH...
I DON'T WANNA MOVE...
THEN LET'S DECIDE WHO GOES BY PLAYING ROCK-PAPER-SCISSORS.
ROCK, PAPER, SCISSORS!
I'LL BE RIGHT BACK...
I LOST...
THUD
OKAY!
...
CHOP
CHOP...
CHOP
HUH? WHAT'S WRONG?
I JUST WANT TO GO WITH YOU!
TEE-HEE

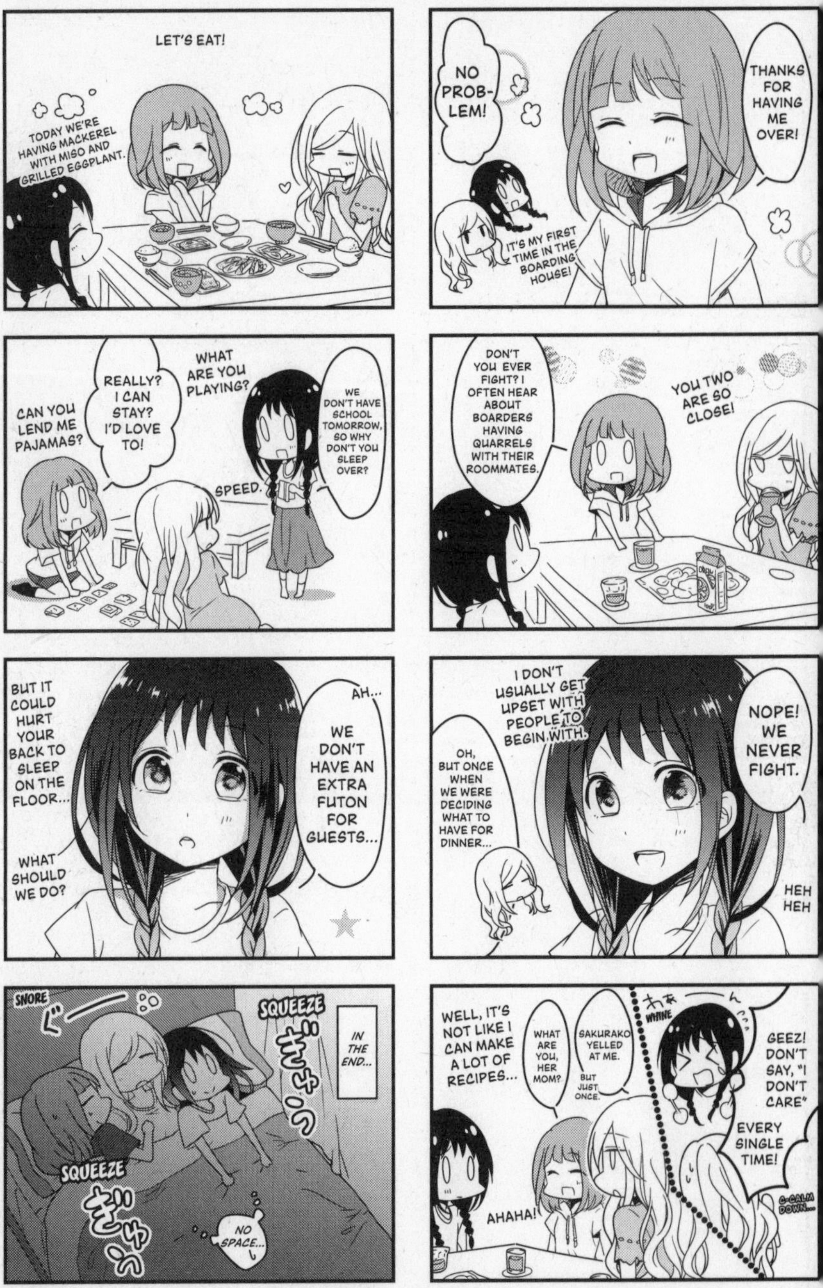
THANKS FOR HAVING ME OVER!
NO PROB-LEM!
IT'S MY FIRST TIME IN THE BOARDING HOUSE!
LET'S EAT!
TODAY WE'RE HAVING MACKEREL WITH MISO AND GRILLED EGGPLANT.
YOU TWO ARE SO CLOSE!
DON'T YOU EVER FIGHT? I OFTEN HEAR ABOUT BOARDERS HAVING QUARRELS WITH THEIR ROOMMATES.
WE DON'T HAVE SCHOOL TOMORROW, SO WHY DON'T YOU SLEEP OVER?
WHAT ARE YOU PLAYING?
REALLY? I CAN STAY? I'D LOVE TO!
SPEED.
CAN YOU LEND ME PAJAMAS?
NOPE! WE NEVER FIGHT.
I DON'T USUALLY GET UPSET WITH PEOPLE TO BEGIN WITH.
OH, BUT ONCE WHEN WE WERE DECIDING WHAT TO HAVE FOR DINNER...
HEH HEH
AH...
WE DON'T HAVE AN EXTRA FUTON FOR GUESTS...
BUT IT COULD HURT YOUR BACK TO SLEEP ON THE FLOOR...
WHAT SHOULD WE DO?
GEEZ! DON'T SAY, "I DON'T CARE" EVERY SINGLE TIME!
わあーん
WHINE
SAKURAKO YELLED AT ME.
BUT JUST ONCE.
WHAT ARE YOU, HER MOM?
WELL, IT'S NOT LIKE I CAN MAKE A LOT OF RECIPES...
C-CALM DOWN...
AHAHA!
SQUEEZE
ぎゅう
IN THE END...
SNORE
ぐー
SQUEEZE
ぎゅう
NO SPACE...

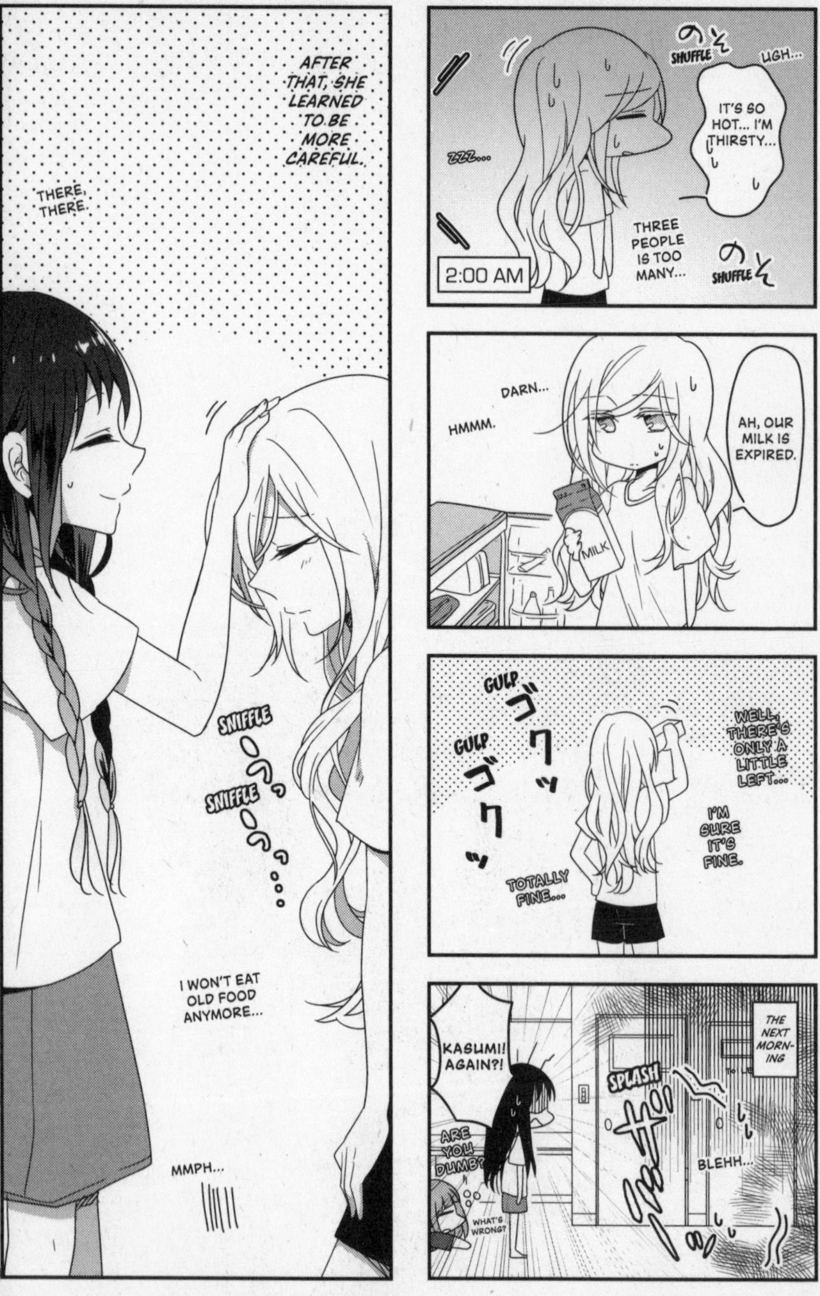
UGH...
SHUFFLE のそ
IT'S SO HOT... I'M THIRSTY...
ZZZ...
THREE PEOPLE IS TOO MANY...
SHUFFLE のそ
2:00 AM
AH, OUR MILK IS EXPIRED.
DARN...
HMMM.
MILK
WELL, THERE'S ONLY A LITTLE LEFT...
I'M SURE IT'S FINE.
GULP ゴクッ
GULP ゴクッ
TOTALLY FINE...
THE NEXT MORNING
BLEHH...
SPLASH
KASUMI! AGAIN?!
ARE YOU DUMB?
WHAT'S WRONG?
AFTER THAT, SHE LEARNED TO BE MORE CAREFUL.
THERE, THERE.
SNIFFLE
SNIFFLE
I WON'T EAT OLD FOOD ANYMORE...
MMPH...

Illustration gallery

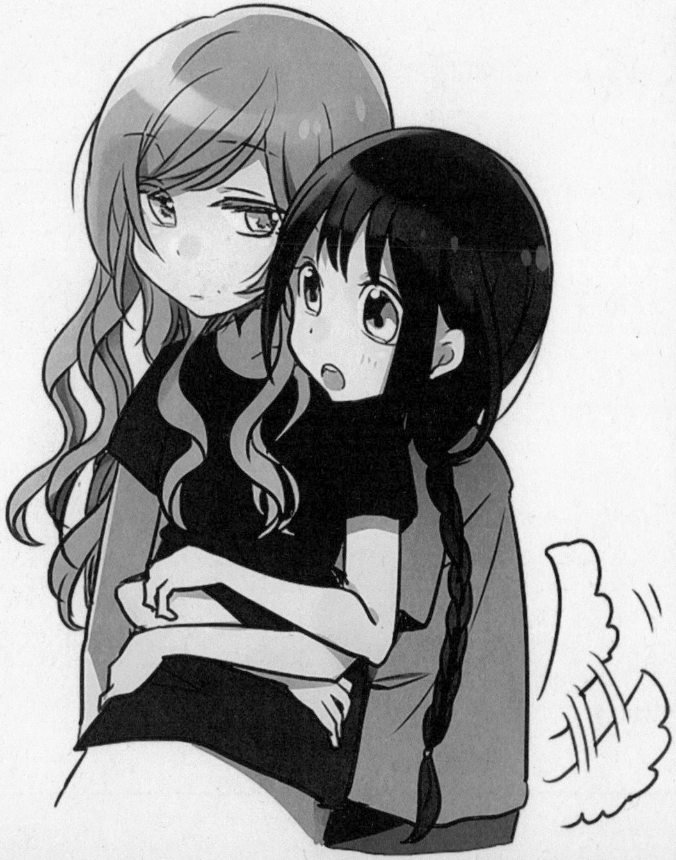

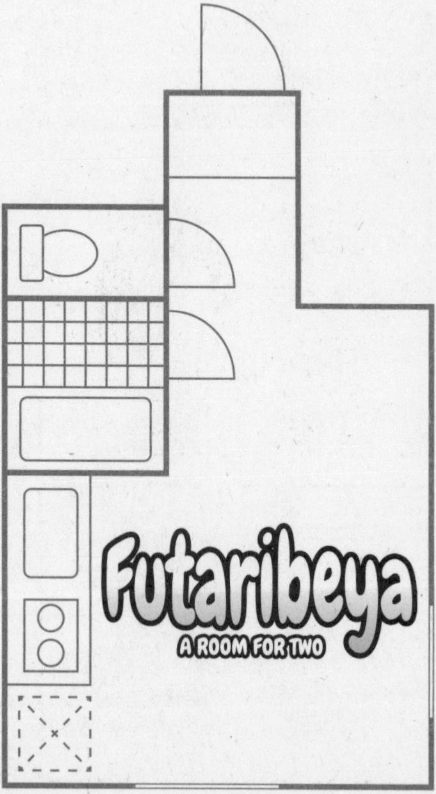
Futaribeya
A ROOM FOR TWO

Chapter 5

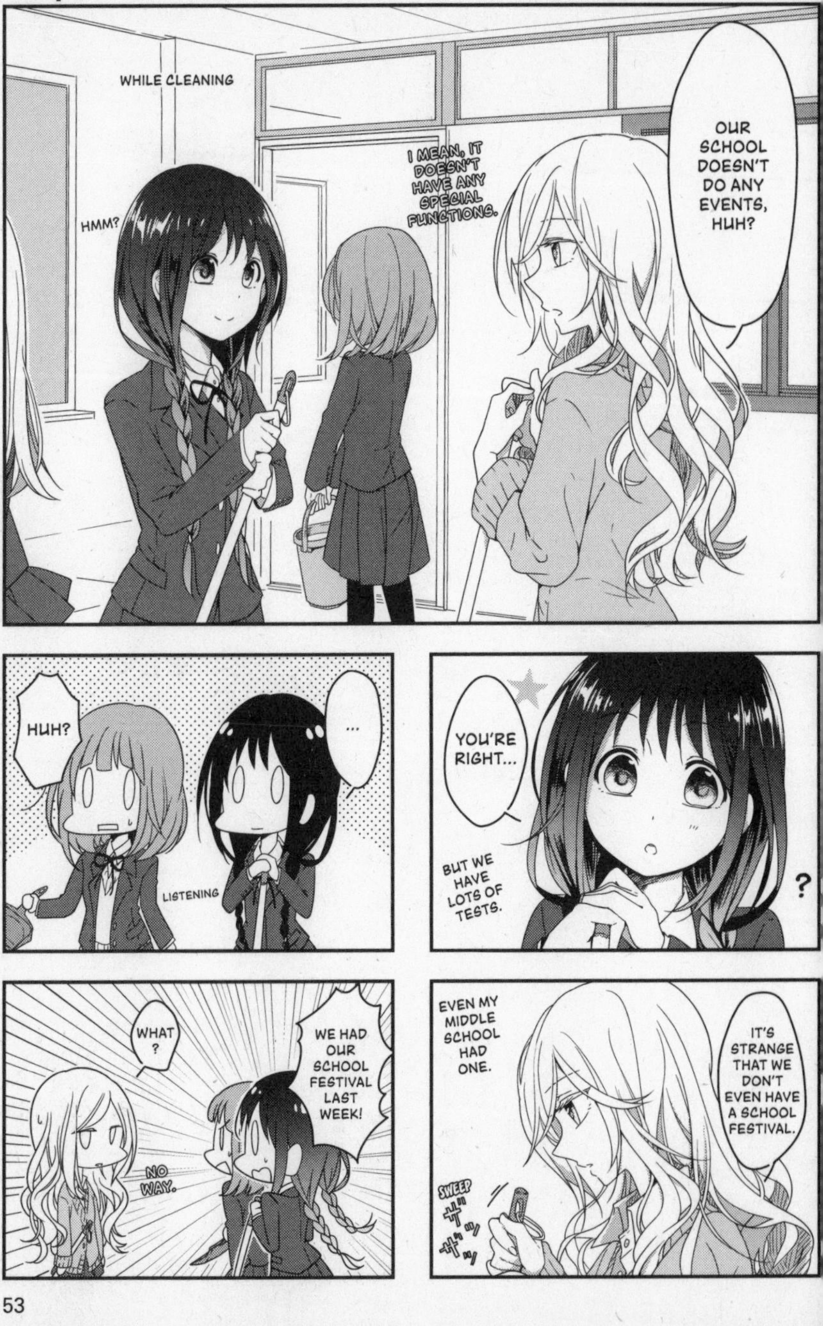

OUR SCHOOL DOESN'T DO ANY EVENTS, HUH?
I MEAN, IT DOESN'T HAVE ANY SPECIAL FUNCTIONS.
WHILE CLEANING
HMM?
YOU'RE RIGHT...
BUT WE HAVE LOTS OF TESTS.
?
...
HUH?
LISTENING
IT'S STRANGE THAT WE DON'T EVEN HAVE A SCHOOL FESTIVAL.
EVEN MY MIDDLE SCHOOL HAD ONE.
SWEEP
WE HAD OUR SCHOOL FESTIVAL LAST WEEK!
WHAT?
NO WAY.

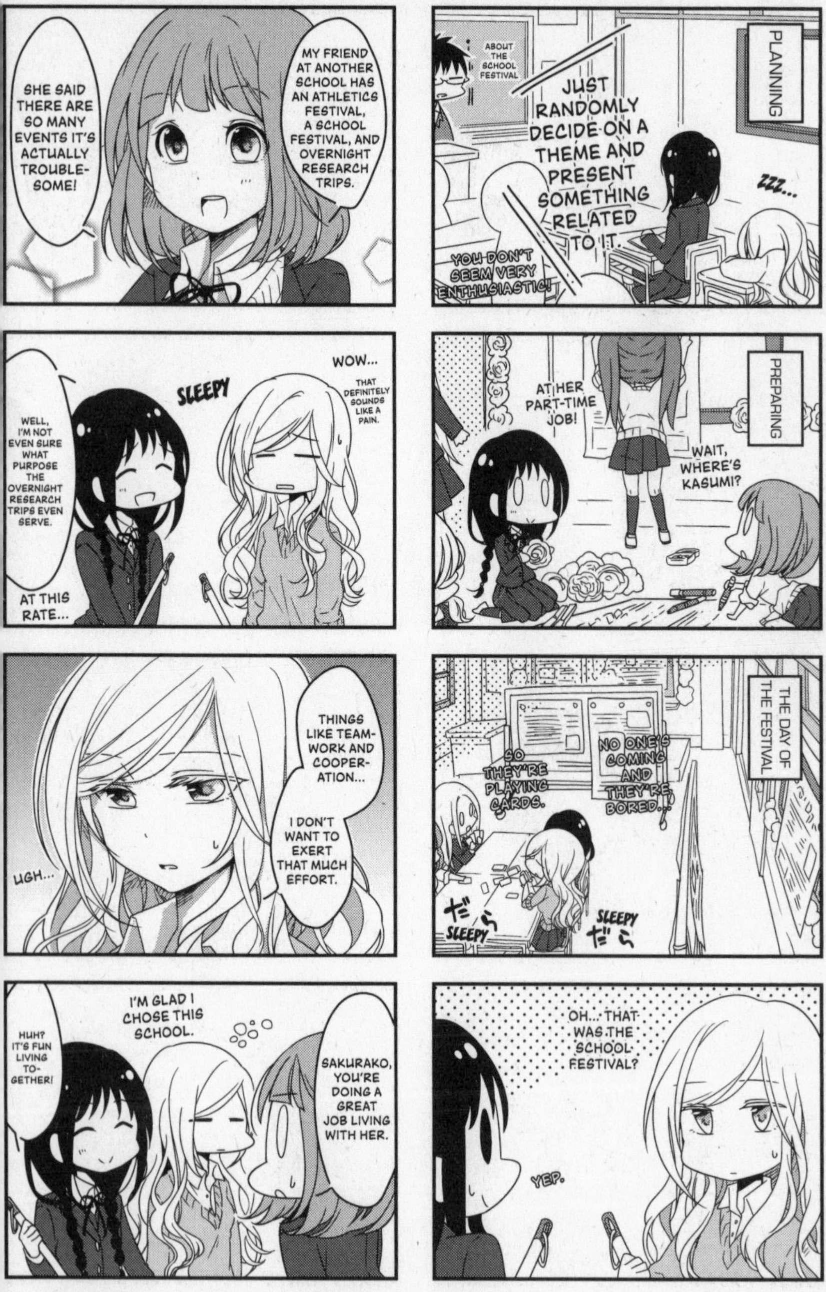
PLANNING
ABOUT THE SCHOOL FESTIVAL
JUST RANDOMLY DECIDE ON A THEME AND PRESENT SOMETHING RELATED TO IT.
ZZZ...
YOU DON'T SEEM VERY ENTHUSIASTIC!
PREPARING
WAIT, WHERE'S KASUMI?
AT HER PART-TIME JOB!
THE DAY OF THE FESTIVAL
NO ONE'S COMING AND THEY'RE BORED...
SO THEY'RE PLAYING CARDS.
だら SLEEPY
だら SLEEPY
OH... THAT WAS THE SCHOOL FESTIVAL?
YEP.
MY FRIEND AT ANOTHER SCHOOL HAS AN ATHLETICS FESTIVAL, A SCHOOL FESTIVAL, AND OVERNIGHT RESEARCH TRIPS.
SHE SAID THERE ARE SO MANY EVENTS IT'S ACTUALLY TROUBLE-SOME!
WOW...
THAT DEFINITELY SOUNDS LIKE A PAIN.
SLEEPY
WELL, I'M NOT EVEN SURE WHAT PURPOSE THE OVERNIGHT RESEARCH TRIPS EVEN SERVE.
AT THIS RATE...
THINGS LIKE TEAM-WORK AND COOPER-ATION...
I DON'T WANT TO EXERT THAT MUCH EFFORT.
UGH...
SAKURAKO, YOU'RE DOING A GREAT JOB LIVING WITH HER.
I'M GLAD I CHOSE THIS SCHOOL.
HUH? IT'S FUN LIVING TO-GETHER!

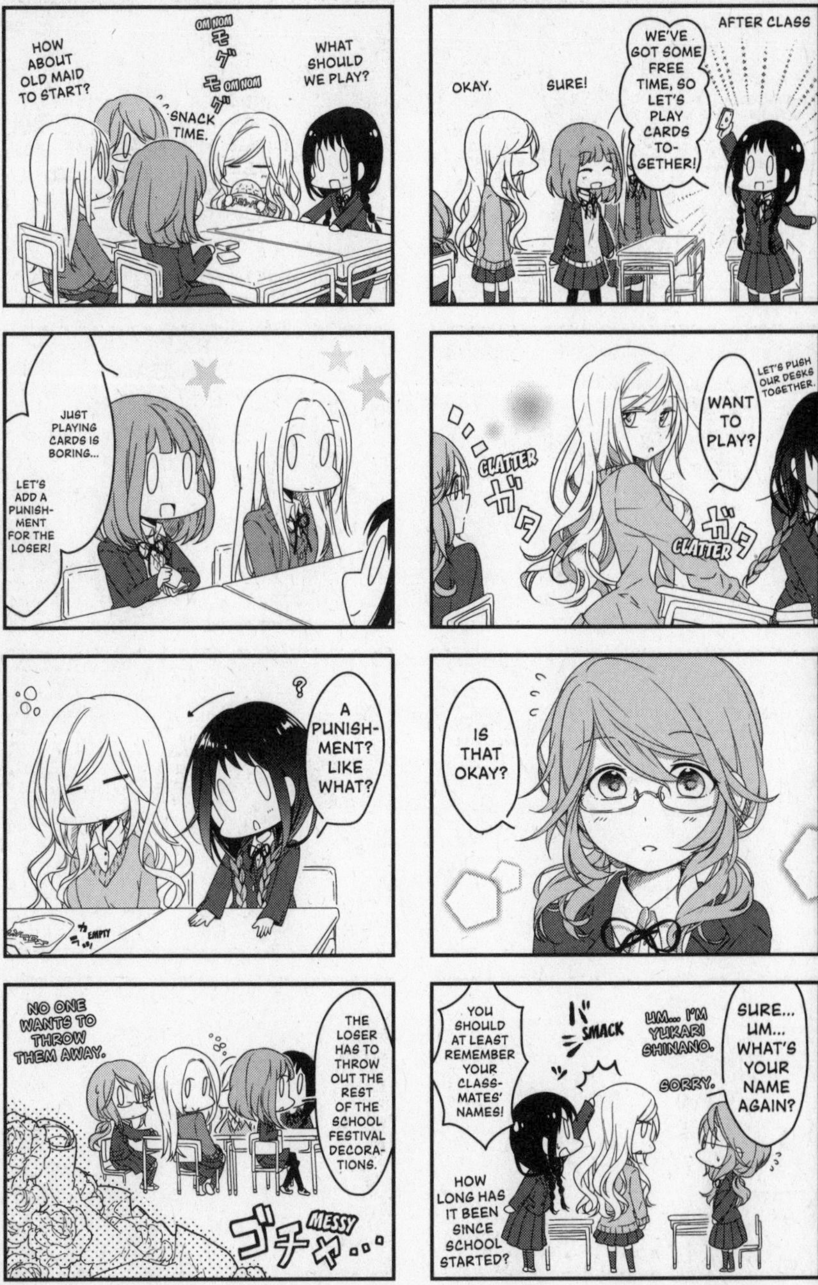
AFTER CLASS
WE'VE GOT SOME FREE TIME, SO LET'S PLAY CARDS TOGETHER!
SURE!
OKAY.
LET'S PUSH OUR DESKS TOGETHER.
WANT TO PLAY?
ガタ CLATTER
ガタ CLATTER
IS THAT OKAY?
SURE... UM... WHAT'S YOUR NAME AGAIN?
SORRY.
UM... I'M YUKARI SHINANO.
バ SMACK
YOU SHOULD AT LEAST REMEMBER YOUR CLASSMATES' NAMES!
HOW LONG HAS IT BEEN SINCE SCHOOL STARTED?
WHAT SHOULD WE PLAY?
OM NOM モグ
モグ OM NOM
SNACK TIME.
HOW ABOUT OLD MAID TO START?
JUST PLAYING CARDS IS BORING...
LET'S ADD A PUNISHMENT FOR THE LOSER!
A PUNISHMENT? LIKE WHAT?
カラ EMPTY
THE LOSER HAS TO THROW OUT THE REST OF THE SCHOOL FESTIVAL DECORATIONS.
NO ONE WANTS TO THROW THEM AWAY.
ゴチャ... MESSY

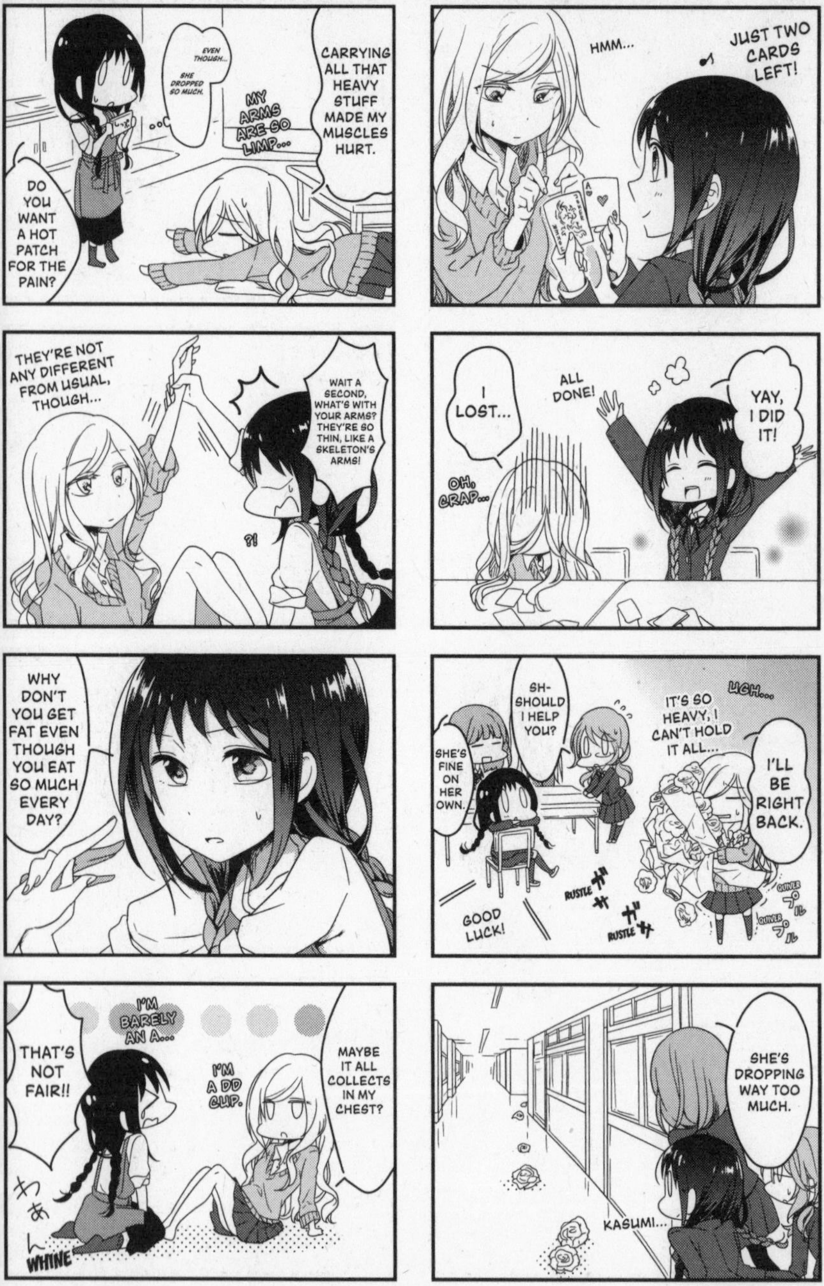
JUST TWO CARDS LEFT!
HMM...
YAY, I DID IT!
ALL DONE!
I LOST...
OH, CRAP...
UGH...
IT'S SO HEAVY, I CAN'T HOLD IT ALL...
I'LL BE RIGHT BACK.
QUIVER
QUIVER
SH-SHOULD I HELP YOU?
SHE'S FINE ON HER OWN.
RUSTLE
RUSTLE
GOOD LUCK!
SHE'S DROPPING WAY TOO MUCH.
KASUMI...
CARRYING ALL THAT HEAVY STUFF MADE MY MUSCLES HURT.
MY ARMS ARE SO LIMP...
EVEN THOUGH... SHE DROPPED SO MUCH.
DO YOU WANT A HOT PATCH FOR THE PAIN?
WAIT A SECOND, WHAT'S WITH YOUR ARMS? THEY'RE SO THIN, LIKE A SKELETON'S ARMS!
?!
THEY'RE NOT ANY DIFFERENT FROM USUAL, THOUGH...
WHY DON'T YOU GET FAT EVEN THOUGH YOU EAT SO MUCH EVERY DAY?
MAYBE IT ALL COLLECTS IN MY CHEST?
I'M A DD CUP.
I'M BARELY AN A...
THAT'S NOT FAIR!!
わあん
WHINE

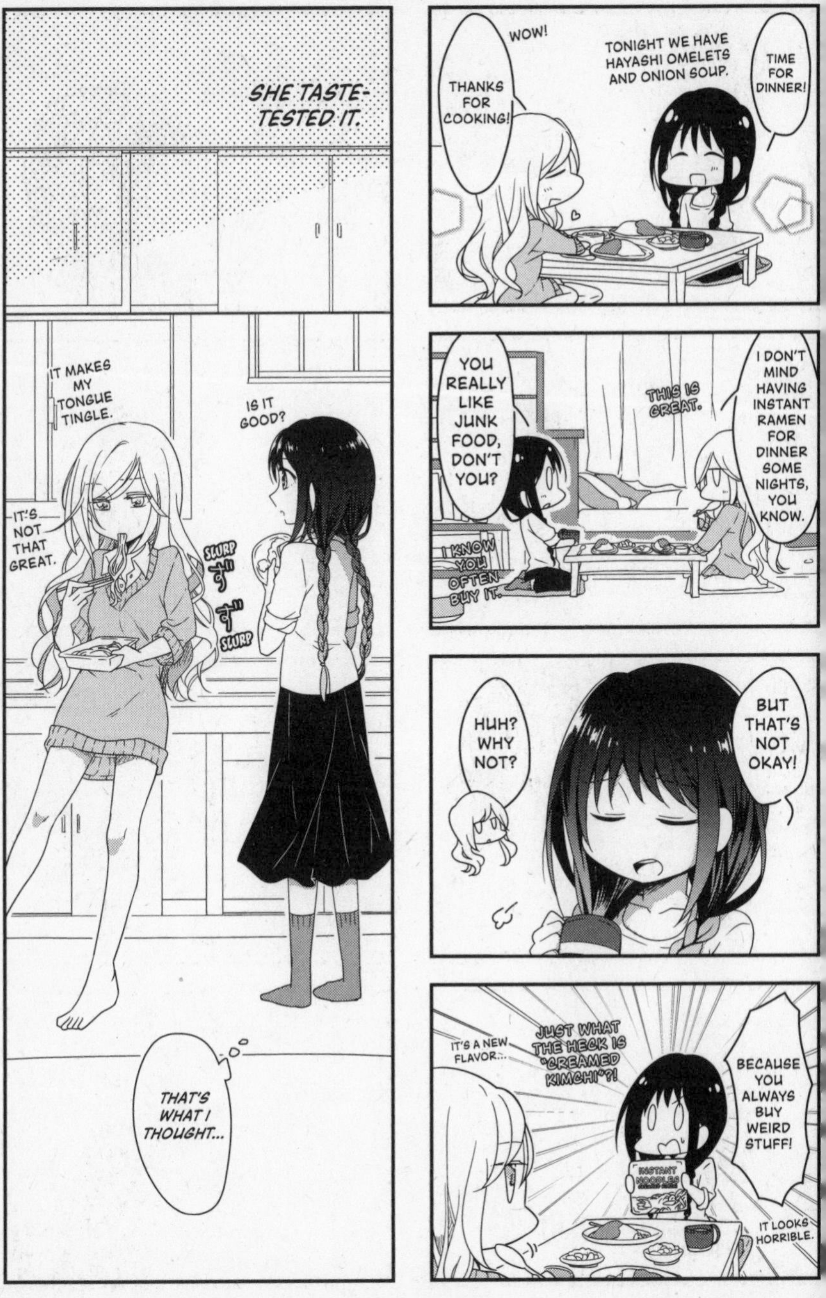
TIME FOR DINNER!
TONIGHT WE HAVE HAYASHI OMELETS AND ONION SOUP.
WOW!
THANKS FOR COOKING!
I DON'T MIND HAVING INSTANT RAMEN FOR DINNER SOME NIGHTS, YOU KNOW.
THIS IS GREAT.
YOU REALLY LIKE JUNK FOOD, DON'T YOU?
I KNOW YOU OFTEN BUY IT.
BUT THAT'S NOT OKAY!
HUH? WHY NOT?
BECAUSE YOU ALWAYS BUY WEIRD STUFF!
JUST WHAT THE HECK IS "CREAMED KIMCHI"?!
IT'S A NEW FLAVOR...
INSTANT NOODLES
IT LOOKS HORRIBLE.
SHE TASTE-TESTED IT.
IS IT GOOD?
IT MAKES MY TONGUE TINGLE.
SLURP ず
ず SLURP
IT'S NOT THAT GREAT.
THAT'S WHAT I THOUGHT...

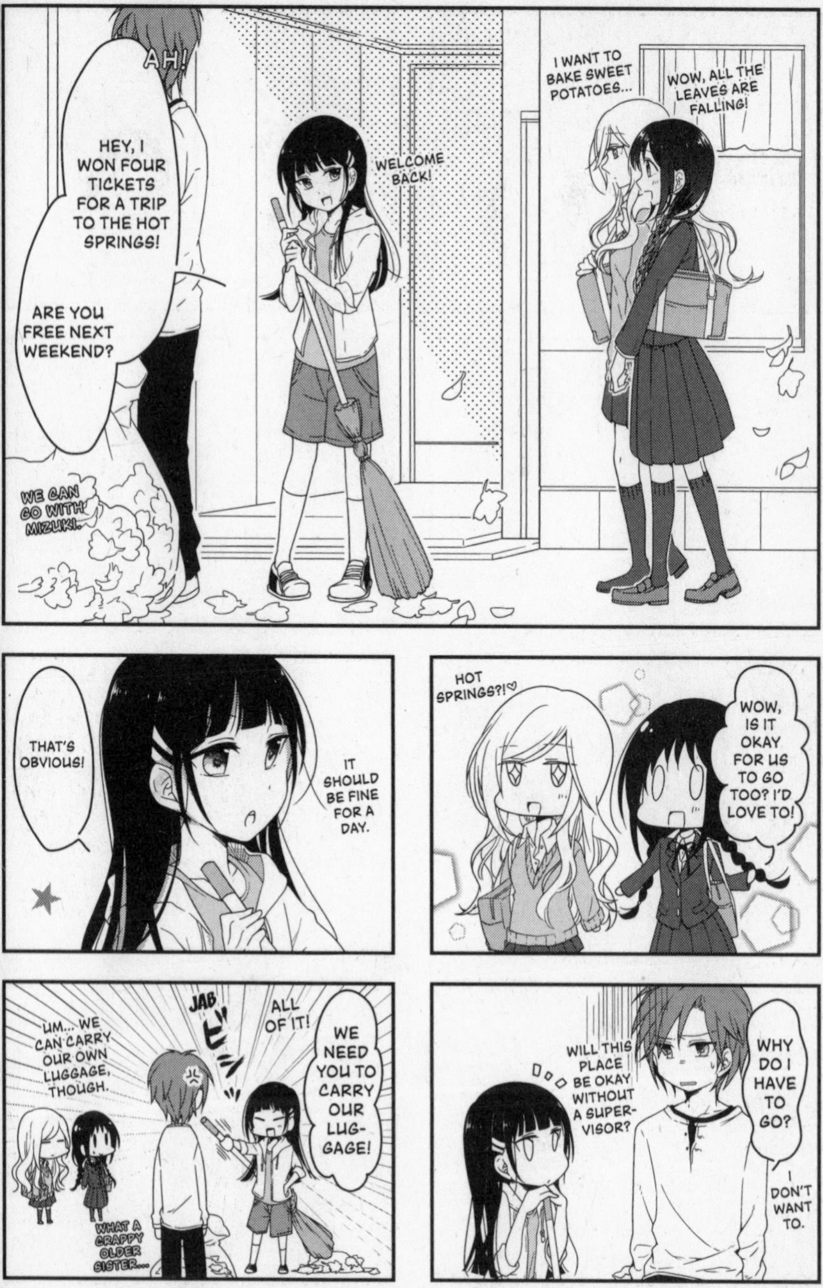
WOW, ALL THE LEAVES ARE FALLING!
I WANT TO BAKE SWEET POTATOES...
WELCOME BACK!
AH!
HEY, I WON FOUR TICKETS FOR A TRIP TO THE HOT SPRINGS!
ARE YOU FREE NEXT WEEKEND?
WE CAN GO WITH MIZUKI.
WOW, IS IT OKAY FOR US TO GO TOO? I'D LOVE TO!
HOT SPRINGS?!♡
IT SHOULD BE FINE FOR A DAY.
THAT'S OBVIOUS!
WHY DO I HAVE TO GO?
I DON'T WANT TO.
WILL THIS PLACE BE OKAY WITHOUT A SUPERVISOR?
WE NEED YOU TO CARRY OUR LUGGAGE!
ALL OF IT!
JAB
UM... WE CAN CARRY OUR OWN LUGGAGE, THOUGH.
WHAT A CRAPPY OLDER SISTER...

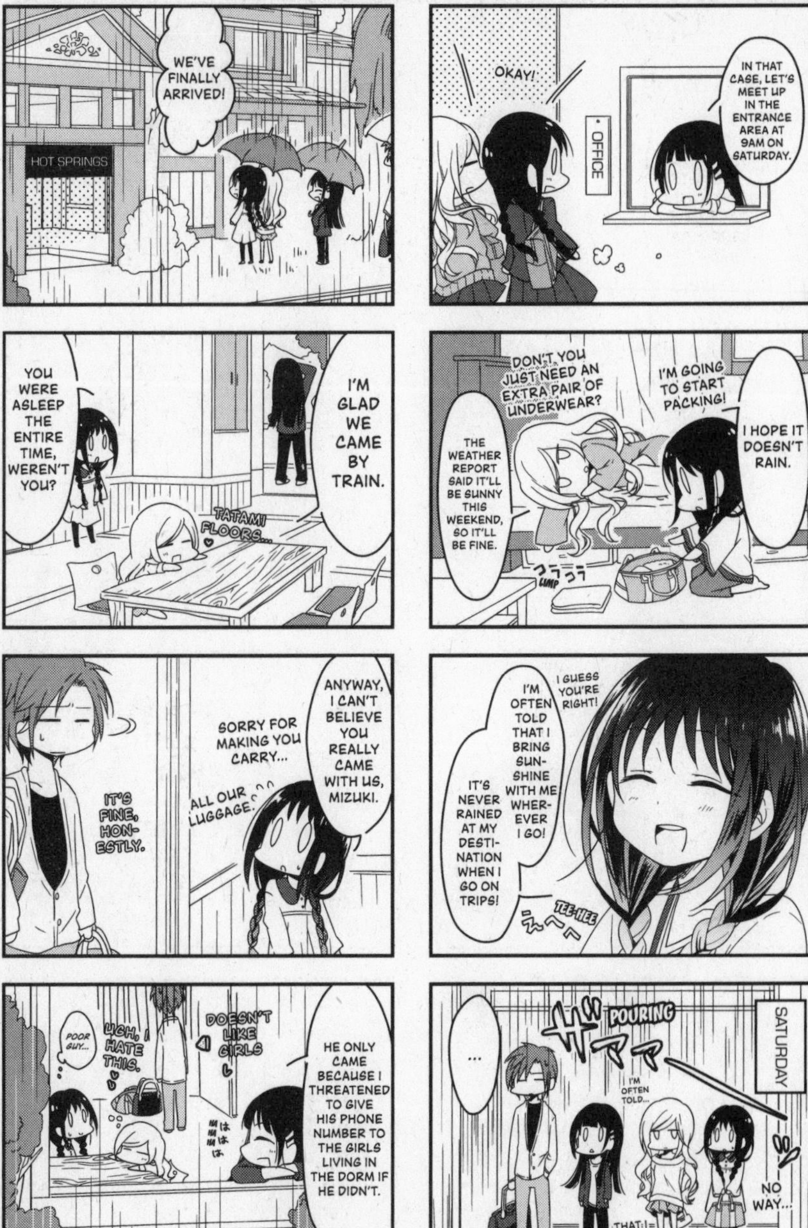
IN THAT CASE, LET'S MEET UP IN THE ENTRANCE AREA AT 9AM ON SATURDAY.
OFFICE
OKAY!
I HOPE IT DOESN'T RAIN.
I'M GOING TO START PACKING!
DON'T YOU JUST NEED AN EXTRA PAIR OF UNDERWEAR?
THE WEATHER REPORT SAID IT'LL BE SUNNY THIS WEEKEND, SO IT'LL BE FINE.
LUMP
I GUESS YOU'RE RIGHT!
I'M OFTEN TOLD THAT I BRING SUNSHINE WITH ME WHEREVER I GO!
IT'S NEVER RAINED AT MY DESTINATION WHEN I GO ON TRIPS!
TEE-HEE
SATURDAY
POURING
...
I'M OFTEN TOLD...
NO WAY...
THAT I BRING RAIN...
WE'VE FINALLY ARRIVED!
HOT SPRINGS
I'M GLAD WE CAME BY TRAIN.
YOU WERE ASLEEP THE ENTIRE TIME, WEREN'T YOU?
TATAMI FLOORS...
ANYWAY, I CAN'T BELIEVE YOU REALLY CAME WITH US, MIZUKI.
SORRY FOR MAKING YOU CARRY...
ALL OUR LUGGAGE.
IT'S FINE, HONESTLY.
HE ONLY CAME BECAUSE I THREATENED TO GIVE HIS PHONE NUMBER TO THE GIRLS LIVING IN THE DORM IF HE DIDN'T.
DOESN'T LIKE GIRLS
UGH, HATE THIS.
POOR GUY...

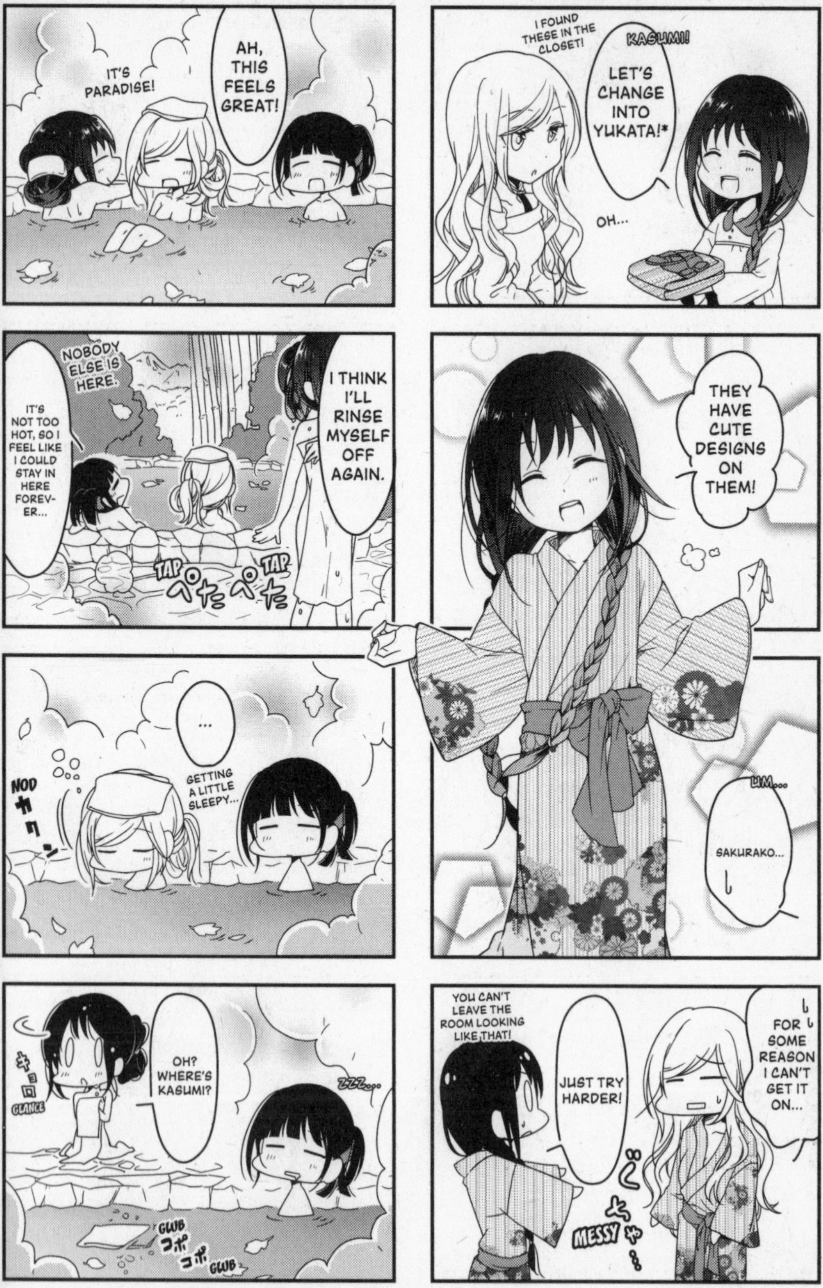
KASUMI!
LET'S CHANGE INTO YUKATA!*
I FOUND THESE IN THE CLOSET!
OH...
THEY HAVE CUTE DESIGNS ON THEM!
UM...
SAKURAKO...
FOR SOME REASON I CAN'T GET IT ON...
JUST TRY HARDER!
YOU CAN'T LEAVE THE ROOM LOOKING LIKE THAT!
MESSY
AH, THIS FEELS GREAT!
IT'S PARADISE!
I THINK I'LL RINSE MYSELF OFF AGAIN.
NOBODY ELSE IS HERE.
IT'S NOT TOO HOT, SO I FEEL LIKE I COULD STAY IN HERE FOREV- ER...
TAP TAP
...
GETTING A LITTLE SLEEPY...
NOD
ZZZ...
OH? WHERE'S KASUMI?
GLANCE
GLUB GLUB

* A LIGHT COTTON KIMONO

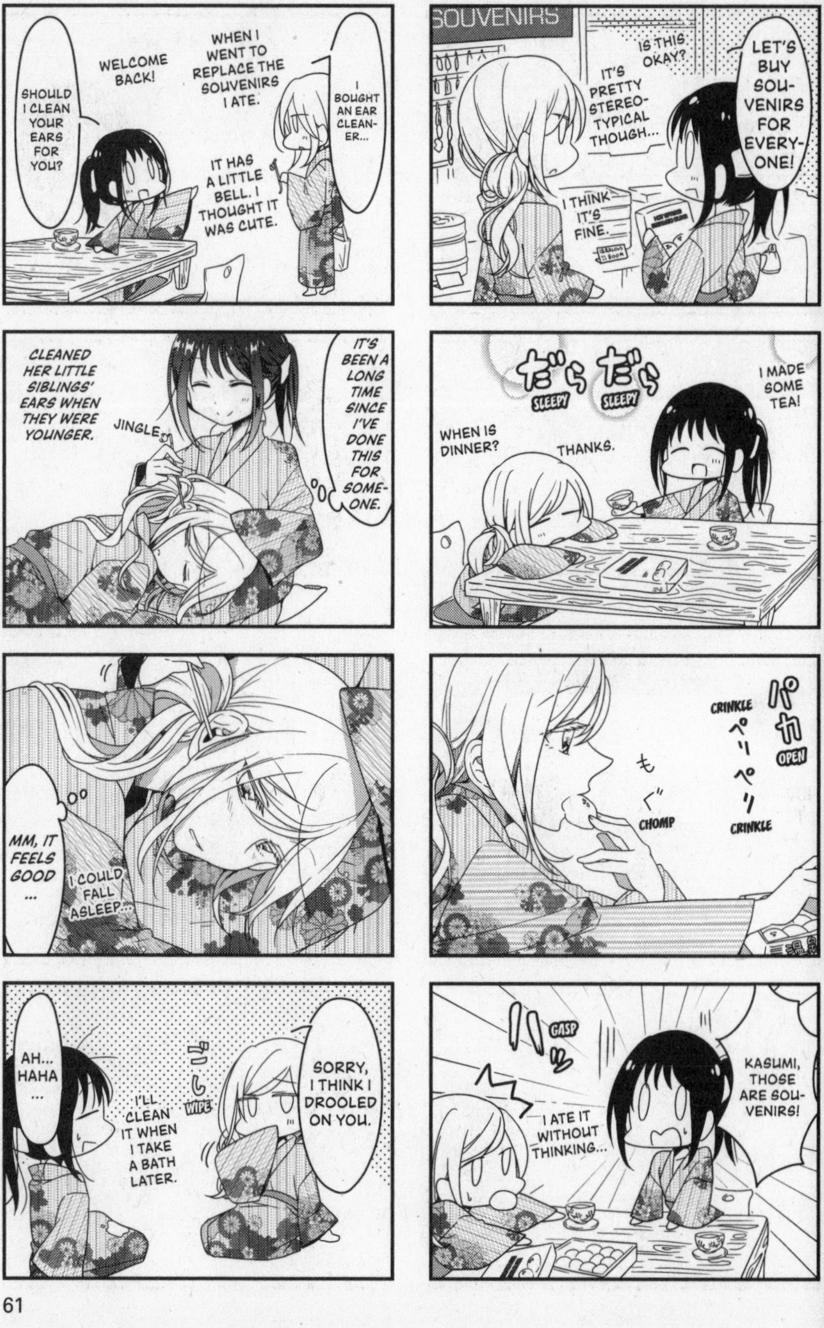
SOUVENIRS
LET'S BUY SOUVENIRS FOR EVERYONE!
IS THIS OKAY?
IT'S PRETTY STEREOTYPICAL THOUGH...
I THINK IT'S FINE.
I MADE SOME TEA!
だら だら
SLEEPY SLEEPY
THANKS.
WHEN IS DINNER?
パカ
OPEN
ペリペリ
CRINKLE
CRINKLE
もぐ
CHOMP
KASUMI, THOSE ARE SOUVENIRS!
ハッ
GASP
I ATE IT WITHOUT THINKING...
WHEN I WENT TO REPLACE THE SOUVENIRS I ATE.
I BOUGHT AN EAR CLEANER...
IT HAS A LITTLE BELL. I THOUGHT IT WAS CUTE.
WELCOME BACK!
SHOULD I CLEAN YOUR EARS FOR YOU?
IT'S BEEN A LONG TIME SINCE I'VE DONE THIS FOR SOMEONE.
JINGLE
CLEANED HER LITTLE SIBLINGS' EARS WHEN THEY WERE YOUNGER.
MM, IT FEELS GOOD ...
I COULD FALL ASLEEP...
SORRY, I THINK I DROOLED ON YOU.
ごし
WIPE
I'LL CLEAN IT WHEN I TAKE A BATH LATER.
AH... HAHA ...

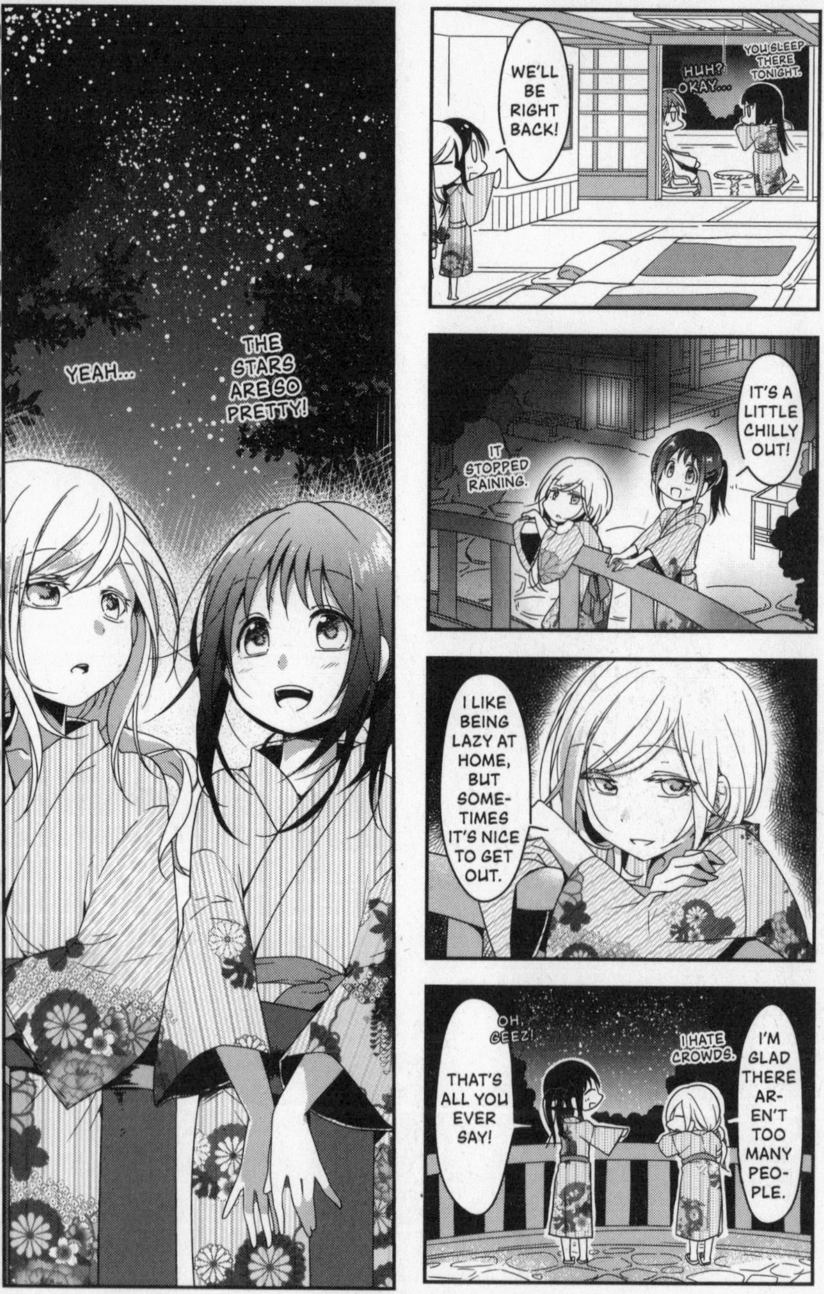
YOU SLEEP THERE TONIGHT.
HUH? OKAY...
WE'LL BE RIGHT BACK!
IT'S A LITTLE CHILLY OUT!
IT STOPPED RAINING.
I LIKE BEING LAZY AT HOME, BUT SOMETIMES IT'S NICE TO GET OUT.
I'M GLAD THERE AREN'T TOO MANY PEOPLE.
I HATE CROWDS.
OH, GEEZ!
THAT'S ALL YOU EVER SAY!
THE STARS ARE SO PRETTY!
YEAH...

Illustration gallery

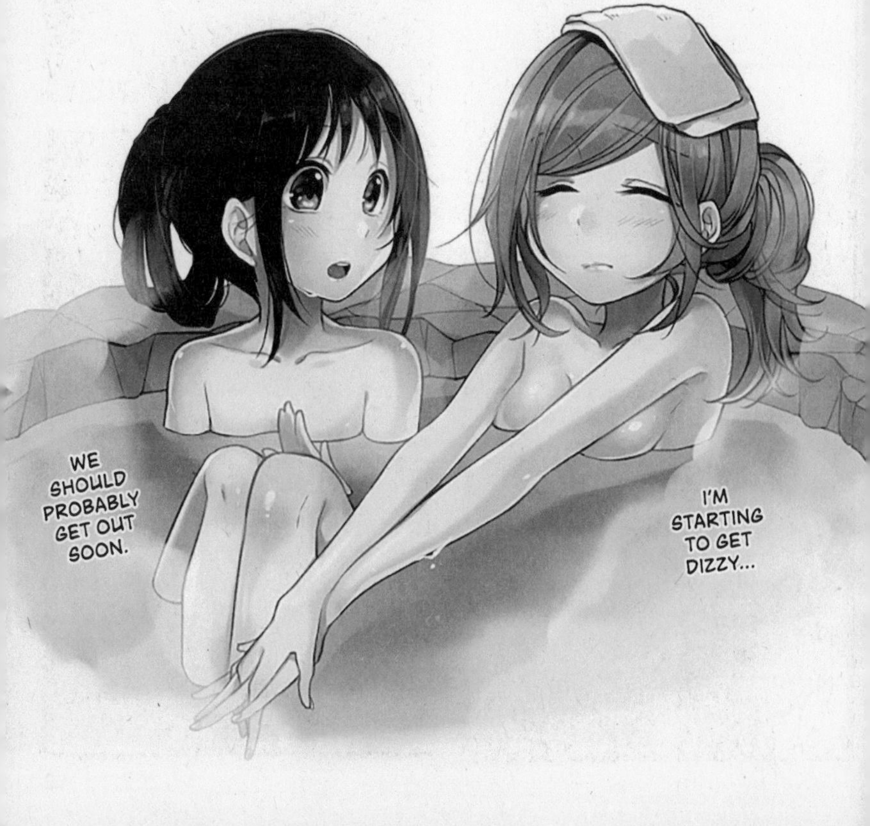
I'M STARTING TO GET DIZZY...
WE SHOULD PROBABLY GET OUT SOON.

Futaribeya
A ROOM FOR TWO

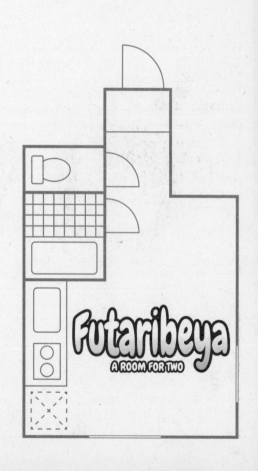

Chapter 6

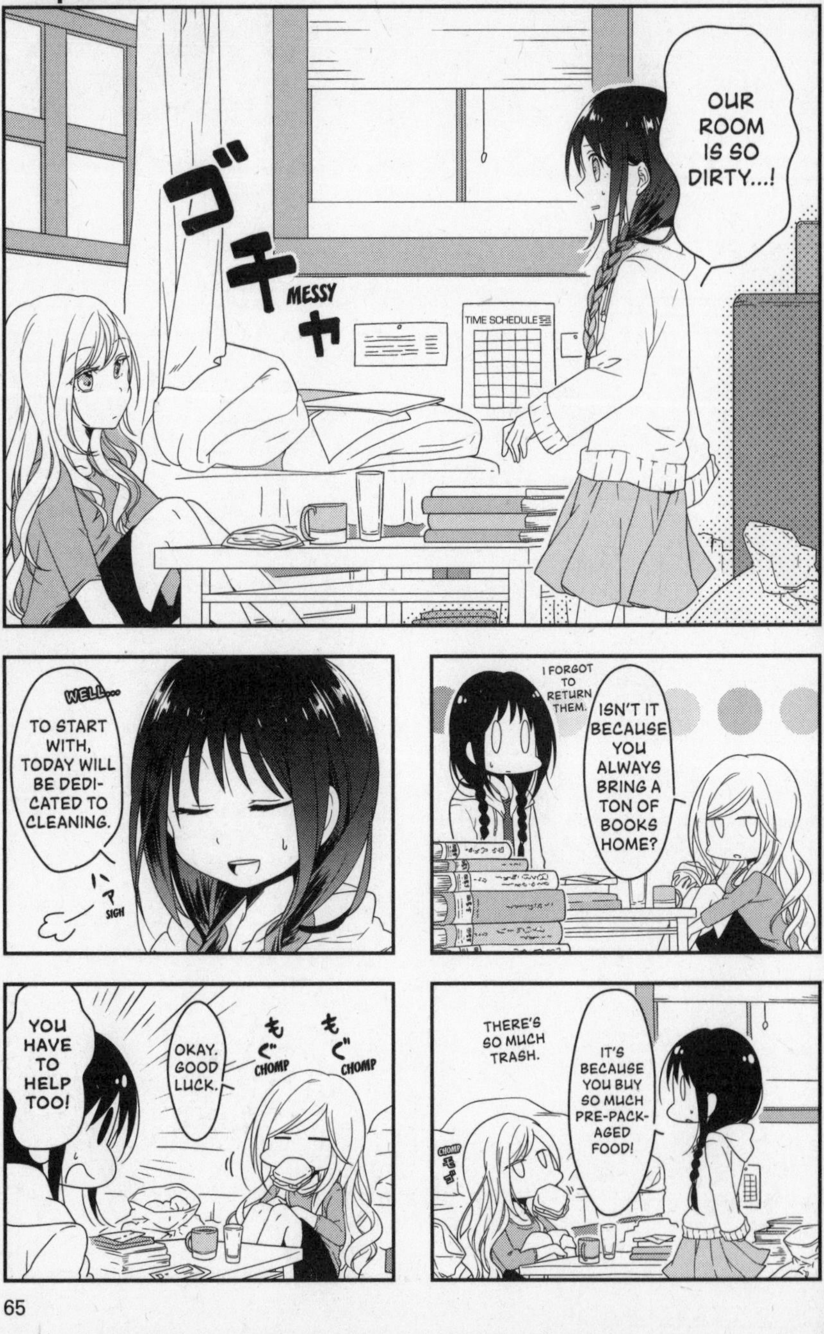

ゴチャ
MESSY
OUR ROOM IS SO DIRTY...!
TIME SCHEDULE
ISN'T IT BECAUSE YOU ALWAYS BRING A TON OF BOOKS HOME?
I FORGOT TO RETURN THEM.
WELL...
TO START WITH, TODAY WILL BE DEDICATED TO CLEANING.
ハァ
SIGH
THERE'S SO MUCH TRASH.
IT'S BECAUSE YOU BUY SO MUCH PRE-PACKAGED FOOD!
CHOMP
もぐ もぐ
CHOMP CHOMP
OKAY. GOOD LUCK.
YOU HAVE TO HELP TOO!

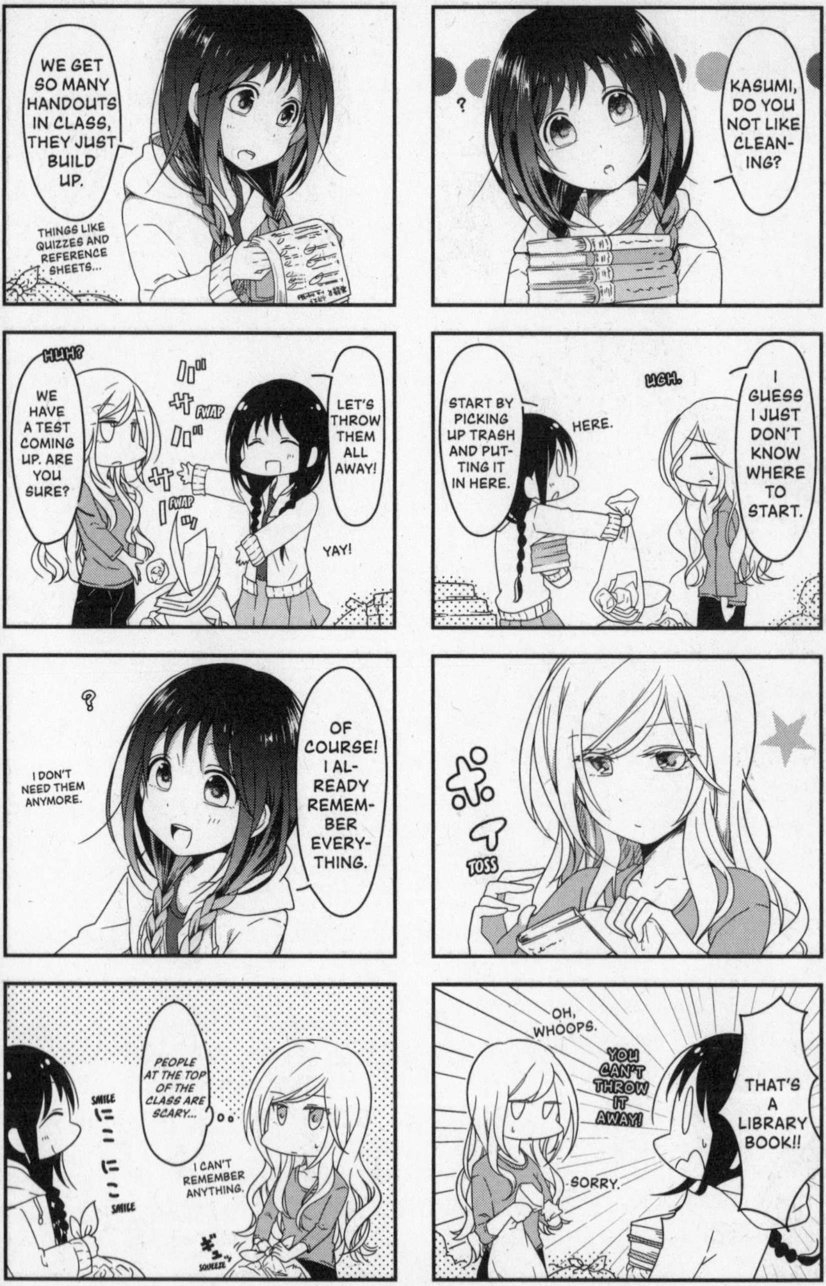
?
KASUMI, DO YOU NOT LIKE CLEAN-ING?
WE GET SO MANY HANDOUTS IN CLASS, THEY JUST BUILD UP.
THINGS LIKE QUIZZES AND REFERENCE SHEETS...
I GUESS I JUST DON'T KNOW WHERE TO START.
UGH.
START BY PICKING UP TRASH AND PUT-TING IT IN HERE.
HERE.
LET'S THROW THEM ALL AWAY!
FWAP
FWAP
YAY!
HUH?
WE HAVE A TEST COMING UP. ARE YOU SURE?
TOSS
OF COURSE! I AL-READY REMEM-BER EVERY-THING.
?
I DON'T NEED THEM ANYMORE.
THAT'S A LIBRARY BOOK!!
YOU CAN'T THROW IT AWAY!
OH, WHOOPS.
SORRY.
PEOPLE AT THE TOP OF THE CLASS ARE SCARY...
SMILE
SMILE
I CAN'T REMEMBER ANYTHING.
SQUEEZE

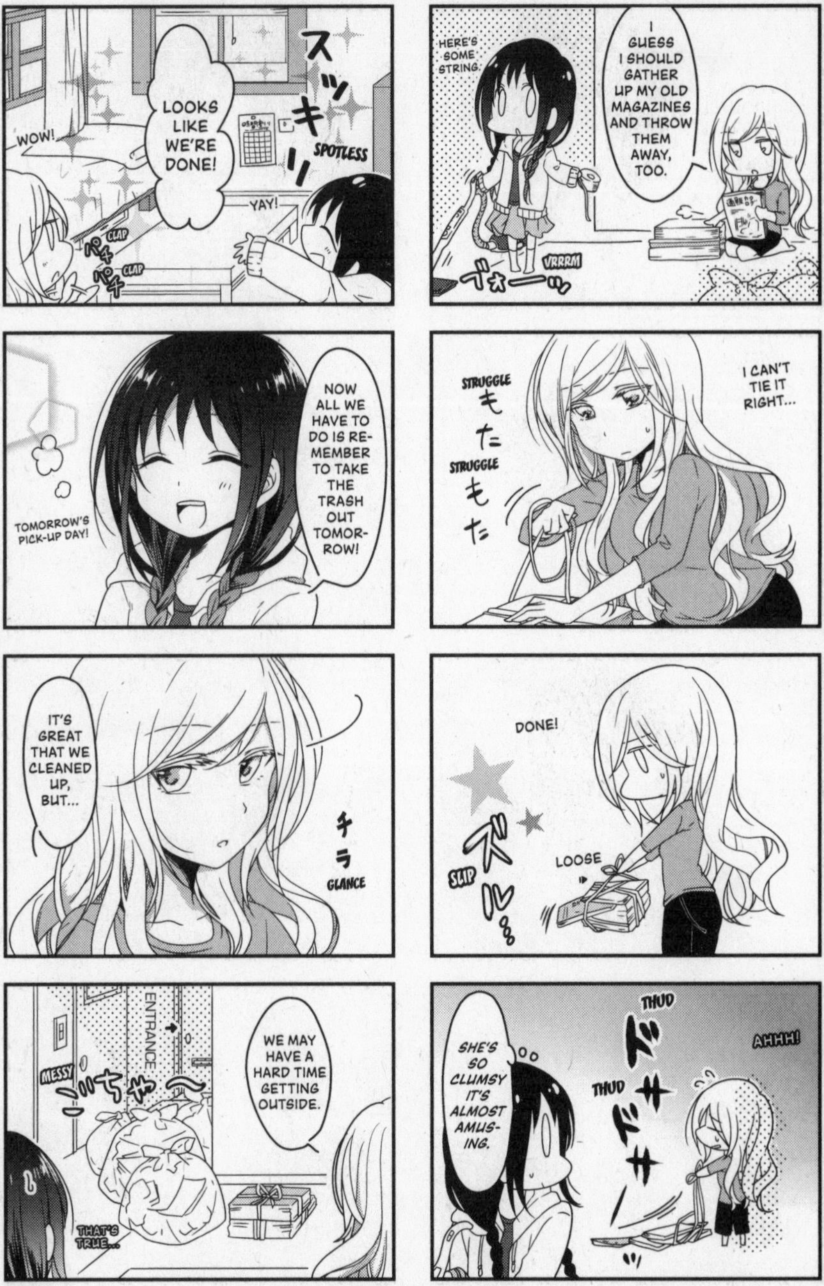
I GUESS I SHOULD GATHER UP MY OLD MAGAZINES AND THROW THEM AWAY, TOO.
HERE'S SOME STRING.
ヴォーーッ VRRRM
I CAN'T TIE IT RIGHT...
もたもた STRUGGLE STRUGGLE
DONE!
LOOSE
ズル… SLIP
AHHH!
ドサドサッ THUD THUD
SHE'S SO CLUMSY IT'S ALMOST AMUSING.
スッキリ SPOTLESS
LOOKS LIKE WE'RE DONE!
WOW!
YAY!
パチパチ CLAP CLAP
NOW ALL WE HAVE TO DO IS REMEMBER TO TAKE THE TRASH OUT TOMORROW!
TOMORROW'S PICK-UP DAY!
チラ GLANCE
IT'S GREAT THAT WE CLEANED UP, BUT...
WE MAY HAVE A HARD TIME GETTING OUTSIDE.
ENTRANCE
ごちゃ～ MESSY
THAT'S TRUE...

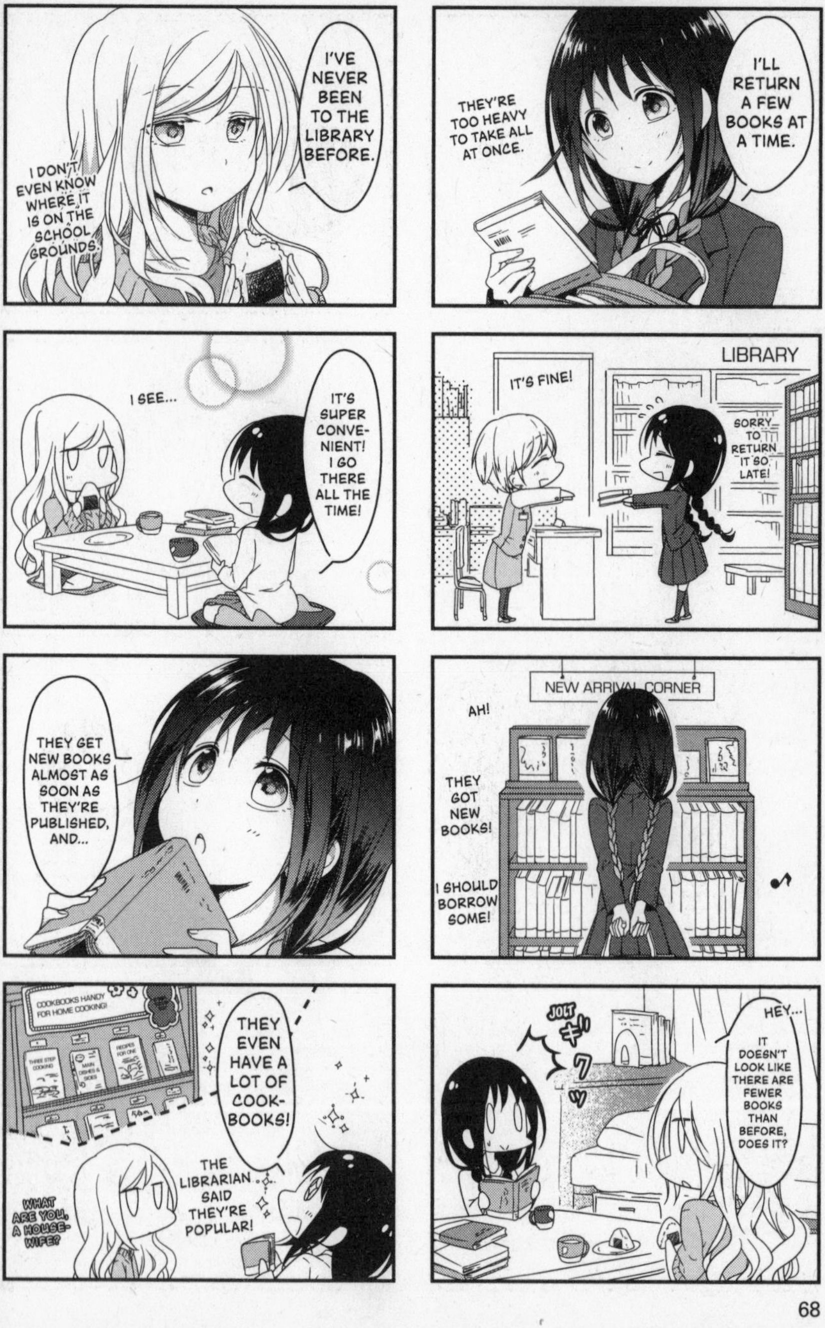
I'LL RETURN A FEW BOOKS AT A TIME.
THEY'RE TOO HEAVY TO TAKE ALL AT ONCE.
LIBRARY
SORRY TO RETURN IT SO LATE!
IT'S FINE!
NEW ARRIVAL CORNER
AH!
THEY GOT NEW BOOKS!
I SHOULD BORROW SOME!
HEY...
IT DOESN'T LOOK LIKE THERE ARE FEWER BOOKS THAN BEFORE, DOES IT?
JOLT
I'VE NEVER BEEN TO THE LIBRARY BEFORE.
I DON'T EVEN KNOW WHERE IT IS ON THE SCHOOL GROUNDS.
IT'S SUPER CONVENIENT! I GO THERE ALL THE TIME!
I SEE...
THEY GET NEW BOOKS ALMOST AS SOON AS THEY'RE PUBLISHED, AND...
THEY EVEN HAVE A LOT OF COOK-BOOKS!
COOKBOOKS HANDY FOR HOME COOKING!
THREE STEP COOKING
MAIN DISHES & SIDES
RECIPES FOR ONE
THE LIBRARIAN SAID THEY'RE POPULAR!
WHAT ARE YOU, A HOUSE-WIFE?

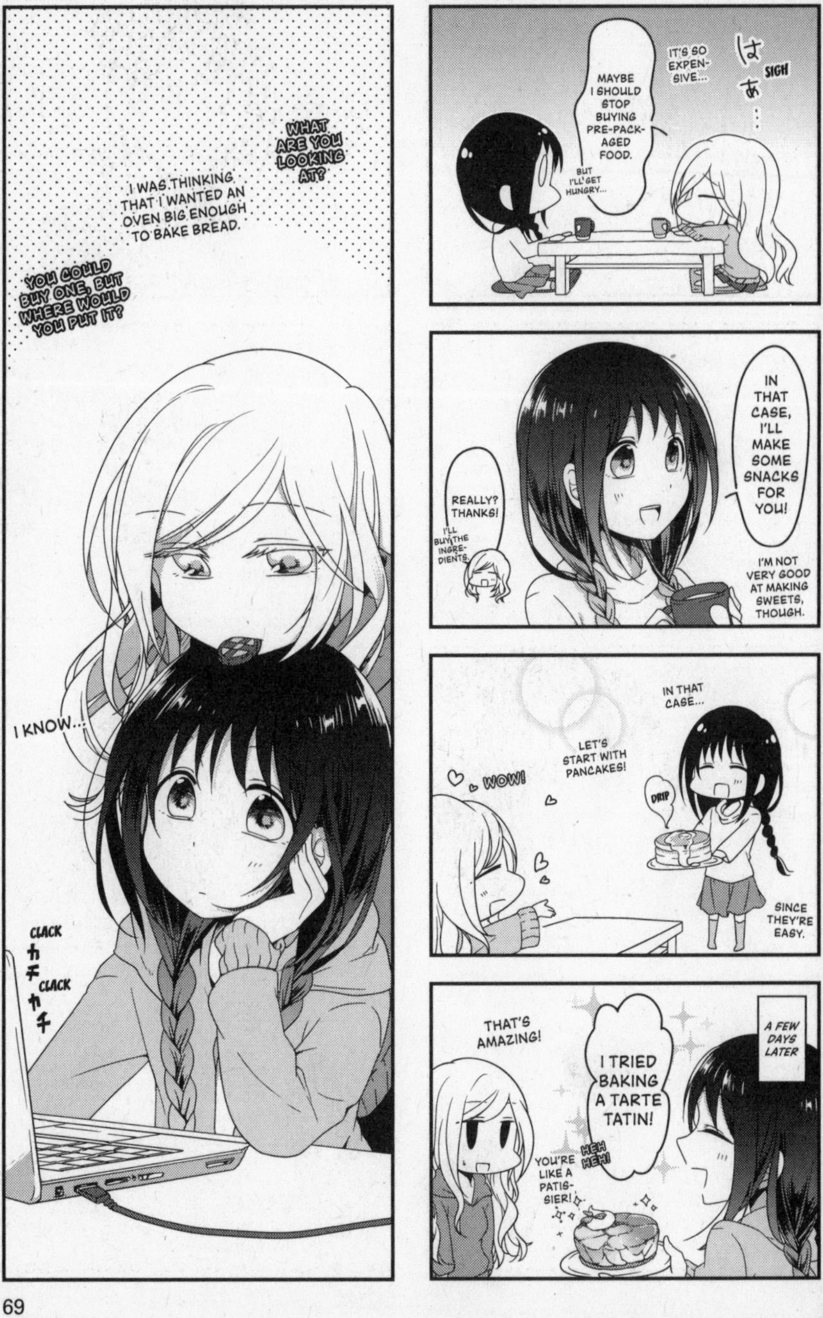
はあ…
SIGH
IT'S SO EXPEN-SIVE...
MAYBE I SHOULD STOP BUYING PRE-PACK-AGED FOOD.
BUT I'LL GET HUNGRY...
IN THAT CASE, I'LL MAKE SOME SNACKS FOR YOU!
I'M NOT VERY GOOD AT MAKING SWEETS, THOUGH.
REALLY? THANKS!
I'LL BUY THE INGRE-DIENTS.
IN THAT CASE...
LET'S START WITH PANCAKES!
SINCE THEY'RE EASY.
DRIP
WOW!
A FEW DAYS LATER
I TRIED BAKING A TARTE TATIN!
HEH HEH!
THAT'S AMAZING!
YOU'RE LIKE A PATIS-SIER!
WHAT ARE YOU LOOKING AT?
I WAS THINKING THAT I WANTED AN OVEN BIG ENOUGH TO BAKE BREAD.
YOU COULD BUY ONE, BUT WHERE WOULD YOU PUT IT?
I KNOW...
カチ
CLACK
カチ
CLACK

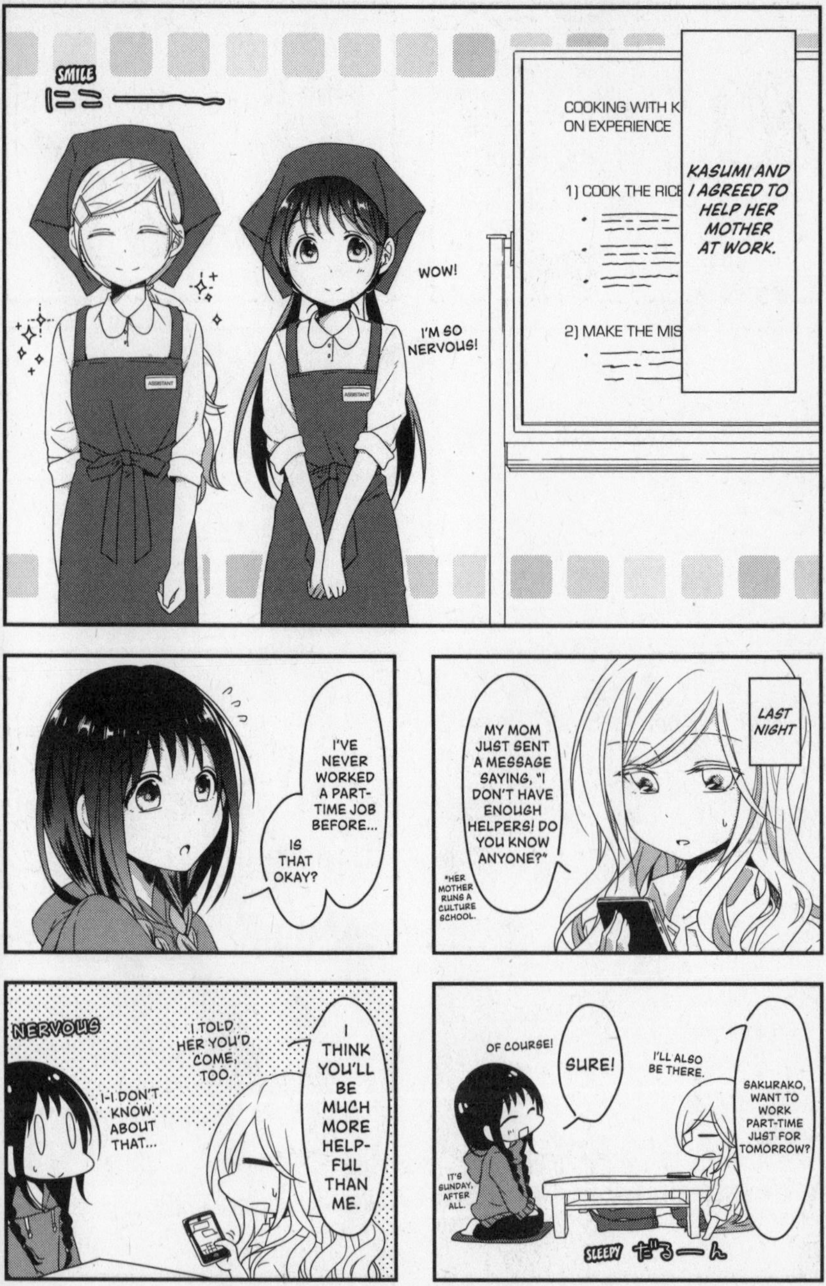
KASUMI AND I AGREED TO HELP HER MOTHER AT WORK.
COOKING WITH K
ON EXPERIENCE
1) COOK THE RICE
2) MAKE THE MIS
WOW!
I'M SO NERVOUS!
SMILE にこーー
LAST NIGHT
MY MOM JUST SENT A MESSAGE SAYING, "I DON'T HAVE ENOUGH HELPERS! DO YOU KNOW ANYONE?"*
*HER MOTHER RUNS A CULTURE SCHOOL.
I'VE NEVER WORKED A PART-TIME JOB BEFORE...
IS THAT OKAY?
SAKURAKO, WANT TO WORK PART-TIME JUST FOR TOMORROW?
I'LL ALSO BE THERE.
SURE!
OF COURSE!
IT'S SUNDAY, AFTER ALL.
SLEEPY だるーん
I THINK YOU'LL BE MUCH MORE HELPFUL THAN ME.
I TOLD HER YOU'D COME, TOO.
I-I DON'T KNOW ABOUT THAT...
NERVOUS

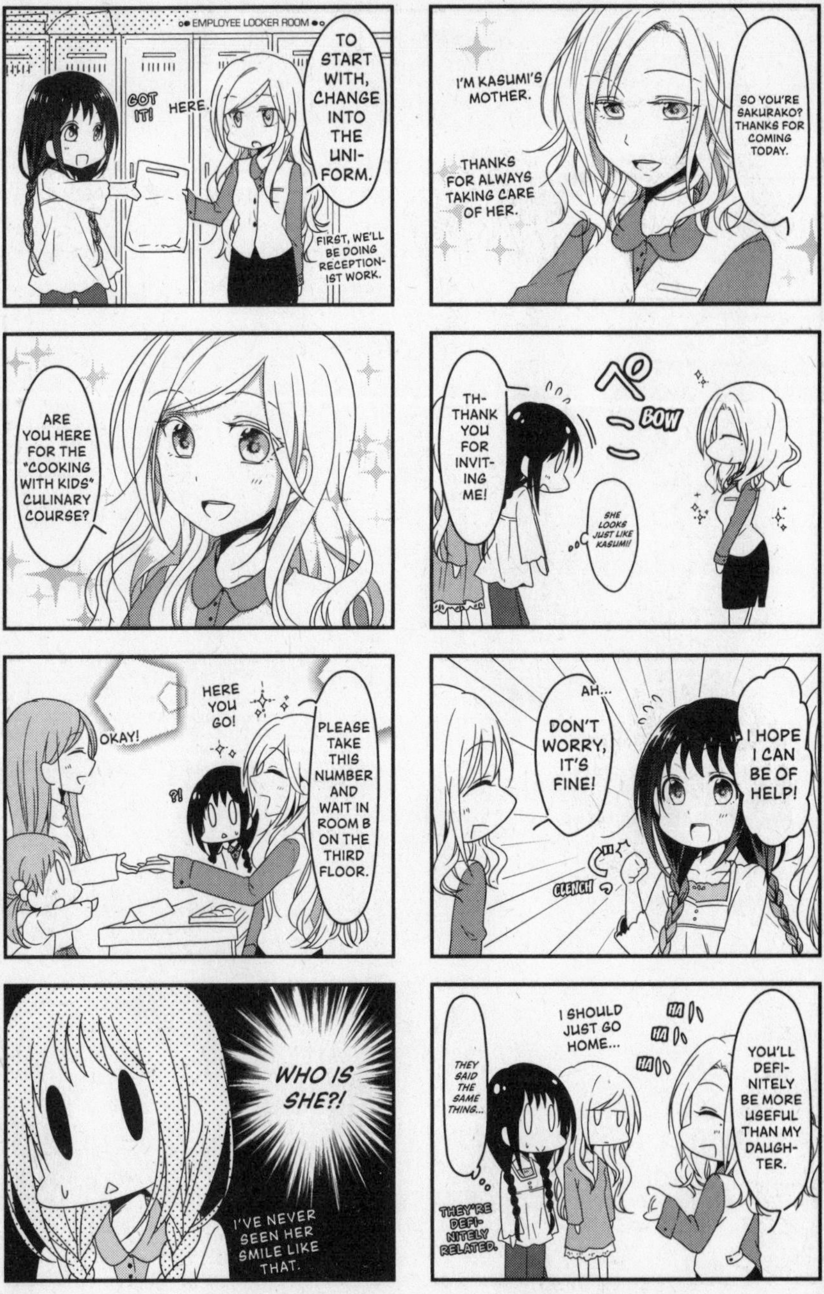
SO YOU'RE SAKURAKO? THANKS FOR COMING TODAY.
I'M KASUMI'S MOTHER.
THANKS FOR ALWAYS TAKING CARE OF HER.
ぺ
BOW
SHE LOOKS JUST LIKE KASUMI!!
TH-THANK YOU FOR INVITING ME!
I HOPE I CAN BE OF HELP!
AH...
DON'T WORRY, IT'S FINE!
CLENCH
YOU'LL DEFINITELY BE MORE USEFUL THAN MY DAUGHTER.
HA
HA
HA
I SHOULD JUST GO HOME...
THEY SAID THE SAME THING...
THEY'RE DEFINITELY RELATED.
EMPLOYEE LOCKER ROOM
TO START WITH, CHANGE INTO THE UNIFORM.
FIRST, WE'LL BE DOING RECEPTIONIST WORK.
HERE.
GOT IT!
ARE YOU HERE FOR THE "COOKING WITH KIDS" CULINARY COURSE?
PLEASE TAKE THIS NUMBER AND WAIT IN ROOM B ON THE THIRD FLOOR.
HERE YOU GO!
?!
OKAY!
WHO IS SHE?!
I'VE NEVER SEEN HER SMILE LIKE THAT.

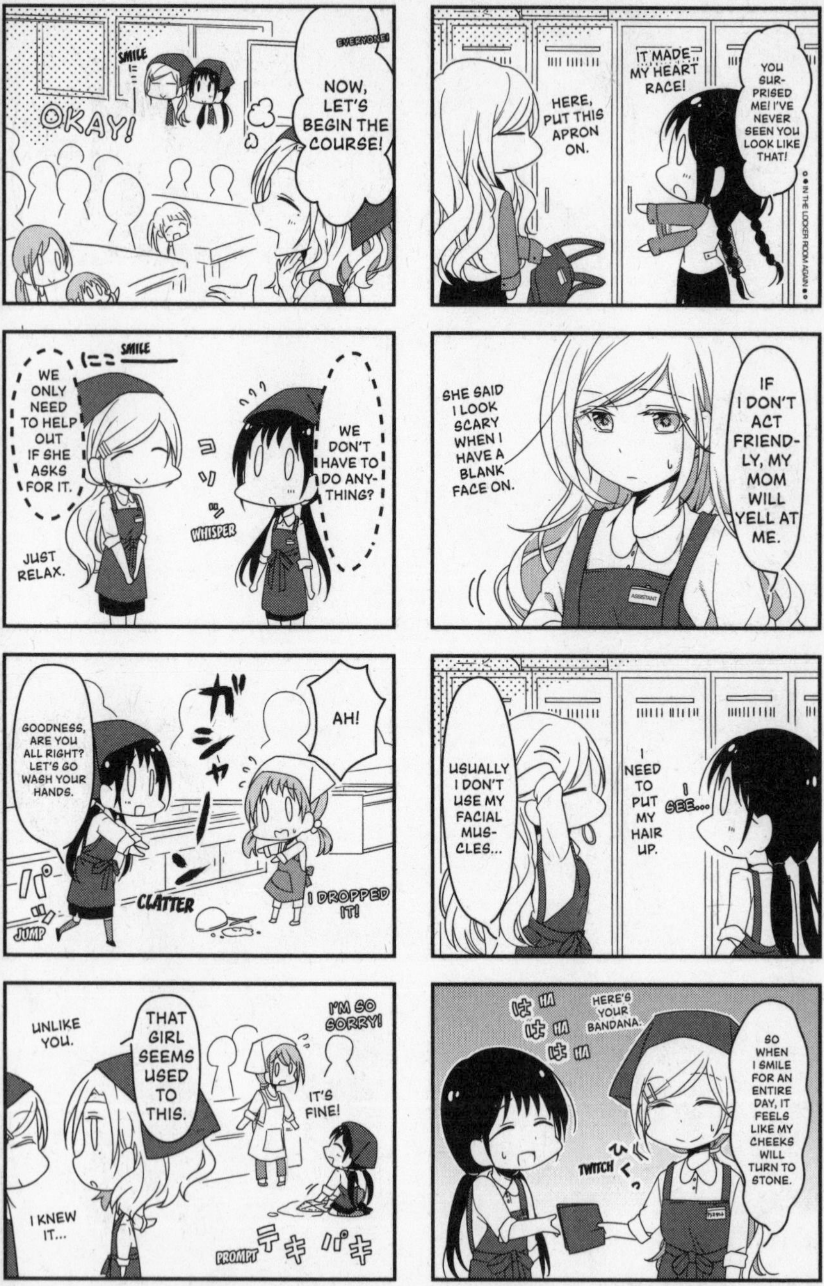
YOU SUR-PRISED ME! I'VE NEVER SEEN YOU LOOK LIKE THAT!
IT MADE MY HEART RACE!
HERE, PUT THIS APRON ON.
IN THE LOCKER ROOM AGAIN
IF I DON'T ACT FRIEND-LY, MY MOM WILL YELL AT ME.
SHE SAID I LOOK SCARY WHEN I HAVE A BLANK FACE ON.
I SEE...
I NEED TO PUT MY HAIR UP.
USUALLY I DON'T USE MY FACIAL MUS-CLES...
SO WHEN I SMILE FOR AN ENTIRE DAY, IT FEELS LIKE MY CHEEKS WILL TURN TO STONE.
HERE'S YOUR BANDANA.
HA HA HA
TWITCH
EVERYONE!
NOW, LET'S BEGIN THE COURSE!
SMILE
OKAY!
WE DON'T HAVE TO DO ANY-THING?
WHISPER
SMILE
WE ONLY NEED TO HELP OUT IF SHE ASKS FOR IT.
JUST RELAX.
AH!
I DROPPED IT!
CLATTER
GOODNESS, ARE YOU ALL RIGHT? LET'S GO WASH YOUR HANDS.
JUMP
I'M SO SORRY!
IT'S FINE!
PROMPT
THAT GIRL SEEMS USED TO THIS.
UNLIKE YOU.
I KNEW IT...

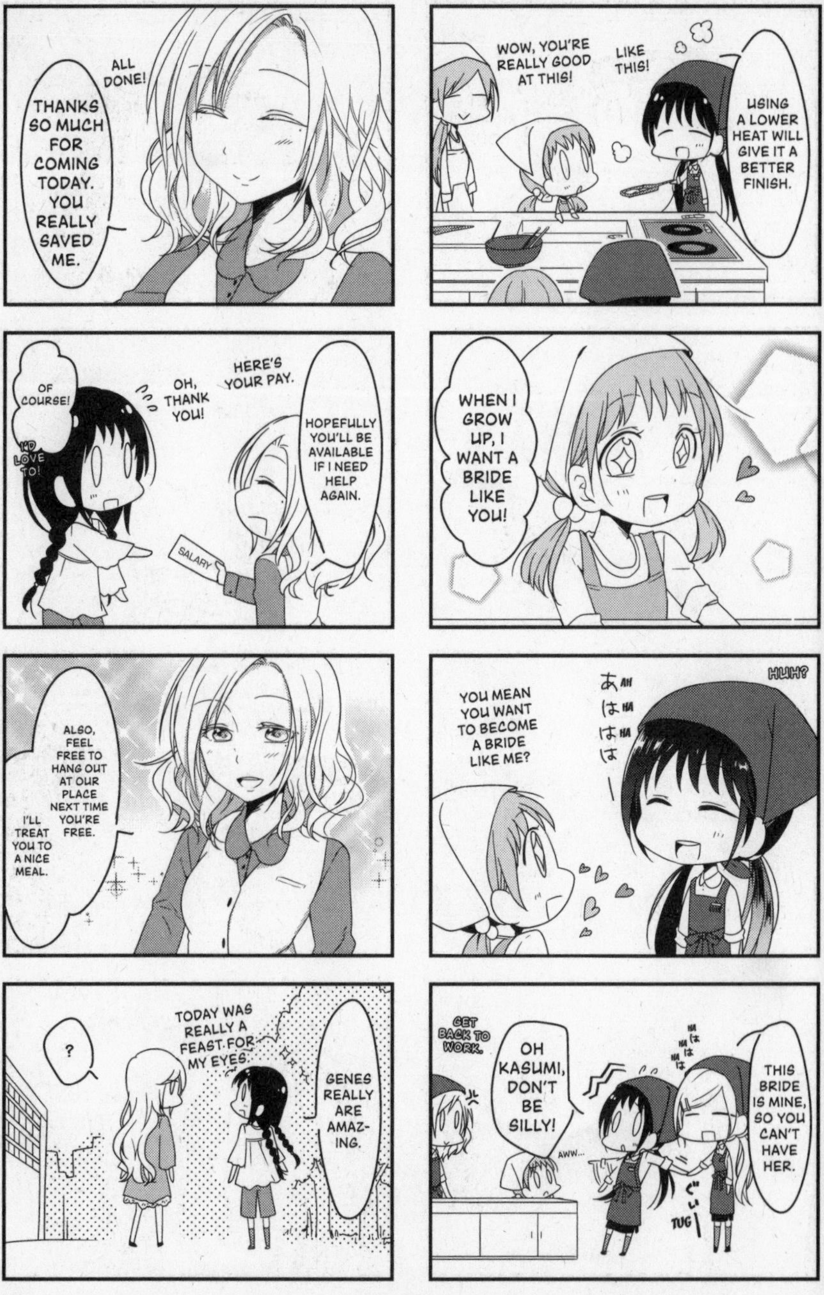
USING A LOWER HEAT WILL GIVE IT A BETTER FINISH.
LIKE THIS!
WOW, YOU'RE REALLY GOOD AT THIS!
ALL DONE!
THANKS SO MUCH FOR COMING TODAY. YOU REALLY SAVED ME.
WHEN I GROW UP, I WANT A BRIDE LIKE YOU!
HOPEFULLY YOU'LL BE AVAILABLE IF I NEED HELP AGAIN.
HERE'S YOUR PAY.
OH, THANK YOU!
OF COURSE!
I'D LOVE TO!
SALARY
HUH?
あはははー
AH HA HA HA
YOU MEAN YOU WANT TO BECOME A BRIDE LIKE ME?
ALSO, FEEL FREE TO HANG OUT AT OUR PLACE NEXT TIME YOU'RE FREE.
I'LL TREAT YOU TO A NICE MEAL.
THIS BRIDE IS MINE, SO YOU CAN'T HAVE HER.
ははは
HA HA HA
ぐい
TUG
OH KASUMI, DON'T BE SILLY!
AWW...
GET BACK TO WORK.
GENES REALLY ARE AMAZ-ING.
TODAY WAS REALLY A FEAST FOR MY EYES.
?

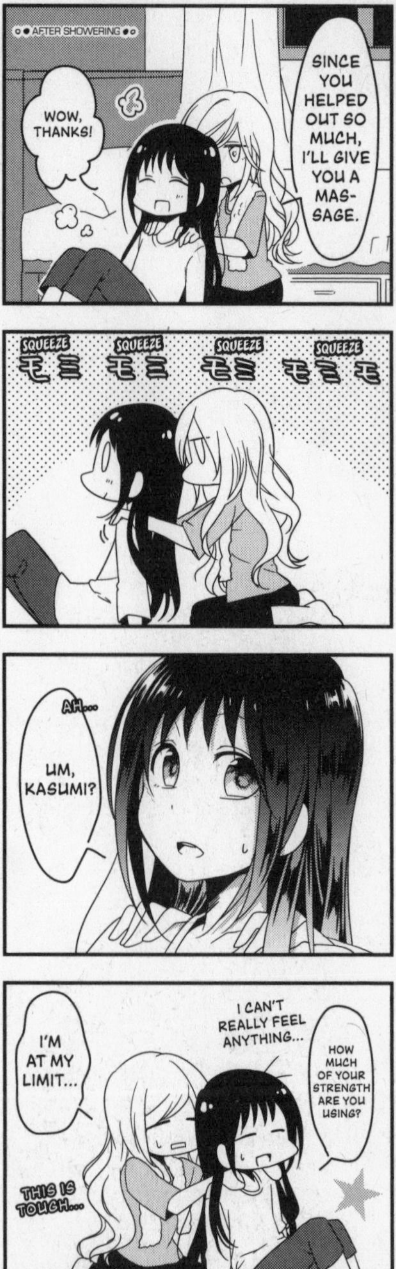
AFTER SHOWERING
SINCE YOU HELPED OUT SO MUCH, I'LL GIVE YOU A MAS-SAGE.
WOW, THANKS!
SQUEEZE モミ
SQUEEZE モミ
SQUEEZE モミ
SQUEEZE モミモ
AH...
UM, KASUMI?
I CAN'T REALLY FEEL ANYTHING...
HOW MUCH OF YOUR STRENGTH ARE YOU USING?
I'M AT MY LIMIT...
THIS IS TOUGH...
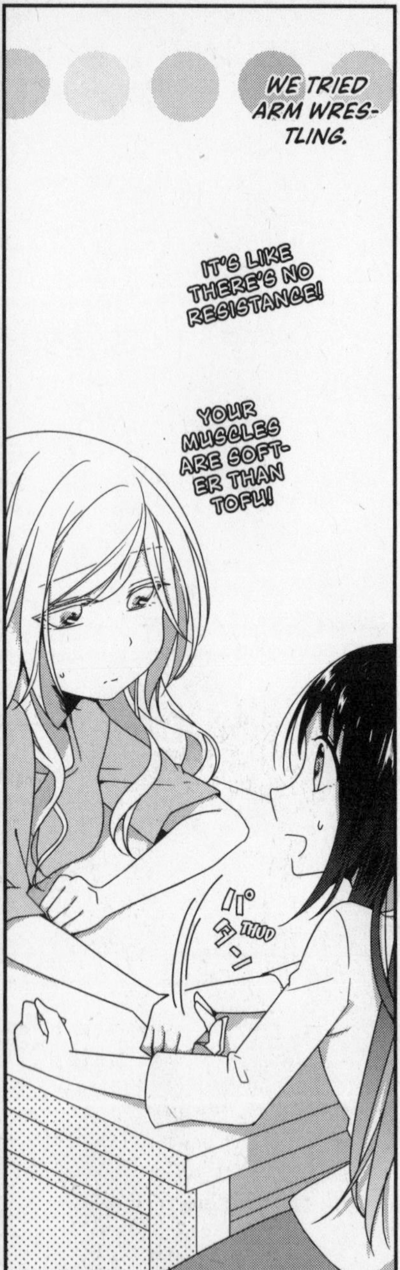
WE TRIED ARM WRES-TLING.
IT'S LIKE THERE'S NO RESISTANCE!
YOUR MUSCLES ARE SOFT-ER THAN TOFU!
パターン THUD

Illustration gallery

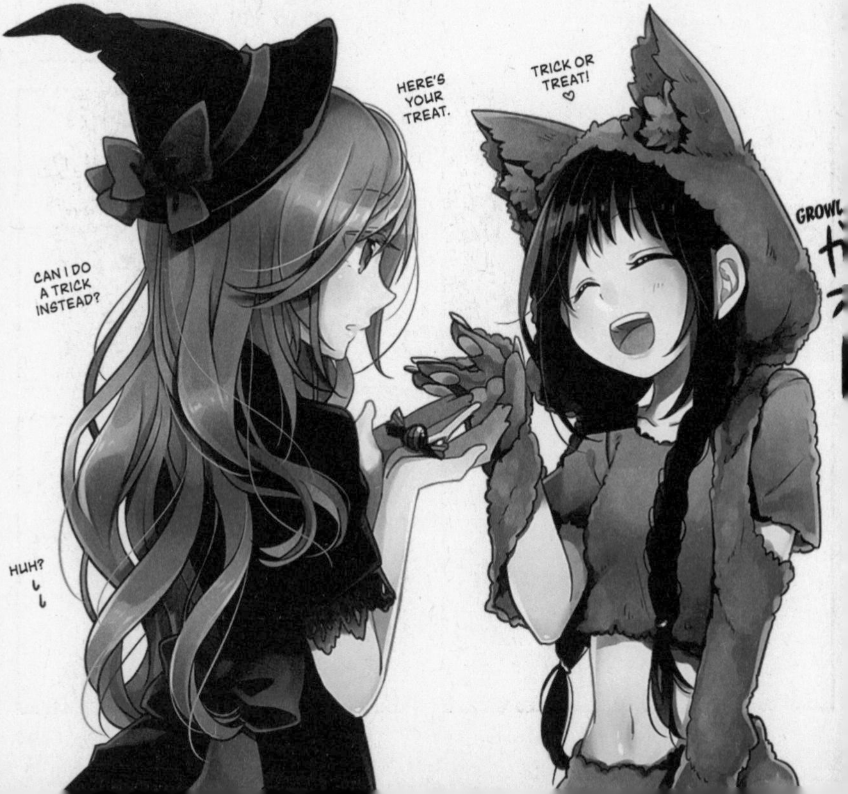
GROWL
TRICK OR TREAT! ♡
HERE'S YOUR TREAT.
CAN I DO A TRICK INSTEAD?
HUH?

Futaribeya
A ROOM FOR TWO

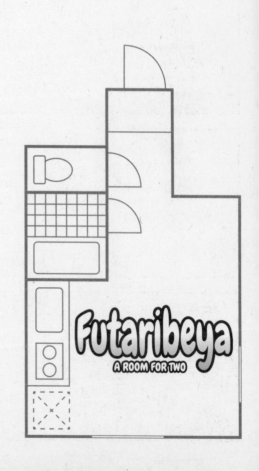

Chapter 7

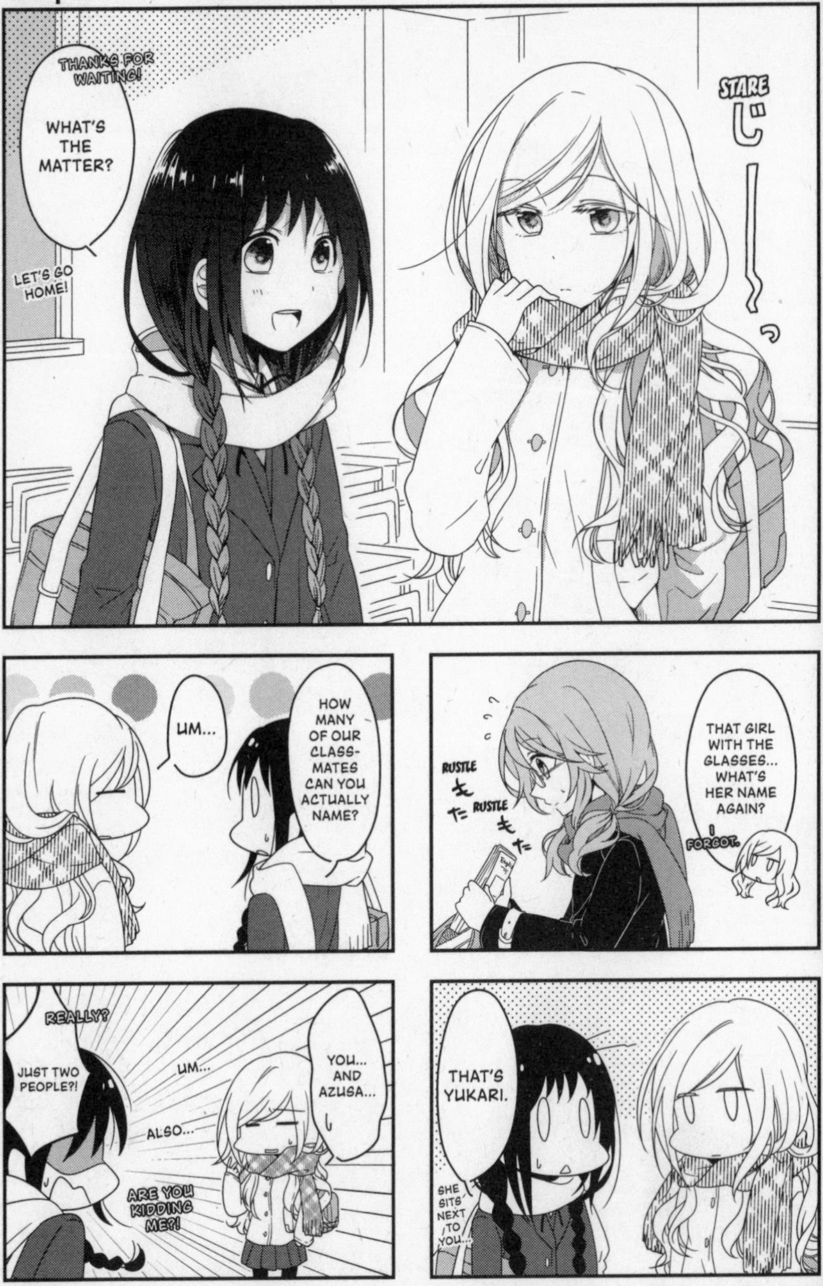
STARE
じ――っ
THANKS FOR WAITING!
WHAT'S THE MATTER?
LET'S GO HOME!
THAT GIRL WITH THE GLASSES... WHAT'S HER NAME AGAIN?
I FORGOT.
RUSTLE
RUSTLE
HOW MANY OF OUR CLASSMATES CAN YOU ACTUALLY NAME?
UM...
THAT'S YUKARI.
SHE SITS NEXT TO YOU...
YOU... AND AZUSA...
UM...
ALSO...
REALLY?
JUST TWO PEOPLE?!
ARE YOU KIDDING ME?!

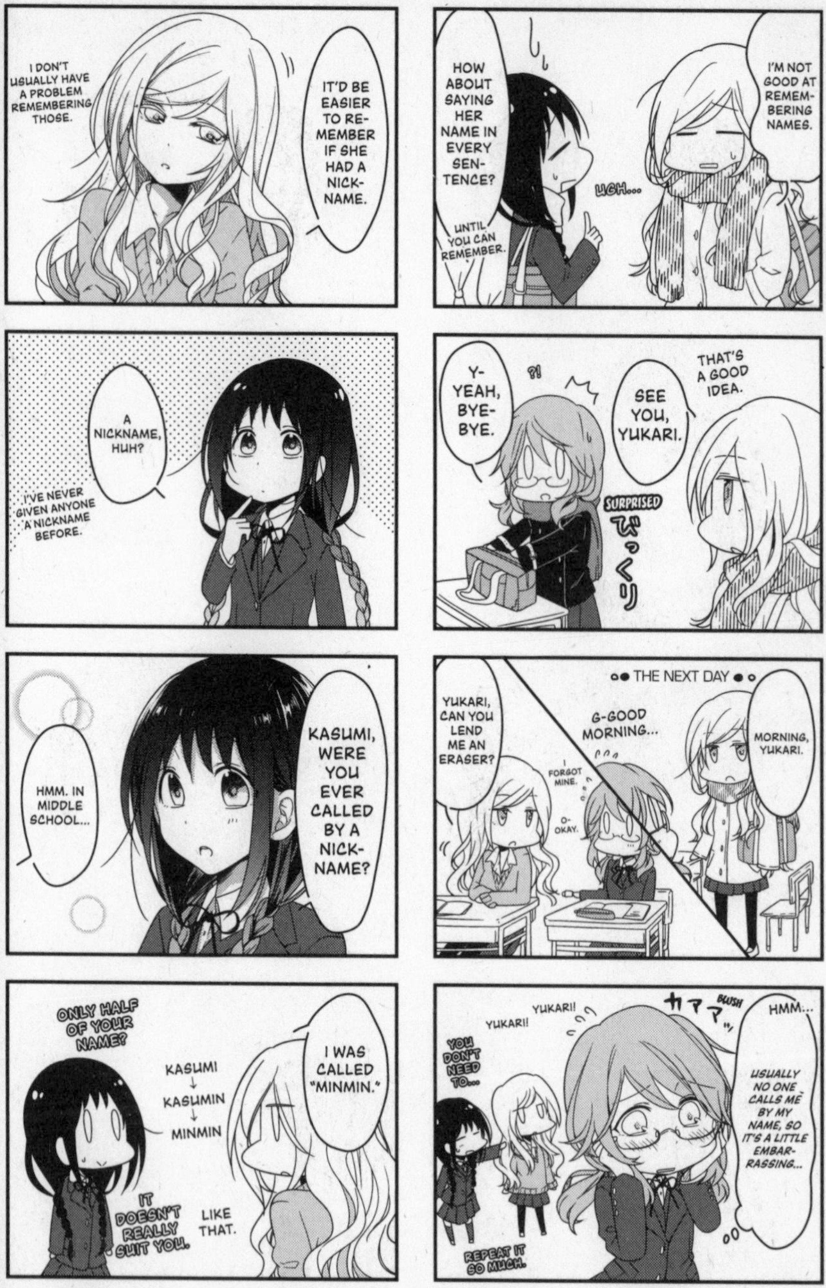
I'M NOT GOOD AT REMEMBERING NAMES.
UGH...
HOW ABOUT SAYING HER NAME IN EVERY SENTENCE?
UNTIL YOU CAN REMEMBER.
THAT'S A GOOD IDEA.
SEE YOU, YUKARI.
?!
Y-YEAH, BYE-BYE.
SURPRISED
びっくり
THE NEXT DAY
MORNING, YUKARI.
G-GOOD MORNING...
YUKARI, CAN YOU LEND ME AN ERASER?
I FORGOT MINE.
O-OKAY.
HMM...
カァァ
BLUSH
USUALLY NO ONE CALLS ME BY MY NAME, SO IT'S A LITTLE EMBARRASSING...
YUKARI!
YUKARI!
YOU DON'T NEED TO...
REPEAT IT SO MUCH.
IT'D BE EASIER TO REMEMBER IF SHE HAD A NICKNAME.
I DON'T USUALLY HAVE A PROBLEM REMEMBERING THOSE.
A NICKNAME, HUH?
I'VE NEVER GIVEN ANYONE A NICKNAME BEFORE.
KASUMI, WERE YOU EVER CALLED BY A NICKNAME?
HMM. IN MIDDLE SCHOOL...
I WAS CALLED "MINMIN."
KASUMI ↓ KASUMIN ↓ MINMIN
ONLY HALF OF YOUR NAME?
LIKE THAT.
IT DOESN'T REALLY SUIT YOU.

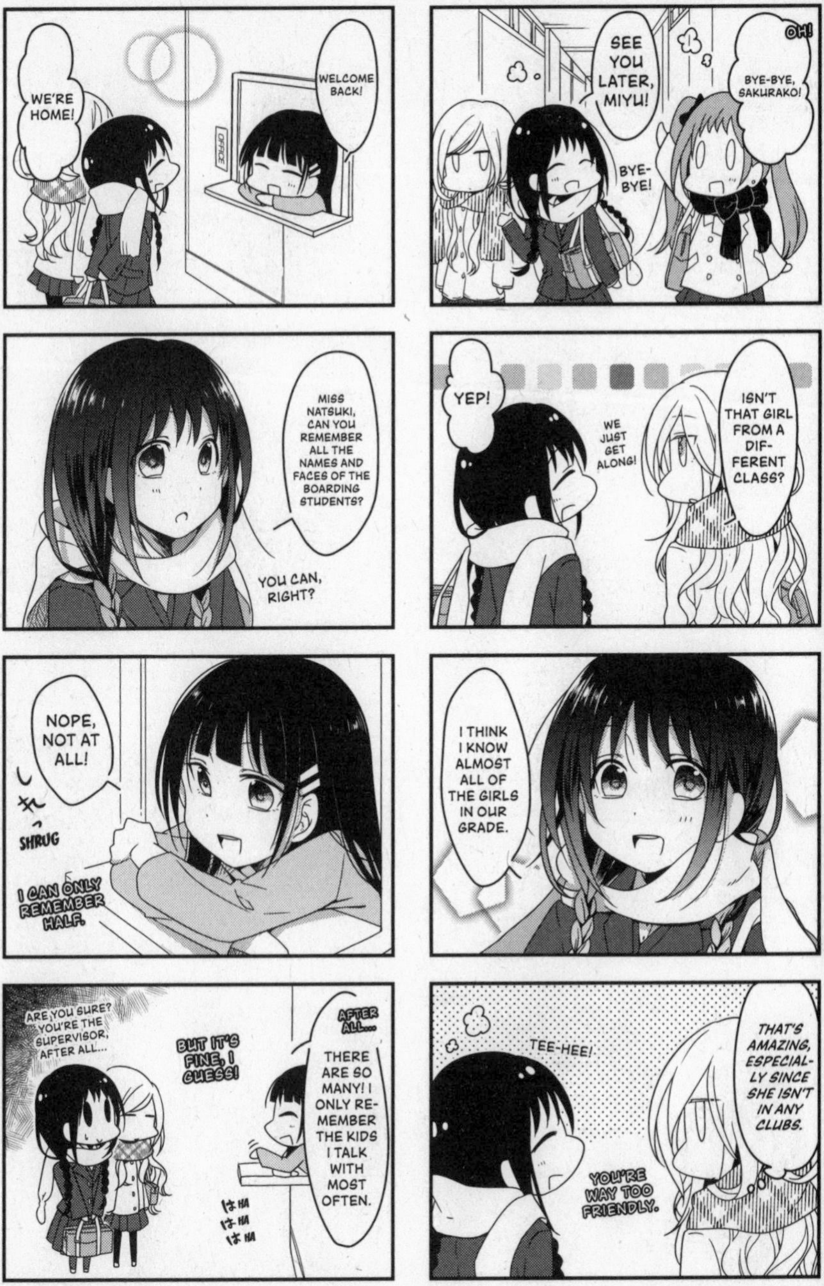
OH!
BYE-BYE, SAKURAKO!
SEE YOU LATER, MIYU!
BYE-BYE!
ISN'T THAT GIRL FROM A DIF-FERENT CLASS?
YEP!
WE JUST GET ALONG!
I THINK I KNOW ALMOST ALL OF THE GIRLS IN OUR GRADE.
THAT'S AMAZING, ESPECIAL-LY SINCE SHE ISN'T IN ANY CLUBS.
TEE-HEE!
YOU'RE WAY TOO FRIENDLY.
WELCOME BACK!
WE'RE HOME!
OFFICE
MISS NATSUKI, CAN YOU REMEMBER ALL THE NAMES AND FACES OF THE BOARDING STUDENTS?
YOU CAN, RIGHT?
NOPE, NOT AT ALL!
しれっ
SHRUG
I CAN ONLY REMEMBER HALF.
AFTER ALL...
THERE ARE SO MANY! I ONLY RE-MEMBER THE KIDS I TALK WITH MOST OFTEN.
は HA は HA は HA
BUT IT'S FINE, I GUESS!
ARE YOU SURE? YOU'RE THE SUPERVISOR, AFTER ALL...

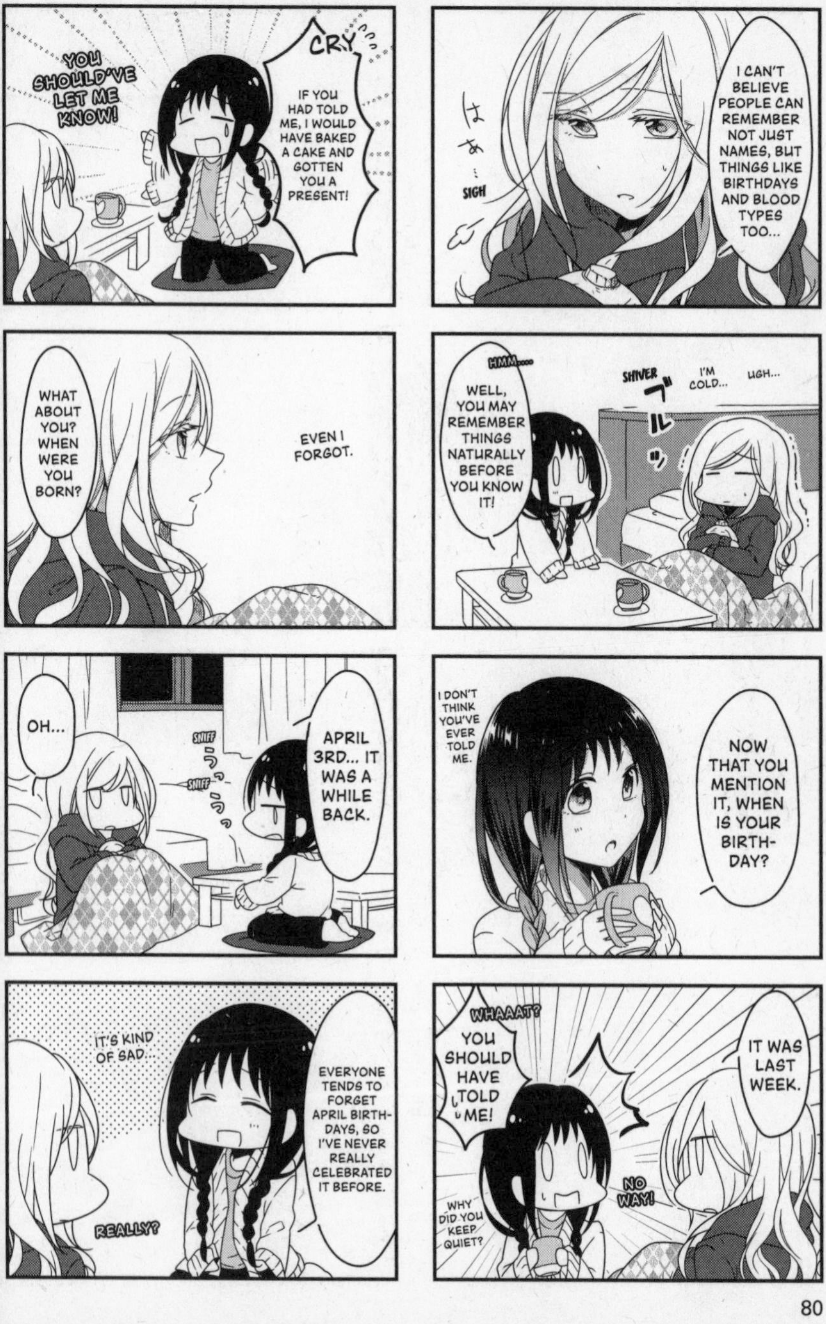

はあ…
SIGH
I CAN'T BELIEVE PEOPLE CAN REMEMBER NOT JUST NAMES, BUT THINGS LIKE BIRTHDAYS AND BLOOD TYPES TOO...
HMM....
WELL, YOU MAY REMEMBER THINGS NATURALLY BEFORE YOU KNOW IT!
SHIVER
ブルッ
I'M COLD...
UGH...
NOW THAT YOU MENTION IT, WHEN IS YOUR BIRTH-DAY?
I DON'T THINK YOU'VE EVER TOLD ME.
IT WAS LAST WEEK.
WHAAAT?
YOU SHOULD HAVE TOLD ME!
NO WAY!
WHY DID YOU KEEP QUIET?
CRY
IF YOU HAD TOLD ME, I WOULD HAVE BAKED A CAKE AND GOTTEN YOU A PRESENT!
YOU SHOULD'VE LET ME KNOW!
EVEN I FORGOT.
WHAT ABOUT YOU? WHEN WERE YOU BORN?
APRIL 3RD... IT WAS A WHILE BACK.
SNIFF
SNIFF
OH...
EVERYONE TENDS TO FORGET APRIL BIRTH-DAYS, SO I'VE NEVER REALLY CELEBRATED IT BEFORE.
IT'S KIND OF SAD...
REALLY?

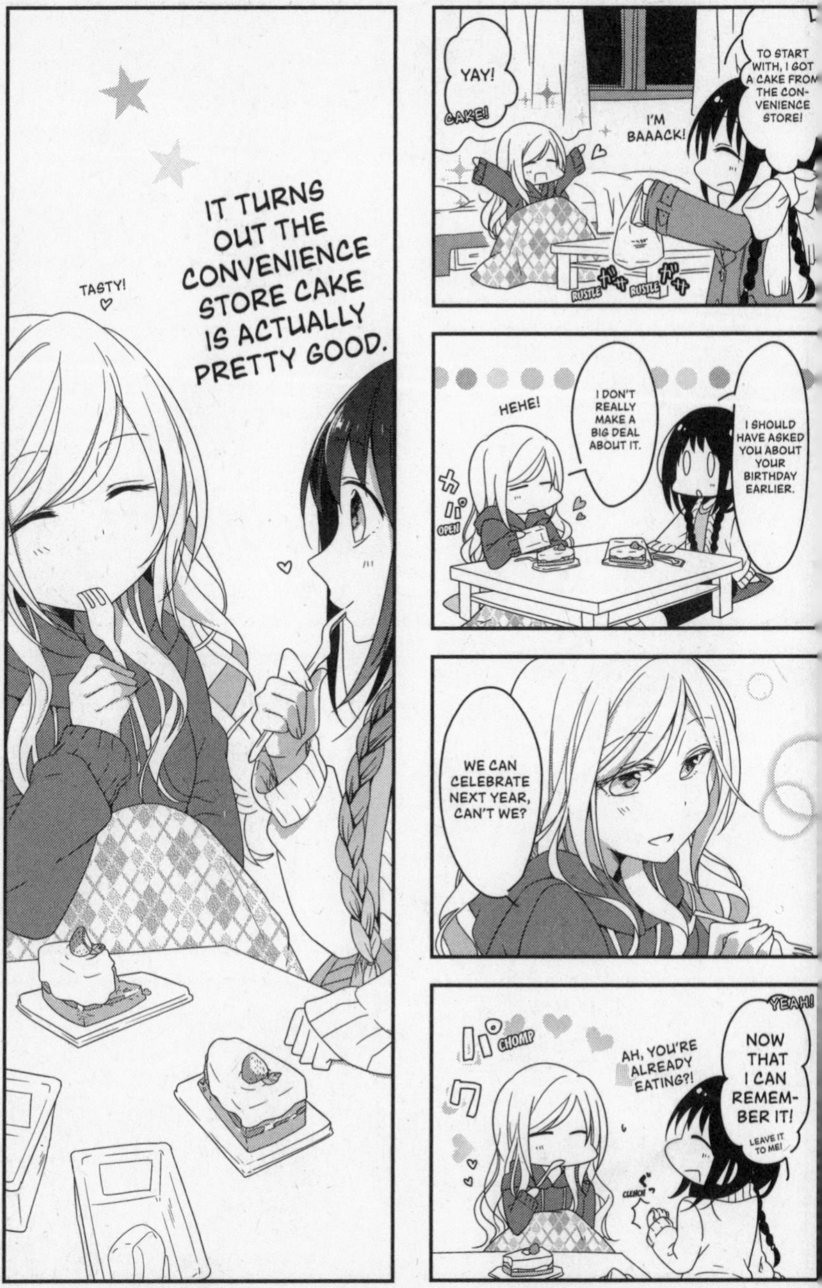
TO START WITH, I GOT A CAKE FROM THE CON-VENIENCE STORE!
I'M BAAACK!
RUSTLE
RUSTLE
YAY!
CAKE!
I SHOULD HAVE ASKED YOU ABOUT YOUR BIRTHDAY EARLIER.
I DON'T REALLY MAKE A BIG DEAL ABOUT IT.
HEHE!
OPEN
WE CAN CELEBRATE NEXT YEAR, CAN'T WE?
YEAH!
NOW THAT I CAN REMEM-BER IT!
LEAVE IT TO ME!
AH, YOU'RE ALREADY EATING?!
CHOMP
CLENCH
IT TURNS OUT THE CONVENIENCE STORE CAKE IS ACTUALLY PRETTY GOOD.
TASTY!

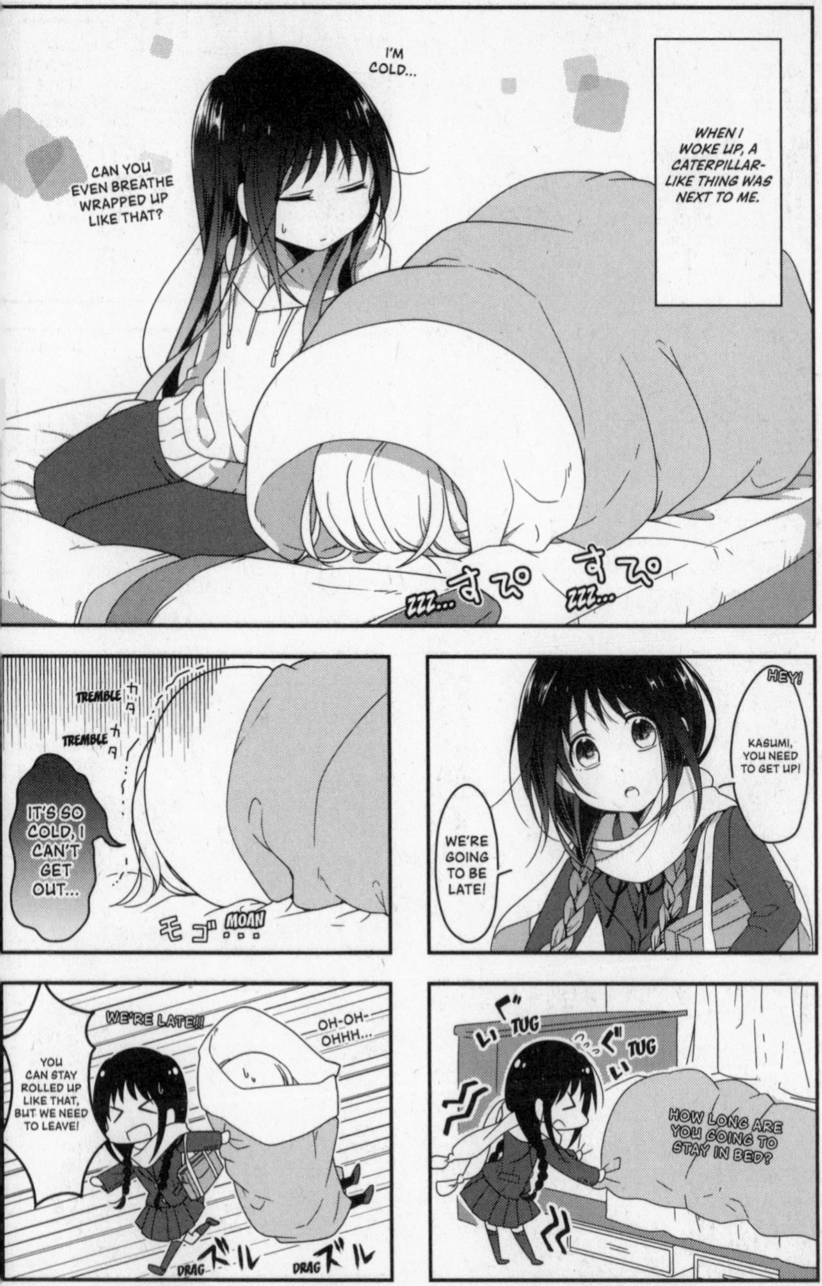
WHEN I WOKE UP, A CATERPILLAR-LIKE THING WAS NEXT TO ME.
I'M COLD...
CAN YOU EVEN BREATHE WRAPPED UP LIKE THAT?
ZZZ... すぴ
ZZZ... すぴ
HEY!
KASUMI, YOU NEED TO GET UP!
WE'RE GOING TO BE LATE!
TREMBLE カタ
TREMBLE カタ
IT'S SO COLD, I CAN'T GET OUT...
モゴ MOAN
ぐい TUG
ぐい TUG
HOW LONG ARE YOU GOING TO STAY IN BED?
WE'RE LATE!!!
OH-OH-OHHH...
YOU CAN STAY ROLLED UP LIKE THAT, BUT WE NEED TO LEAVE!
DRAG ズル
DRAG ズル

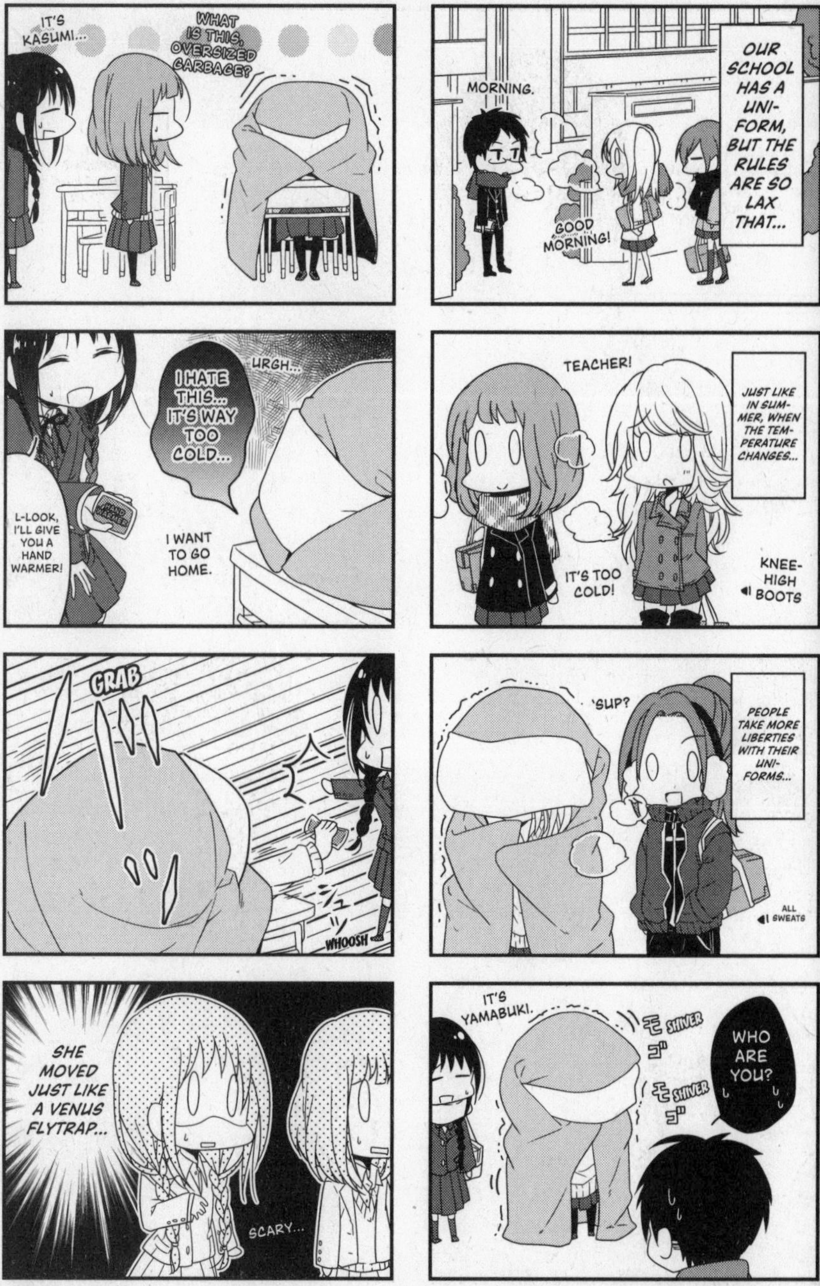

OUR SCHOOL HAS A UNIFORM, BUT THE RULES ARE SO LAX THAT...
MORNING.
GOOD MORNING!
JUST LIKE IN SUMMER, WHEN THE TEMPERATURE CHANGES...
TEACHER!
KNEE-HIGH BOOTS
IT'S TOO COLD!
PEOPLE TAKE MORE LIBERTIES WITH THEIR UNIFORMS...
'SUP?
ALL SWEATS
WHO ARE YOU?
SHIVER
SHIVER
IT'S YAMABUKI.
WHAT IS THIS, OVERSIZED GARBAGE?
IT'S KASUMI...
URGH...
I HATE THIS... IT'S WAY TOO COLD...
I WANT TO GO HOME.
HAND WARMER
L-LOOK, I'LL GIVE YOU A HAND WARMER!
GRAB
WHOOSH
SHE MOVED JUST LIKE A VENUS FLYTRAP...
SCARY...

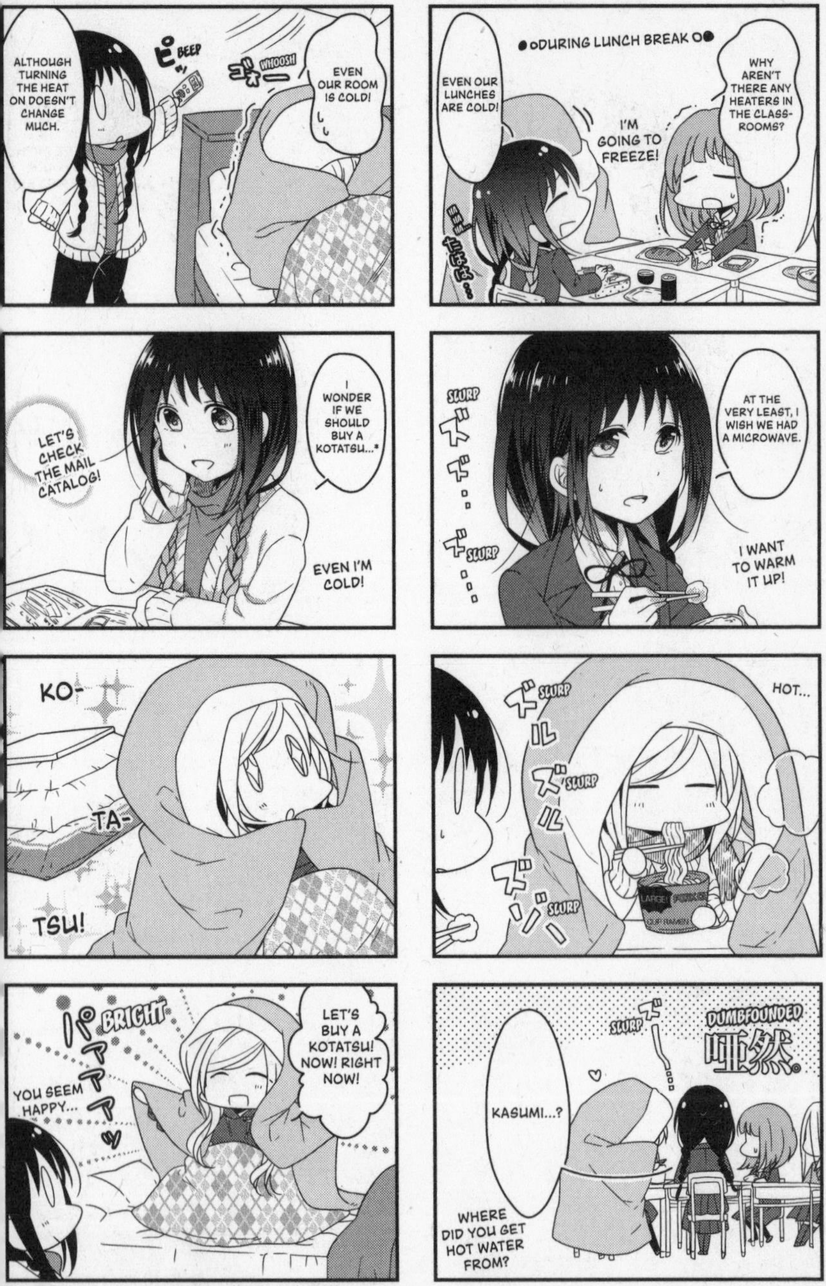
●○DURING LUNCH BREAK○●
WHY AREN'T THERE ANY HEATERS IN THE CLASSROOMS?
I'M GOING TO FREEZE!
EVEN OUR LUNCHES ARE COLD!
HA HA...
たはは…
AT THE VERY LEAST, I WISH WE HAD A MICROWAVE.
I WANT TO WARM IT UP!
SLURP
ズズ…
SLURP
ズ…
HOT...
SLURP
ズル
SLURP
ズル
SLURP
ズゾゾ
LARGE!
CUP RAMEN
DUMBFOUNDED
唖然。
SLURP
ズー…
KASUMI...?
WHERE DID YOU GET HOT WATER FROM?
ALTHOUGH TURNING THE HEAT ON DOESN'T CHANGE MUCH.
BEEP
ピッ
WHOOSH
ゴォー
EVEN OUR ROOM IS COLD!
I WONDER IF WE SHOULD BUY A KOTATSU...*
LET'S CHECK THE MAIL CATALOG!
EVEN I'M COLD!
KO-
TA-
TSU!
LET'S BUY A KOTATSU! NOW! RIGHT NOW!
BRIGHT
パァァァッ
YOU SEEM HAPPY...

*A LOW TABLE WITH A BUILT-IN, HEATED BLANKET

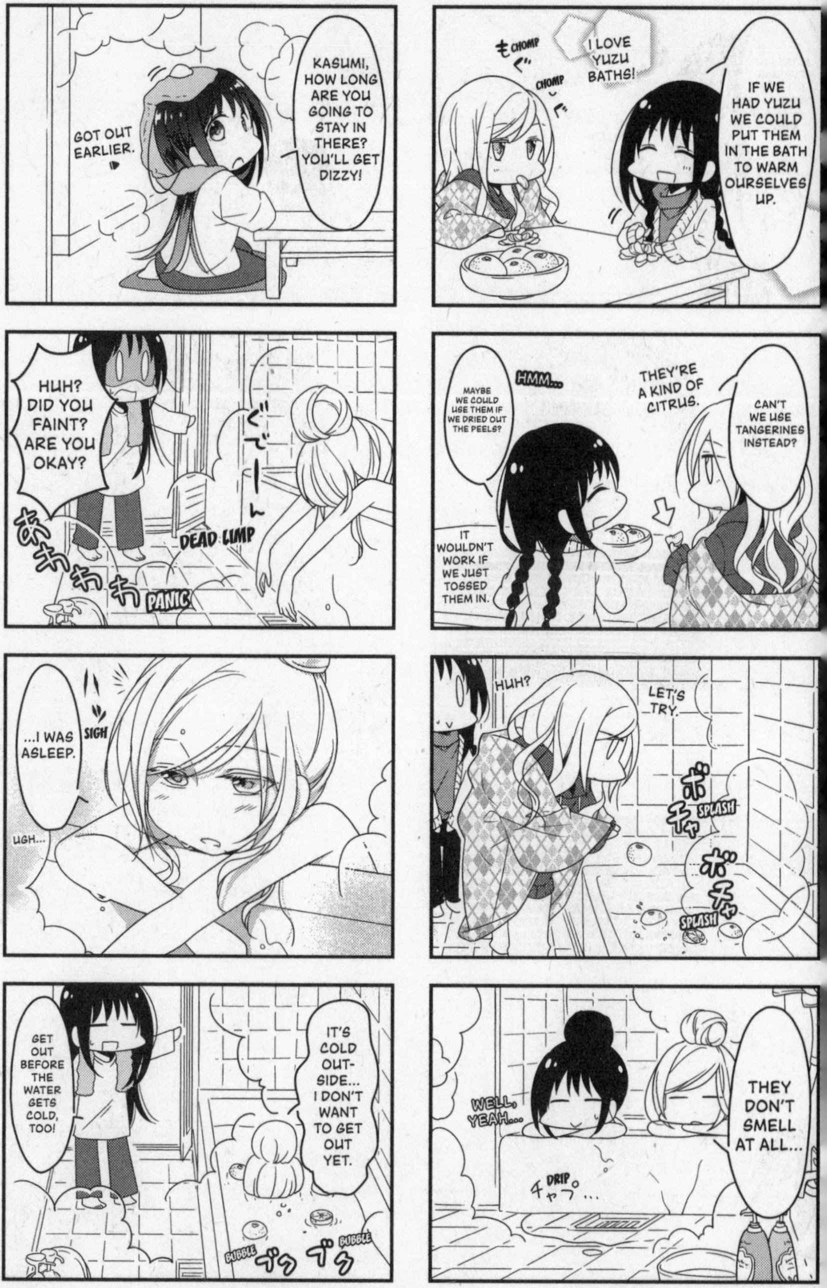
IF WE HAD YUZU WE COULD PUT THEM IN THE BATH TO WARM OURSELVES UP.
I LOVE YUZU BATHS!
もぐ CHOMP
もぐ CHOMP
CAN'T WE USE TANGERINES INSTEAD?
THEY'RE A KIND OF CITRUS.
HMM...
MAYBE WE COULD USE THEM IF WE DRIED OUT THE PEELS?
IT WOULDN'T WORK IF WE JUST TOSSED THEM IN.
LET'S TRY.
HUH?
ボチャ SPLASH
ボチャ SPLASH
THEY DON'T SMELL AT ALL...
WELL, YEAH...
チャプ... DRIP
KASUMI, HOW LONG ARE YOU GOING TO STAY IN THERE? YOU'LL GET DIZZY!
GOT OUT EARLIER.
ぐでーん DEAD LIMP
HUH? DID YOU FAINT? ARE YOU OKAY?
あわわわ PANIC
...I WAS ASLEEP.
SIGH
UGH...
IT'S COLD OUTSIDE... I DON'T WANT TO GET OUT YET.
GET OUT BEFORE THE WATER GETS COLD, TOO!
ブクブク BUBBLE BUBBLE

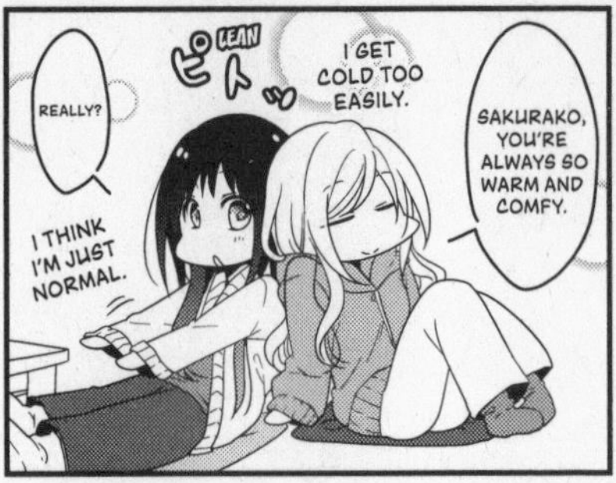
SAKURAKO, YOU'RE ALWAYS SO WARM AND COMFY.
I GET COLD TOO EASILY.
LEAN
REALLY?
I THINK I'M JUST NORMAL.

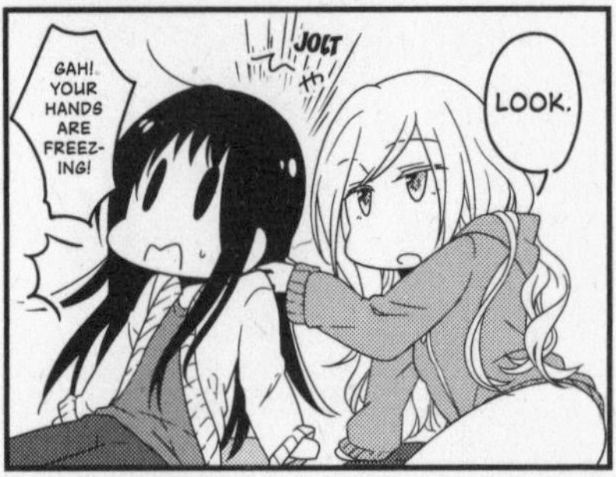
LOOK.
JOLT
GAH! YOUR HANDS ARE FREEZ-ING!

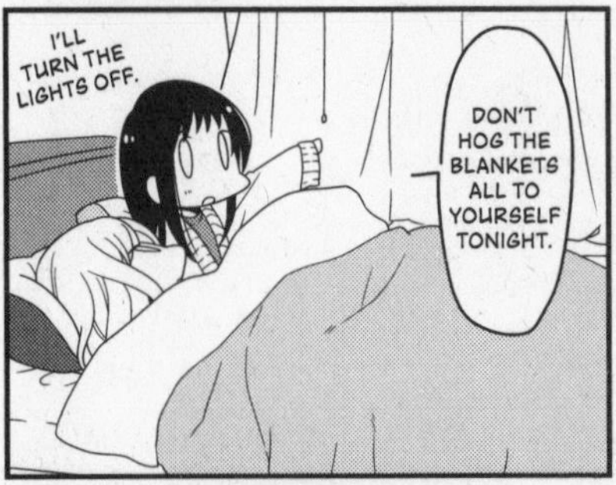
DON'T HOG THE BLANKETS ALL TO YOURSELF TONIGHT.
I'LL TURN THE LIGHTS OFF.

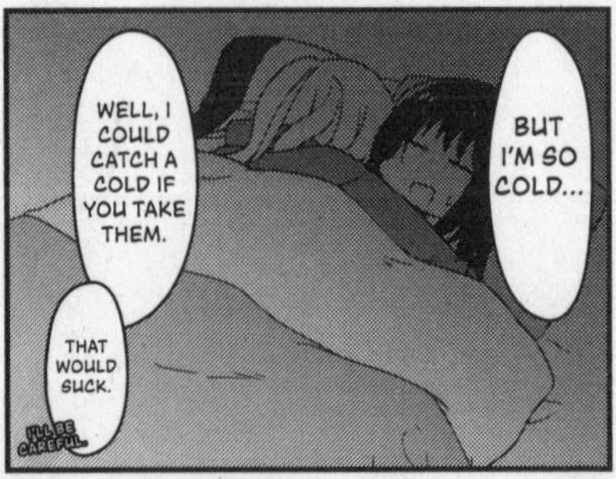
BUT I'M SO COLD...
WELL, I COULD CATCH A COLD IF YOU TAKE THEM.
THAT WOULD SUCK.
I'LL BE CAREFUL.

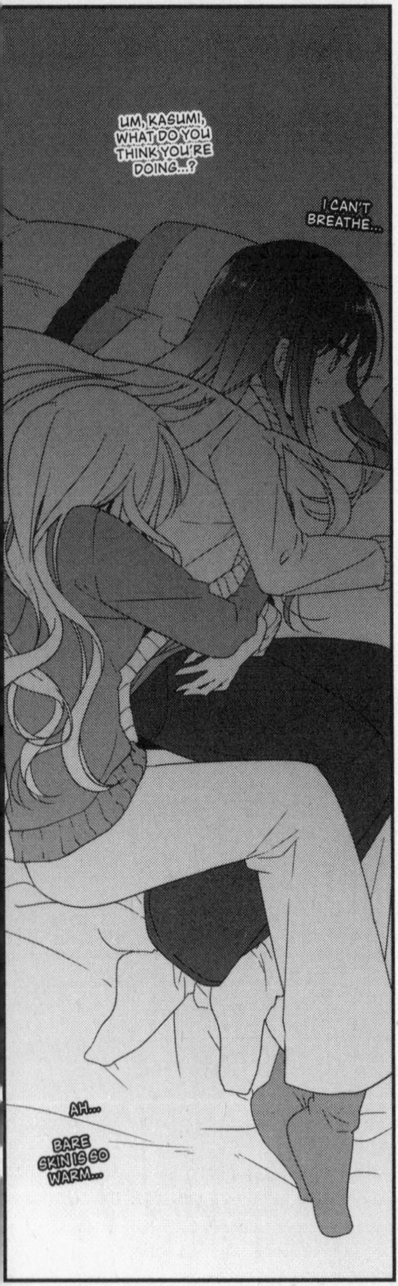
I CAN'T BREATHE...
UM, KASUMI, WHAT DO YOU THINK YOU'RE DOING...?
AH...
BARE SKIN IS SO WARM...

Illustration gallery

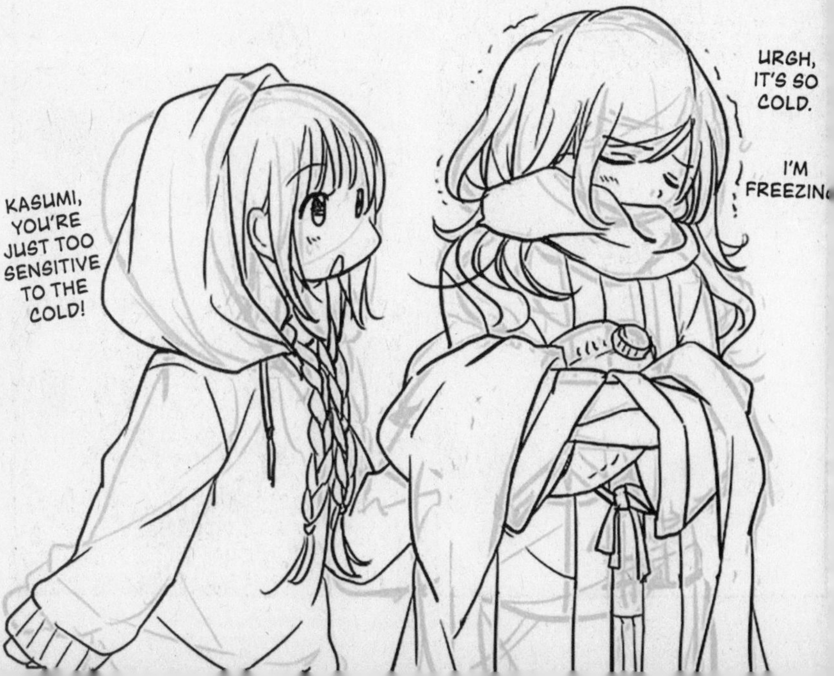
URGH, IT'S SO COLD.
I'M FREEZIN
KASUMI, YOU'RE JUST TOO SENSITIVE TO THE COLD!

Futaribeya
A ROOM FOR TWO

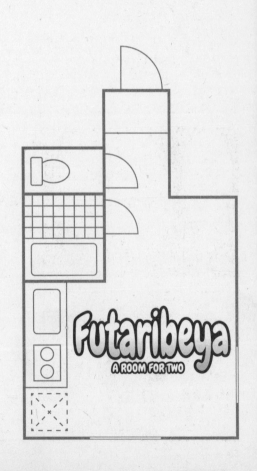

Chapter 8

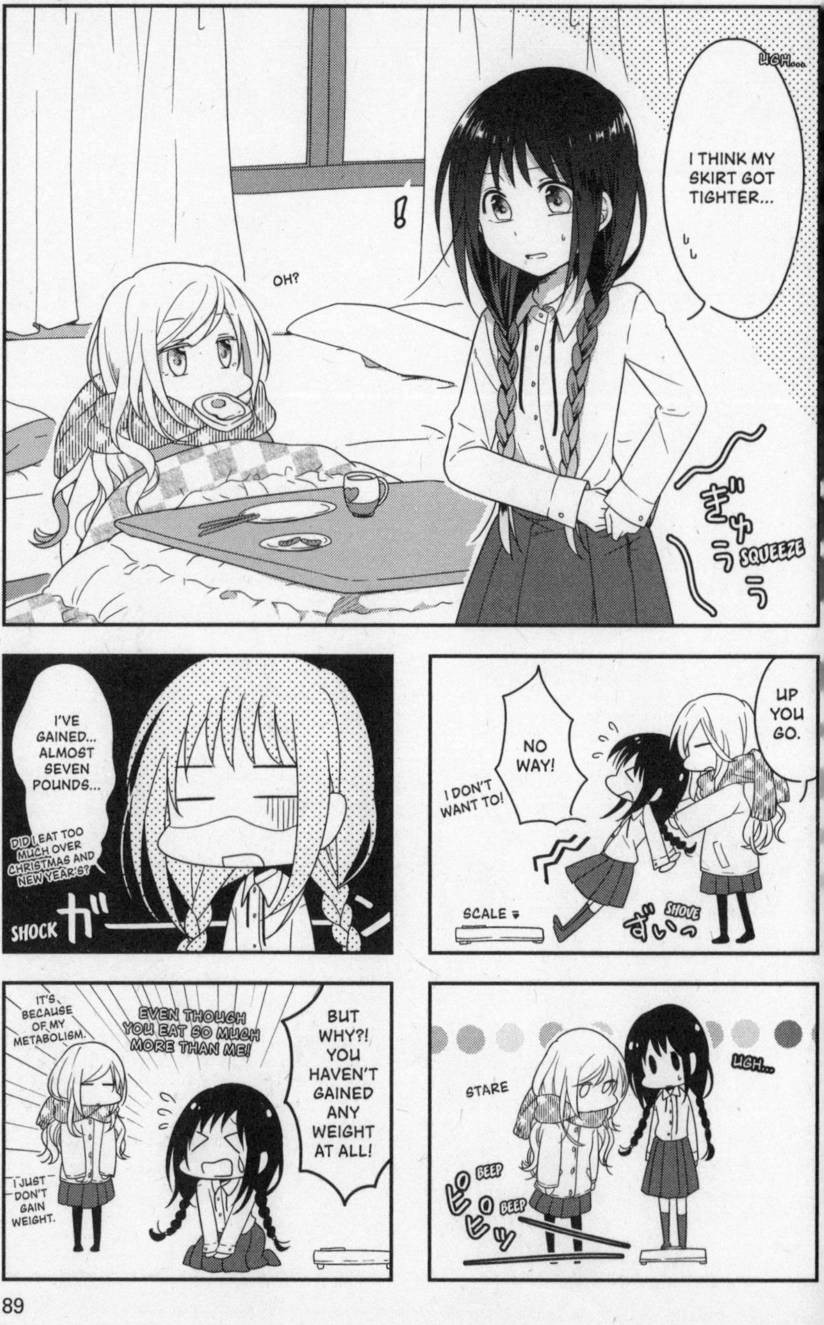
UGH...
I THINK MY SKIRT GOT TIGHTER...
!
OH?
SQUEEZE
UP YOU GO.
NO WAY!
I DON'T WANT TO!
SCALE
SHOVE
I'VE GAINED... ALMOST SEVEN POUNDS...
DID I EAT TOO MUCH OVER CHRISTMAS AND NEW YEAR'S?
SHOCK
STARE
UGH...
BEEP
BEEP
BUT WHY?! YOU HAVEN'T GAINED ANY WEIGHT AT ALL!
EVEN THOUGH YOU EAT SO MUCH MORE THAN ME!
IT'S BECAUSE OF MY METABOLISM.
I JUST DON'T GAIN WEIGHT.

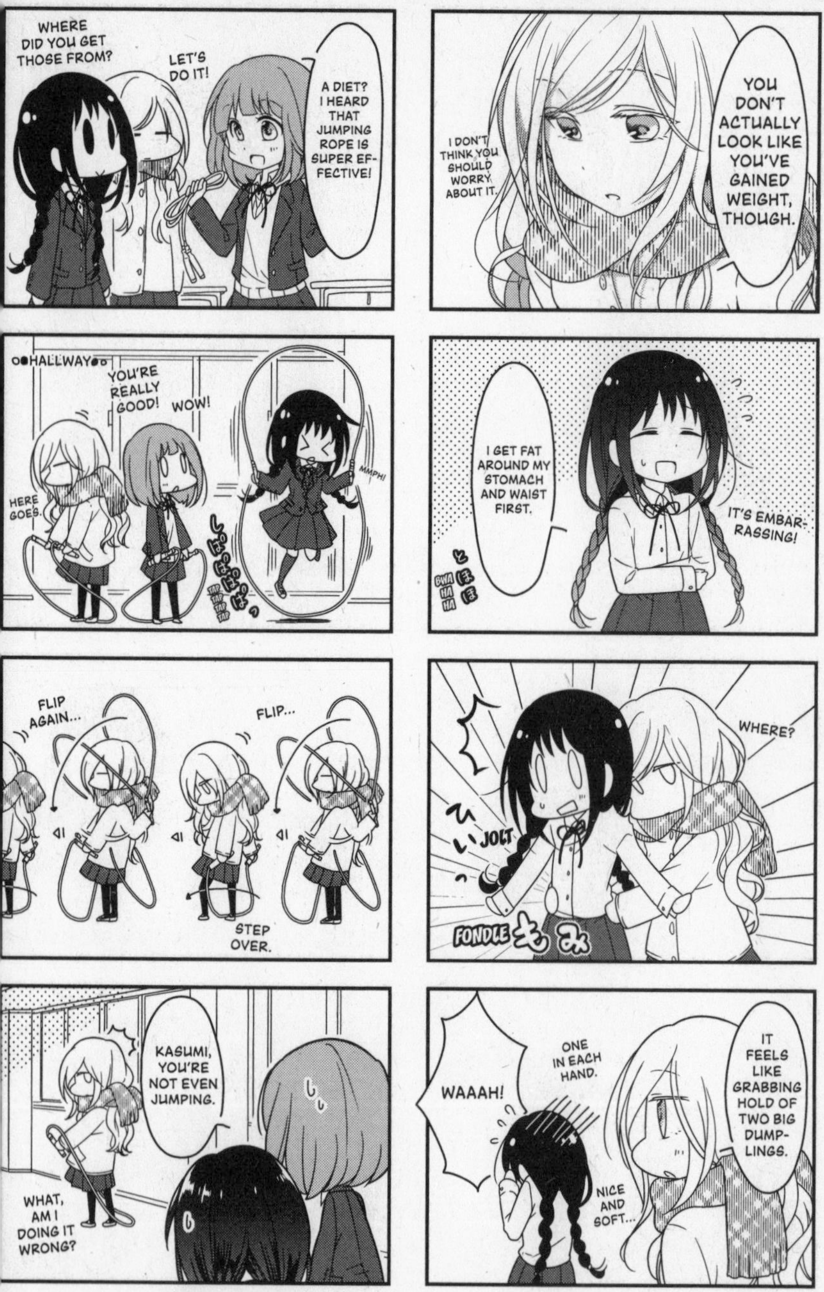

YOU DON'T ACTUALLY LOOK LIKE YOU'VE GAINED WEIGHT, THOUGH.
I DON'T THINK YOU SHOULD WORRY ABOUT IT.
IT'S EMBARRASSING!
I GET FAT AROUND MY STOMACH AND WAIST FIRST.
とほほ BWA HA HA
WHERE?
ひぃ JOLT
FONDLE もみ
IT FEELS LIKE GRABBING HOLD OF TWO BIG DUMPLINGS.
ONE IN EACH HAND.
NICE AND SOFT...
WAAAH!
A DIET? I HEARD THAT JUMPING ROPE IS SUPER EFFECTIVE!
LET'S DO IT!
WHERE DID YOU GET THOSE FROM?
MMPH!
TAP TAP TAP TAP
WOW!
YOU'RE REALLY GOOD!
HALLWAY
HERE GOES.
FLIP...
FLIP AGAIN...
STEP OVER.
KASUMI, YOU'RE NOT EVEN JUMPING.
WHAT, AM I DOING IT WRONG?

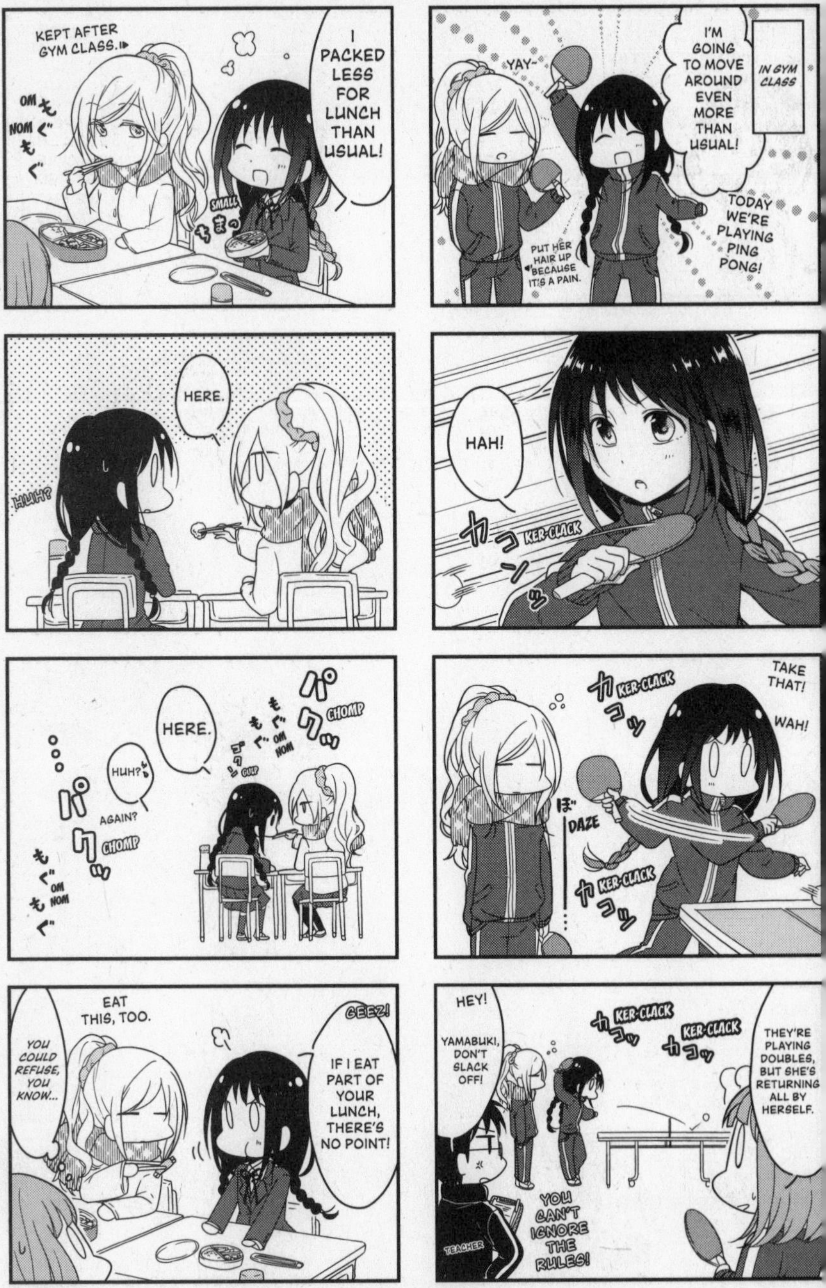
IN GYM CLASS
I'M GOING TO MOVE AROUND EVEN MORE THAN USUAL!
TODAY WE'RE PLAYING PING PONG!
YAY~
PUT HER HAIR UP BECAUSE IT'S A PAIN.
HAH!
KER-CLACK
TAKE THAT!
WAH!
KER-CLACK
DAZE
KER-CLACK
THEY'RE PLAYING DOUBLES, BUT SHE'S RETURNING ALL BY HERSELF.
KER-CLACK
KER-CLACK
HEY!
YAMABUKI, DON'T SLACK OFF!
YOU CAN'T IGNORE THE RULES!
TEACHER
I PACKED LESS FOR LUNCH THAN USUAL!
SMALL
KEPT AFTER GYM CLASS.
OM NOM
HERE.
HUH?
CHOMP
OM NOM
GULP
HERE.
HUH?
AGAIN?
CHOMP
OM NOM
GEEZ!
IF I EAT PART OF YOUR LUNCH, THERE'S NO POINT!
EAT THIS, TOO.
YOU COULD REFUSE, YOU KNOW...

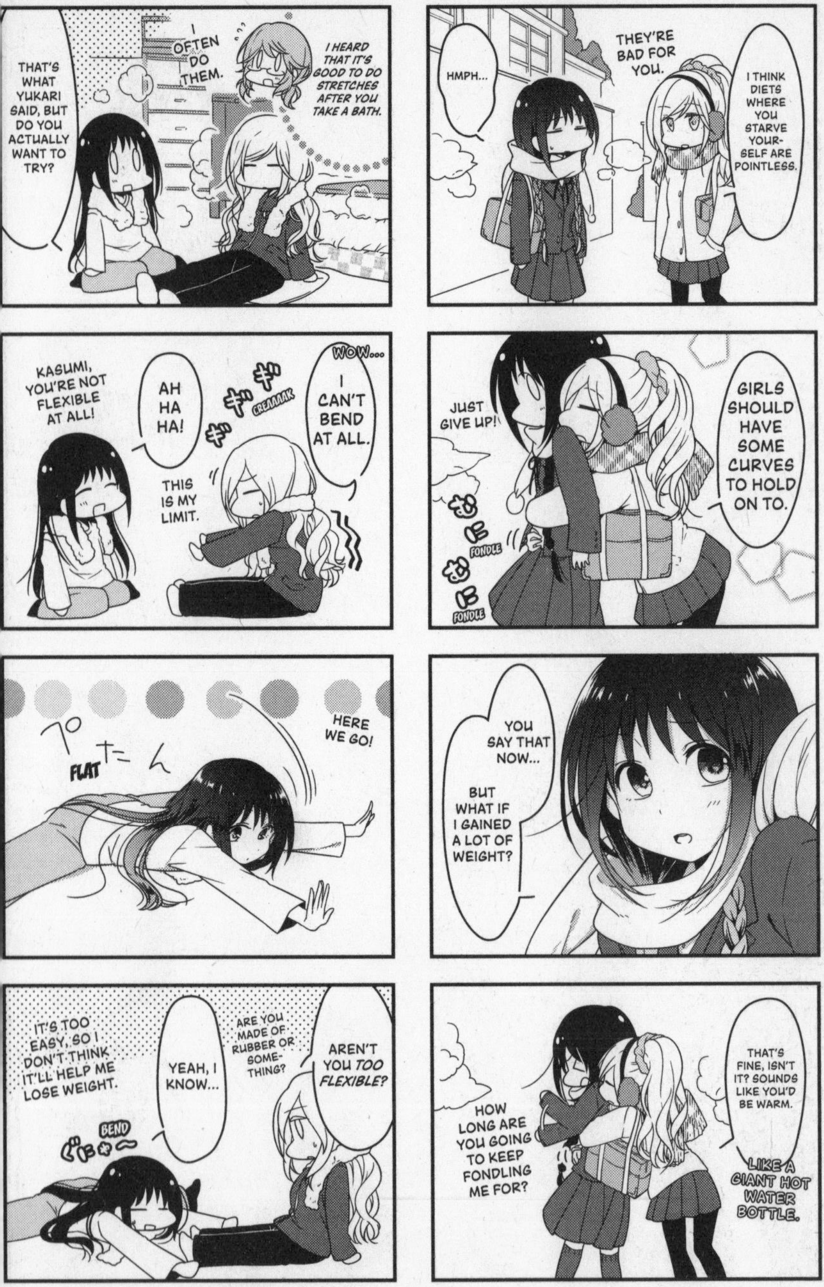
I THINK DIETS WHERE YOU STARVE YOURSELF ARE POINTLESS.
THEY'RE BAD FOR YOU.
HMPH...
GIRLS SHOULD HAVE SOME CURVES TO HOLD ON TO.
JUST GIVE UP!
むに FONDLE
むに FONDLE
YOU SAY THAT NOW...
BUT WHAT IF I GAINED A LOT OF WEIGHT?
THAT'S FINE, ISN'T IT? SOUNDS LIKE YOU'D BE WARM.
LIKE A GIANT HOT WATER BOTTLE.
HOW LONG ARE YOU GOING TO KEEP FONDLING ME FOR?
I HEARD THAT IT'S GOOD TO DO STRETCHES AFTER YOU TAKE A BATH.
I OFTEN DO THEM.
THAT'S WHAT YUKARI SAID, BUT DO YOU ACTUALLY WANT TO TRY?
WOW...
I CAN'T BEND AT ALL.
ギギギ CREAAAAK
AH HA HA!
KASUMI, YOU'RE NOT FLEXIBLE AT ALL!
THIS IS MY LIMIT.
HERE WE GO!
ぺたーん FLAT
ARE YOU MADE OF RUBBER OR SOMETHING?
AREN'T YOU *TOO* FLEXIBLE?
YEAH, I KNOW...
IT'S TOO EASY, SO I DON'T THINK IT'LL HELP ME LOSE WEIGHT.
ぐにゃ〜 BEND

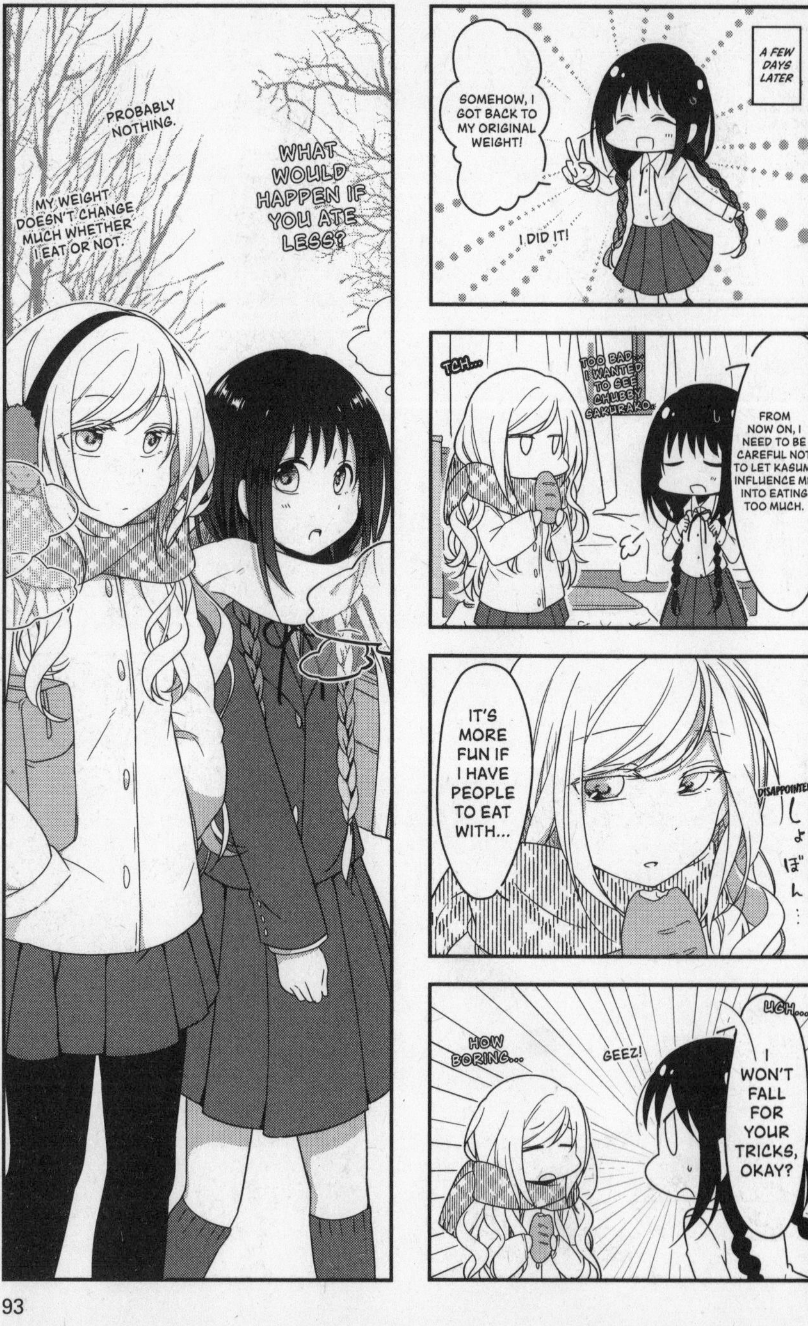
A FEW DAYS LATER
SOMEHOW, I GOT BACK TO MY ORIGINAL WEIGHT!
I DID IT!
FROM NOW ON, I NEED TO BE CAREFUL NOT TO LET KASUMI INFLUENCE ME INTO EATING TOO MUCH.
TOO BAD... I WANTED TO SEE CHUBBY SAKURAKO.
TCH...
DISAPPOINTED
しょぼん…
IT'S MORE FUN IF I HAVE PEOPLE TO EAT WITH...
UGH...
I WON'T FALL FOR YOUR TRICKS, OKAY?
GEEZ!
HOW BORING...
WHAT WOULD HAPPEN IF YOU ATE LESS?
PROBABLY NOTHING.
MY WEIGHT DOESN'T CHANGE MUCH WHETHER I EAT OR NOT.

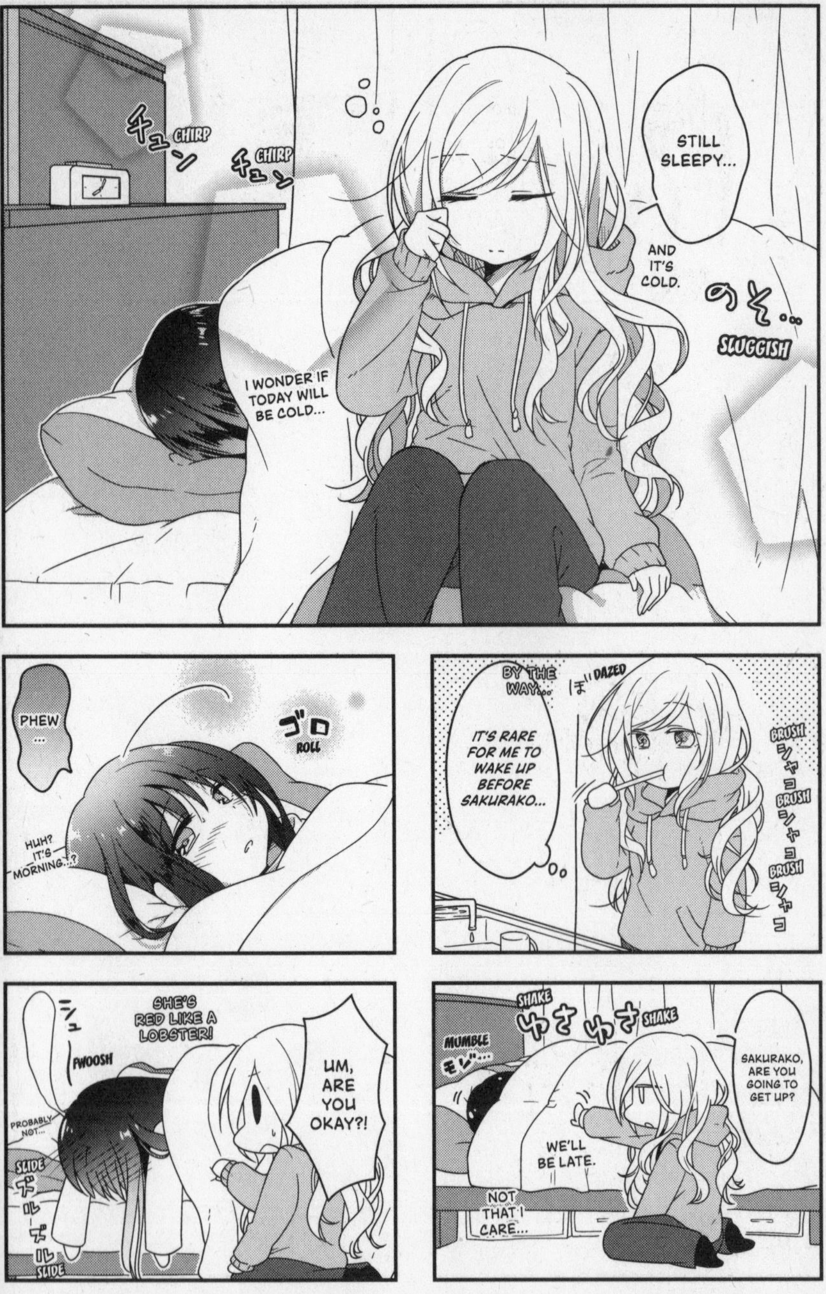
STILL SLEEPY...
AND IT'S COLD.
のそ...
SLUGGISH
チュン CHIRP
チュン CHIRP
I WONDER IF TODAY WILL BE COLD...
BY THE WAY...
ぼ DAZED
BRUSH シャコ BRUSH シャコ BRUSH シャコ
IT'S RARE FOR ME TO WAKE UP BEFORE SAKURAKO...
ゴロ ROLL
PHEW...
HUH? IT'S MORNING...?
SAKURAKO, ARE YOU GOING TO GET UP?
SHAKE ゆさゆさ SHAKE
WE'LL BE LATE.
MUMBLE モゾ...
NOT THAT I CARE...
UM, ARE YOU OKAY?!
SHE'S RED LIKE A LOBSTER!
シュ FWOOSH
PROBABLY NOT...
SLIDE ズルーズル SLIDE

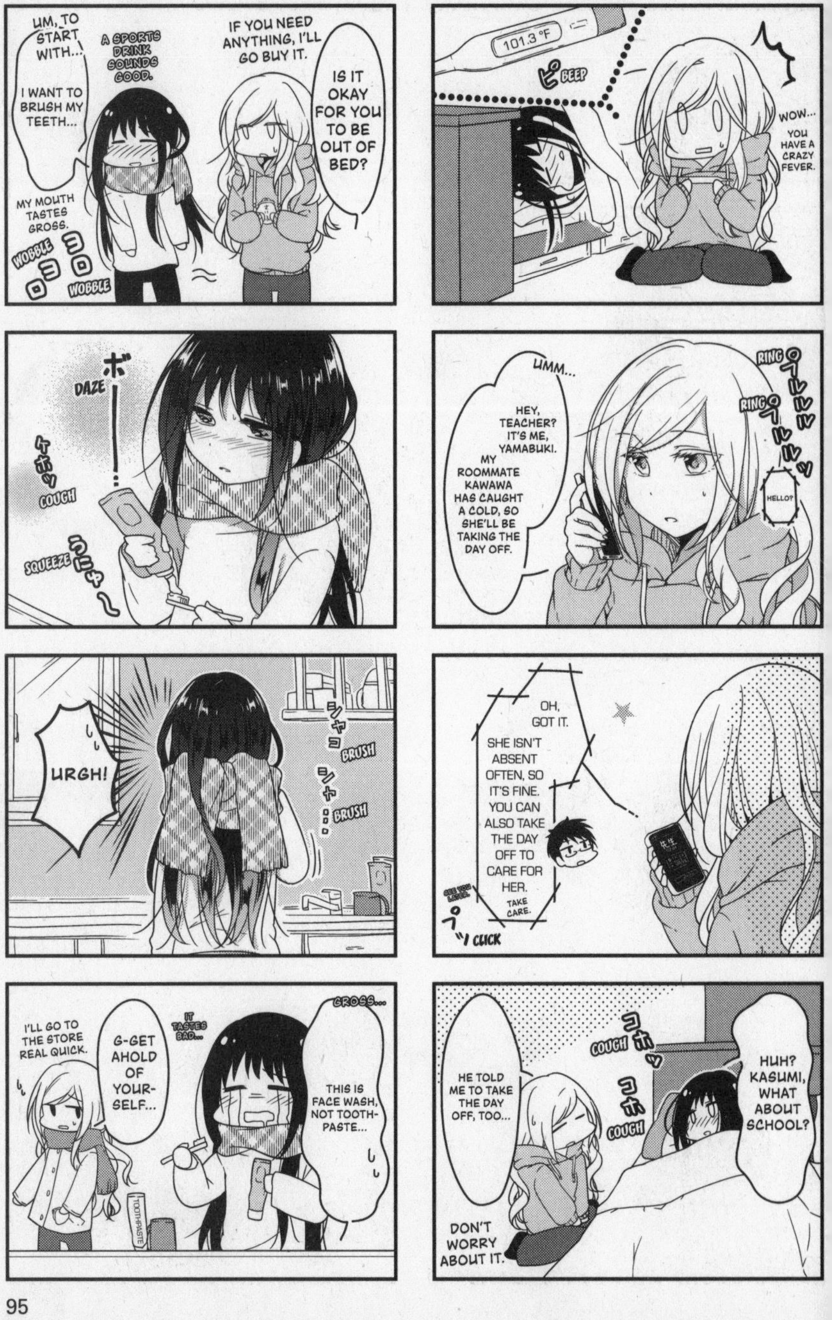
101.3°F
ピ BEEP
WOW... YOU HAVE A CRAZY FEVER.
UMM...
HEY, TEACHER? IT'S ME, YAMABUKI. MY ROOMMATE KAWAWA HAS CAUGHT A COLD, SO SHE'LL BE TAKING THE DAY OFF.
RING プルル RING プルルッ
HELLO?
OH, GOT IT. SHE ISN'T ABSENT OFTEN, SO IT'S FINE. YOU CAN ALSO TAKE THE DAY OFF TO CARE FOR HER.
TAKE CARE.
SEE YOU LATER.
プツ CLICK
先生
HUH? KASUMI, WHAT ABOUT SCHOOL?
COUGH コホッ
コホ COUGH
HE TOLD ME TO TAKE THE DAY OFF, TOO...
DON'T WORRY ABOUT IT.
IF YOU NEED ANYTHING, I'LL GO BUY IT.
IS IT OKAY FOR YOU TO BE OUT OF BED?
UM, TO START WITH...
I WANT TO BRUSH MY TEETH...
A SPORTS DRINK SOUNDS GOOD.
MY MOUTH TASTES GROSS.
WOBBLE ヨロヨロ WOBBLE
ボーー... DAZE
ケホッ COUGH
うにゅ~ SQUEEZE
URGH!
シャコ BRUSH
シャコ... BRUSH
GROSS...
THIS IS FACE WASH, NOT TOOTHPASTE...
IT TASTES BAD...
G-GET AHOLD OF YOURSELF...
I'LL GO TO THE STORE REAL QUICK.
TOOTHPASTE

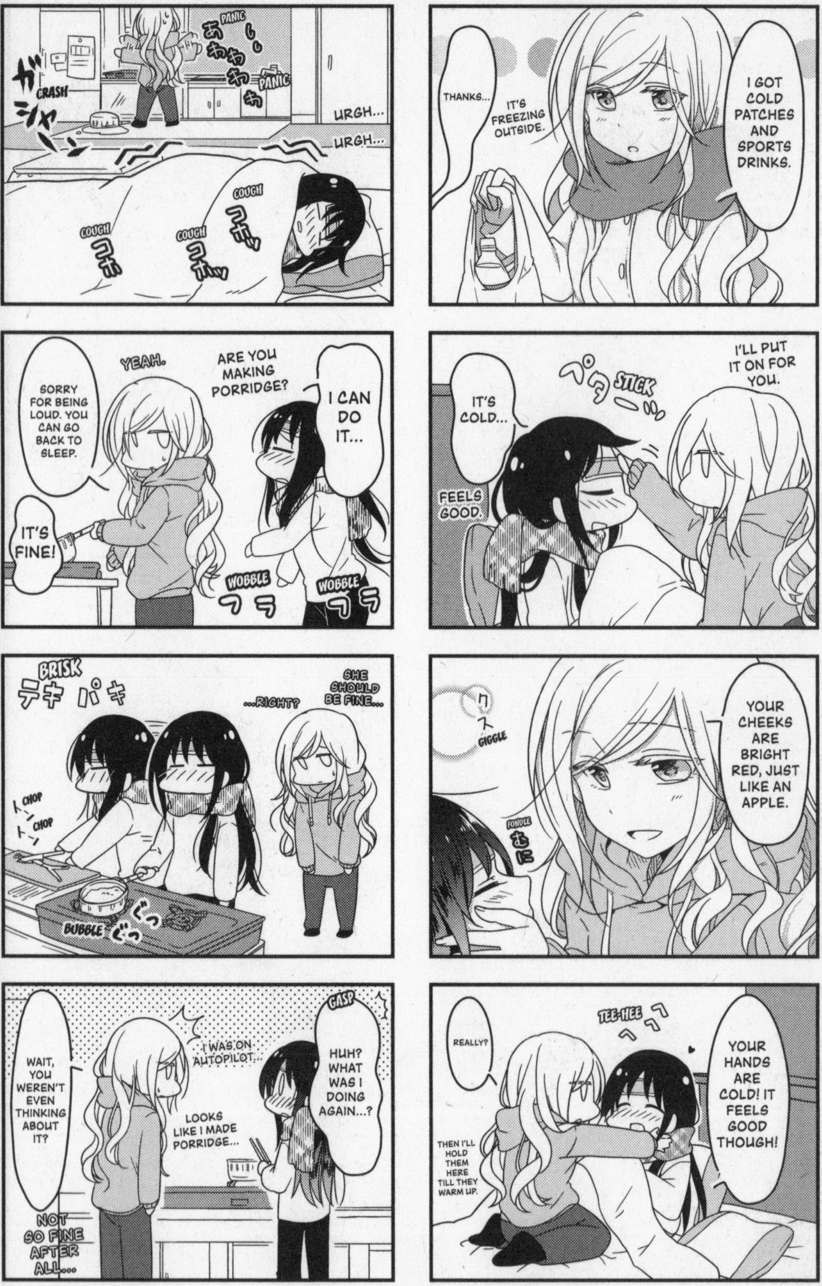
I GOT COLD PATCHES AND SPORTS DRINKS.
IT'S FREEZING OUTSIDE.
THANKS...
I'LL PUT IT ON FOR YOU.
STICK
IT'S COLD...
FEELS GOOD.
YOUR CHEEKS ARE BRIGHT RED, JUST LIKE AN APPLE.
クス
GIGGLE
むに
FONDLE
YOUR HANDS ARE COLD! IT FEELS GOOD THOUGH!
TEE-HEE
へへへ
REALLY?
THEN I'LL HOLD THEM HERE TILL THEY WARM UP.
PANIC
PANIC
CRASH
URGH...
URGH...
COUGH
コホッ
COUGH
コホッ
COUGH
コホ
I CAN DO IT...
ARE YOU MAKING PORRIDGE?
YEAH.
SORRY FOR BEING LOUD. YOU CAN GO BACK TO SLEEP.
IT'S FINE!
WOBBLE
フラ
WOBBLE
フラ
SHE SHOULD BE FINE...
...RIGHT?
BRISK
テキパキ
CHOP
トン
CHOP
トン
BUBBLE
ぐつぐつ
GASP
HUH? WHAT WAS I DOING AGAIN...?
I WAS ON AUTOPILOT...
LOOKS LIKE I MADE PORRIDGE...
WAIT, YOU WEREN'T EVEN THINKING ABOUT IT?
NOT SO FINE AFTER ALL...

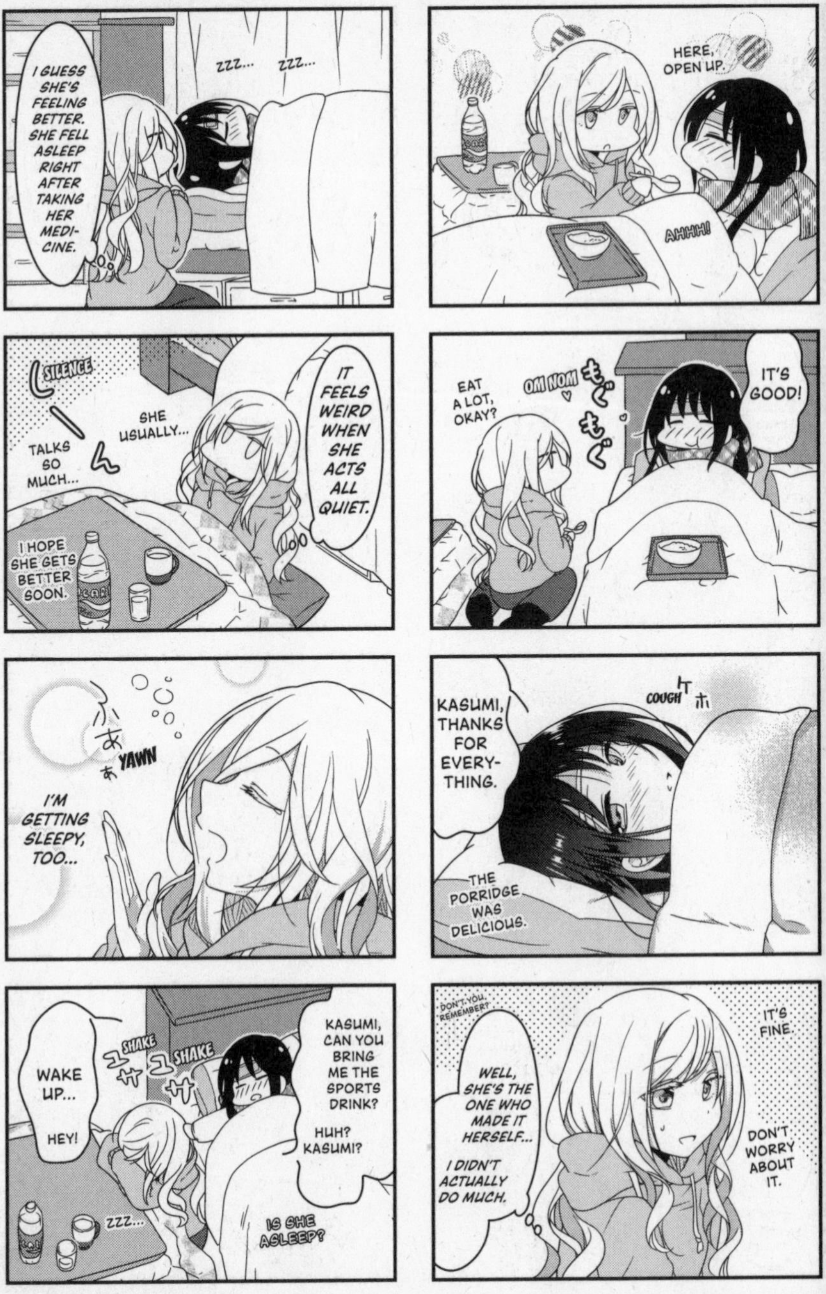

HERE, OPEN UP.
AHHH!
IT'S GOOD!
OM NOM もぐもぐ
EAT A LOT, OKAY?
COUGH ケホ
KASUMI, THANKS FOR EVERYTHING.
THE PORRIDGE WAS DELICIOUS.
IT'S FINE.
DON'T WORRY ABOUT IT.
DON'T YOU REMEMBER?
WELL, SHE'S THE ONE WHO MADE IT HERSELF...
I DIDN'T ACTUALLY DO MUCH.
ZZZ... ZZZ...
I GUESS SHE'S FEELING BETTER. SHE FELL ASLEEP RIGHT AFTER TAKING HER MEDI-CINE.
IT FEELS WEIRD WHEN SHE ACTS ALL QUIET.
SHE USUALLY...
SILENCE しーん
TALKS SO MUCH...
I HOPE SHE GETS BETTER SOON.
ふああ YAWN
I'M GETTING SLEEPY, TOO...
KASUMI, CAN YOU BRING ME THE SPORTS DRINK?
HUH? KASUMI?
IS SHE ASLEEP?
ユサユサ SHAKE SHAKE
WAKE UP...
HEY!
ZZZ...

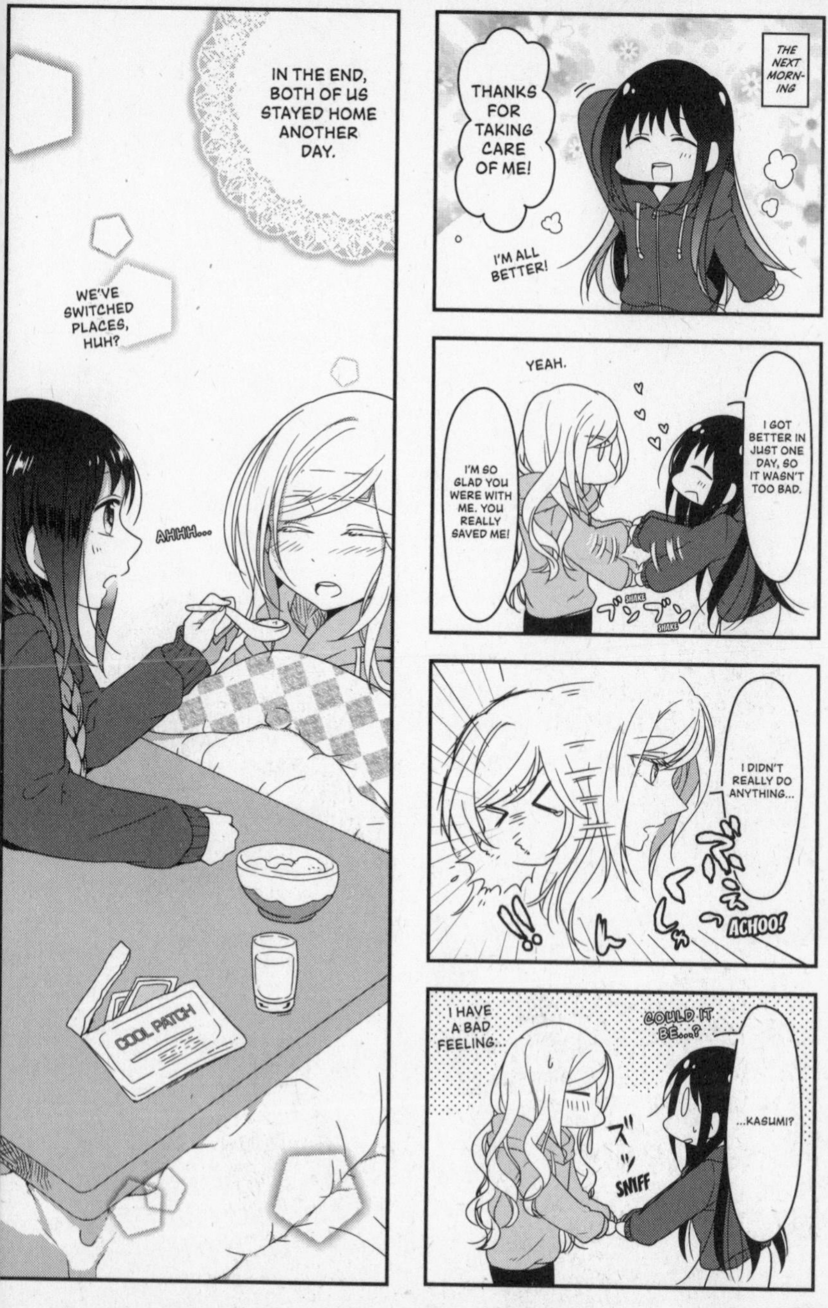
THE NEXT MORNING
THANKS FOR TAKING CARE OF ME!
I'M ALL BETTER!
I GOT BETTER IN JUST ONE DAY, SO IT WASN'T TOO BAD.
YEAH.
I'M SO GLAD YOU WERE WITH ME. YOU REALLY SAVED ME!
SHAKE
SHAKE
I DIDN'T REALLY DO ANYTHING...
ACHOO!
...KASUMI?
COULD IT BE...?
I HAVE A BAD FEELING...
SNIFF
IN THE END, BOTH OF US STAYED HOME ANOTHER DAY.
WE'VE SWITCHED PLACES, HUH?
AHHH...
COOL PATCH

Illustration gallery

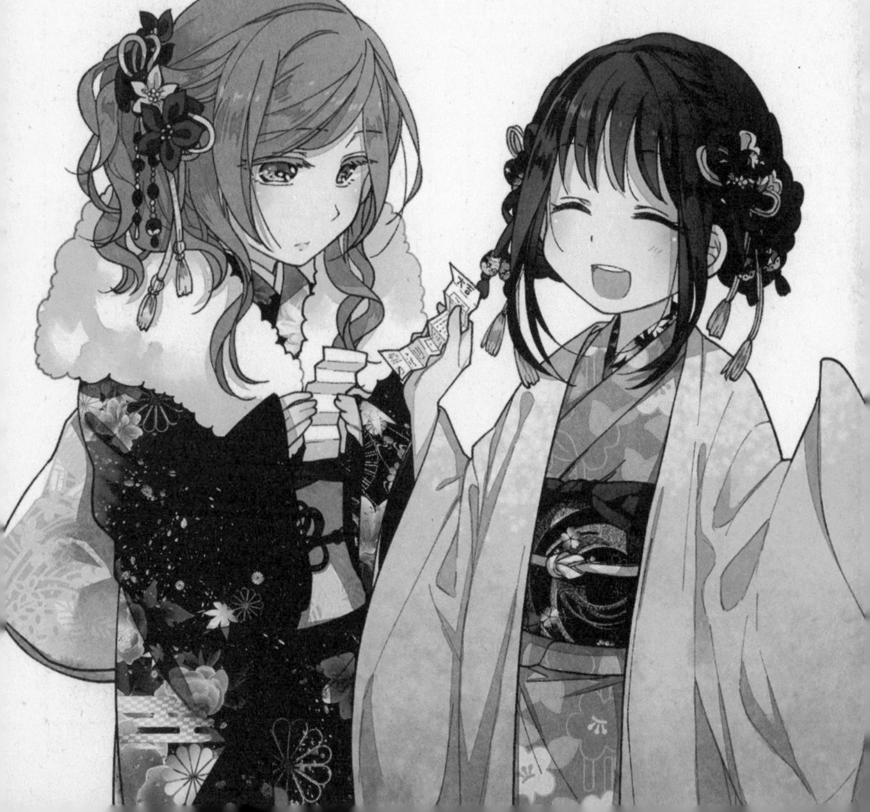

Futaribeya
A ROOM FOR TWO

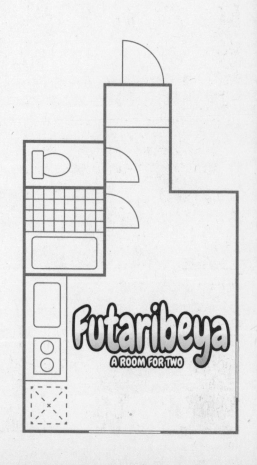

Chapter 9

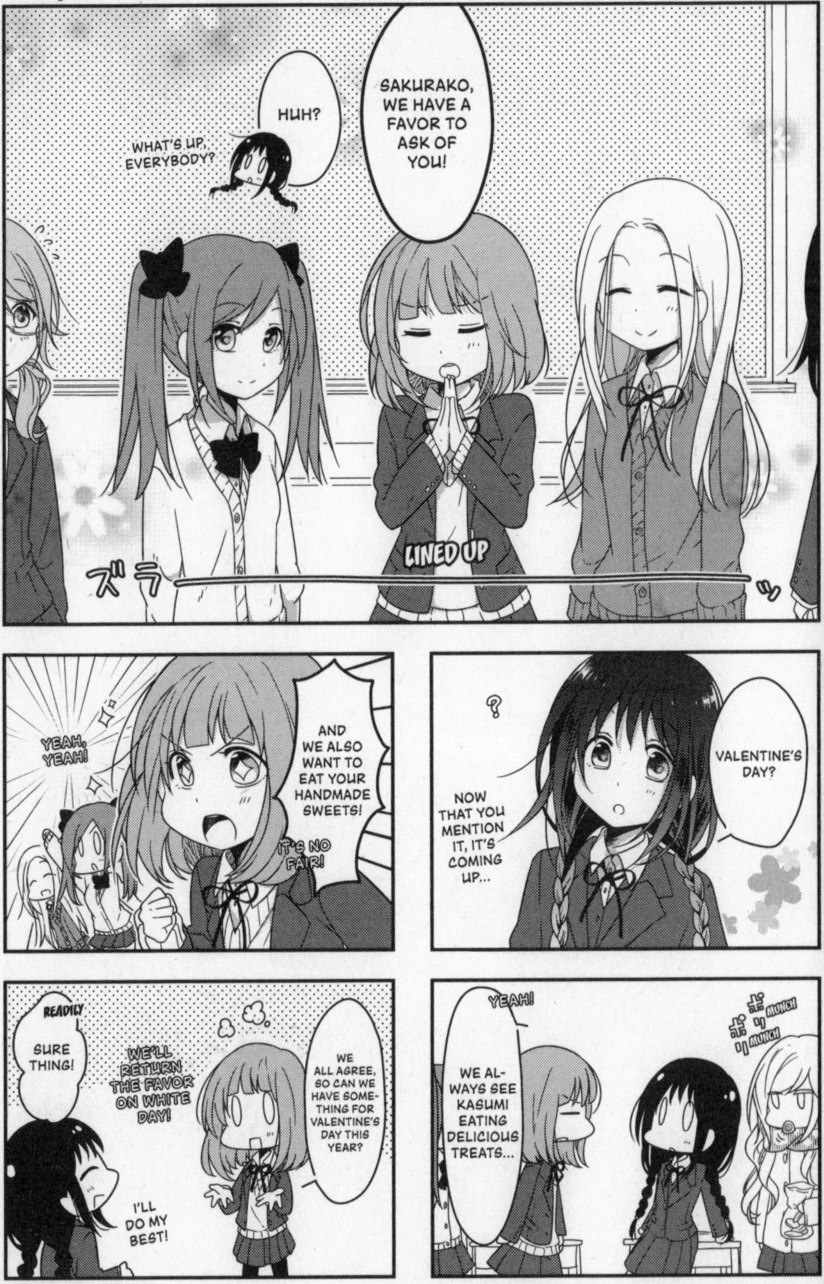
SAKURAKO, WE HAVE A FAVOR TO ASK OF YOU!
HUH?
WHAT'S UP, EVERYBODY?
LINED UP
ズラッ
VALENTINE'S DAY?
?
NOW THAT YOU MENTION IT, IT'S COMING UP...
AND WE ALSO WANT TO EAT YOUR HANDMADE SWEETS!
IT'S NO FAIR!
YEAH, YEAH!
MUNCH MUNCH
WE ALWAYS SEE KASUMI EATING DELICIOUS TREATS...
YEAH!
WE ALL AGREE, SO CAN WE HAVE SOMETHING FOR VALENTINE'S DAY THIS YEAR?
WE'LL RETURN THE FAVOR ON WHITE DAY!
READILY
SURE THING!
I'LL DO MY BEST!

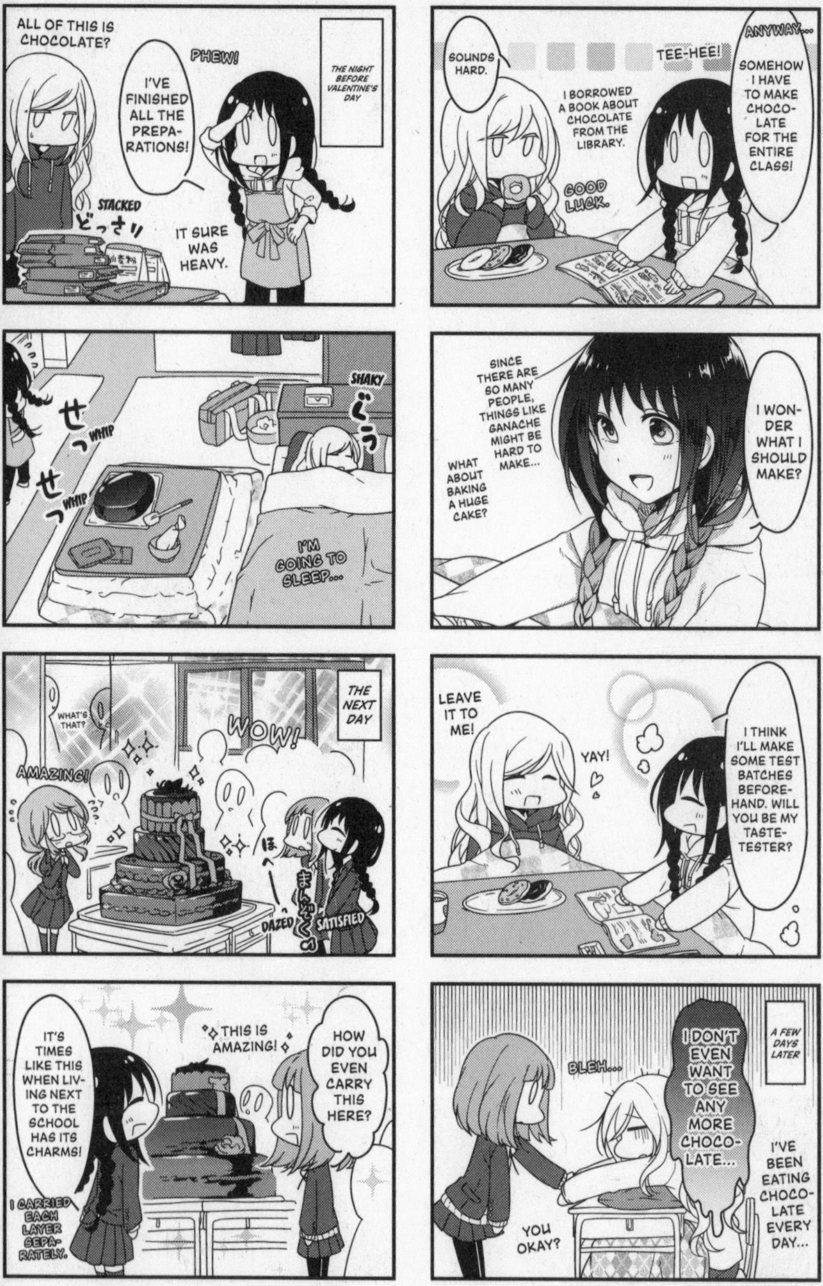
ANYWAY...
SOMEHOW I HAVE TO MAKE CHOCOLATE FOR THE ENTIRE CLASS!
TEE-HEE!
I BORROWED A BOOK ABOUT CHOCOLATE FROM THE LIBRARY.
SOUNDS HARD.
GOOD LUCK.
I WONDER WHAT I SHOULD MAKE?
SINCE THERE ARE SO MANY PEOPLE, THINGS LIKE GANACHE MIGHT BE HARD TO MAKE...
WHAT ABOUT BAKING A HUGE CAKE?
I THINK I'LL MAKE SOME TEST BATCHES BEFOREHAND. WILL YOU BE MY TASTE-TESTER?
YAY!
LEAVE IT TO ME!
A FEW DAYS LATER
I DON'T EVEN WANT TO SEE ANY MORE CHOCOLATE...
I'VE BEEN EATING CHOCOLATE EVERY DAY...
BLEH...
YOU OKAY?
THE NIGHT BEFORE VALENTINE'S DAY
PHEW!
I'VE FINISHED ALL THE PREPARATIONS!
ALL OF THIS IS CHOCOLATE?
IT SURE WAS HEAVY.
STACKED
どっさり
SHAKY
ぐぅ
せっ
WHIP
せっ
WHIP
I'M GOING TO SLEEP...
THE NEXT DAY
WOW!
WHAT'S THAT?
AMAZING!
まんぞく
SATISFIED
ほへー
DAZED
HOW DID YOU EVEN CARRY THIS HERE?
THIS IS AMAZING!
IT'S TIMES LIKE THIS WHEN LIVING NEXT TO THE SCHOOL HAS ITS CHARMS!
I CARRIED EACH LAYER SEPARATELY.

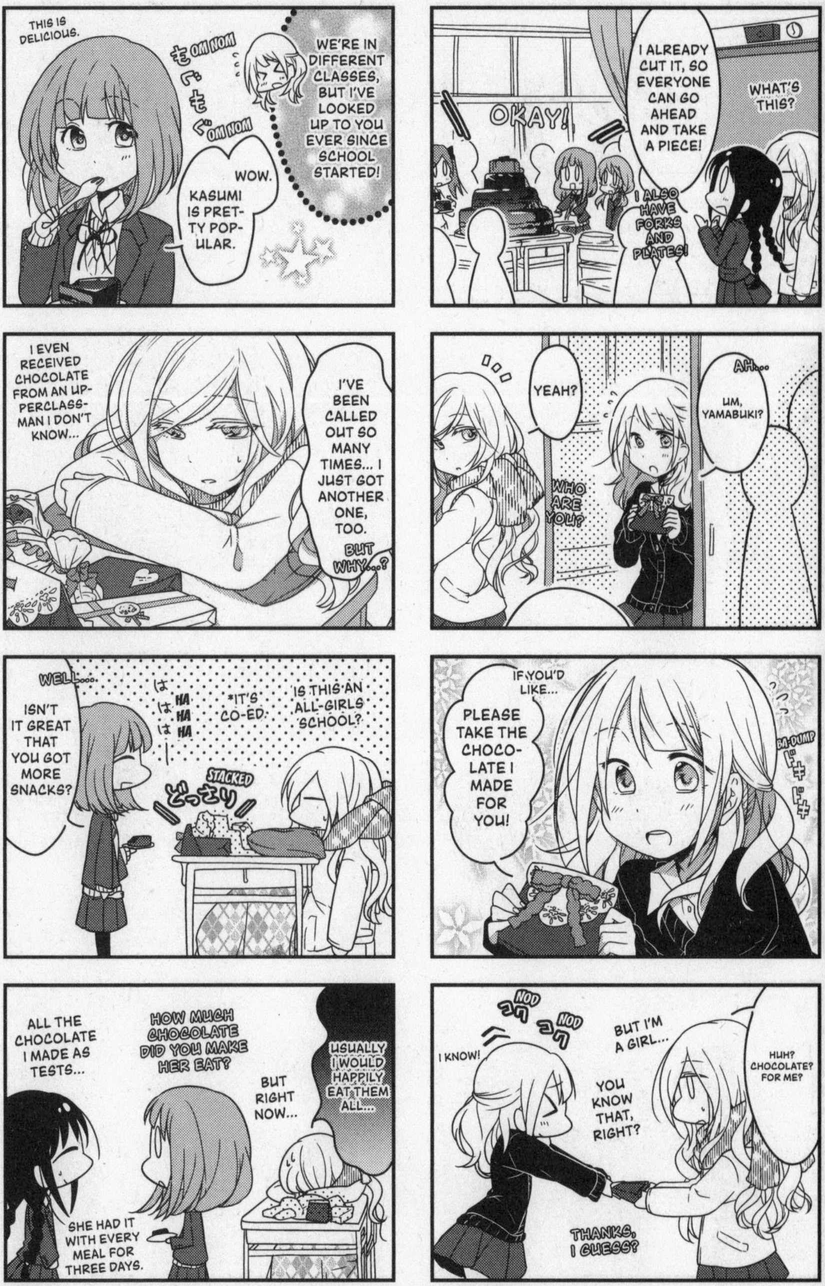
I ALREADY CUT IT, SO EVERYONE CAN GO AHEAD AND TAKE A PIECE!
WHAT'S THIS?
OKAY!
I ALSO HAVE FORKS AND PLATES!
AH...
UM, YAMABUKI?
YEAH?
WHO ARE YOU?
BA-DUMP
ドキ ドキ
IF YOU'D LIKE...
PLEASE TAKE THE CHOCOLATE I MADE FOR YOU!
HUH? CHOCOLATE? FOR ME?
BUT I'M A GIRL...
YOU KNOW THAT, RIGHT?
コク NOD コク NOD
I KNOW!
THANKS, I GUESS?
WE'RE IN DIFFERENT CLASSES, BUT I'VE LOOKED UP TO YOU EVER SINCE SCHOOL STARTED!
もぐ OM NOM もぐ OM NOM
THIS IS DELICIOUS.
WOW.
KASUMI IS PRETTY POPULAR.
I'VE BEEN CALLED OUT SO MANY TIMES... I JUST GOT ANOTHER ONE, TOO.
BUT WHY...?
I EVEN RECEIVED CHOCOLATE FROM AN UPPERCLASSMAN I DON'T KNOW...
IS THIS AN ALL-GIRLS SCHOOL?
*IT'S CO-ED.
ははは— HA HA HA
どっさり STACKED
WELL...
ISN'T IT GREAT THAT YOU GOT MORE SNACKS?
USUALLY I WOULD HAPPILY EAT THEM ALL...
BUT RIGHT NOW...
HOW MUCH CHOCOLATE DID YOU MAKE HER EAT?
ALL THE CHOCOLATE I MADE AS TESTS...
SHE HAD IT WITH EVERY MEAL FOR THREE DAYS.

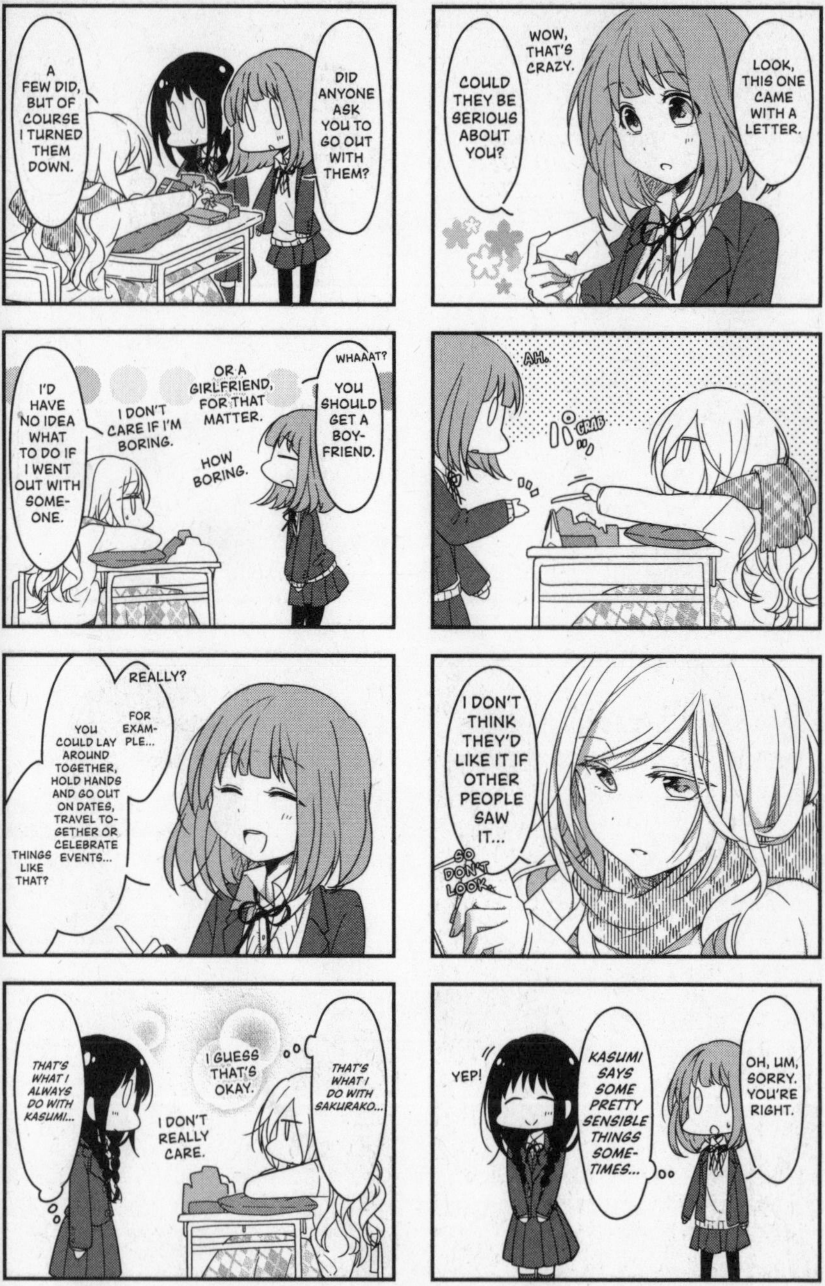
LOOK, THIS ONE CAME WITH A LETTER.
WOW, THAT'S CRAZY.
COULD THEY BE SERIOUS ABOUT YOU?
AH.
GRAB
I DON'T THINK THEY'D LIKE IT IF OTHER PEOPLE SAW IT...
SO DON'T LOOK.
OH, UM, SORRY. YOU'RE RIGHT.
KASUMI SAYS SOME PRETTY SENSIBLE THINGS SOME-TIMES...
YEP!
DID ANYONE ASK YOU TO GO OUT WITH THEM?
A FEW DID, BUT OF COURSE I TURNED THEM DOWN.
WHAAAT?
YOU SHOULD GET A BOY-FRIEND.
OR A GIRLFRIEND, FOR THAT MATTER.
HOW BORING.
I DON'T CARE IF I'M BORING.
I'D HAVE NO IDEA WHAT TO DO IF I WENT OUT WITH SOME-ONE.
REALLY?
FOR EXAM-PLE...
YOU COULD LAY AROUND TOGETHER, HOLD HANDS AND GO OUT ON DATES, TRAVEL TO-GETHER OR CELEBRATE EVENTS...
THINGS LIKE THAT?
THAT'S WHAT I DO WITH SAKURAKO...
I GUESS THAT'S OKAY.
I DON'T REALLY CARE.
THAT'S WHAT I ALWAYS DO WITH KASUMI...

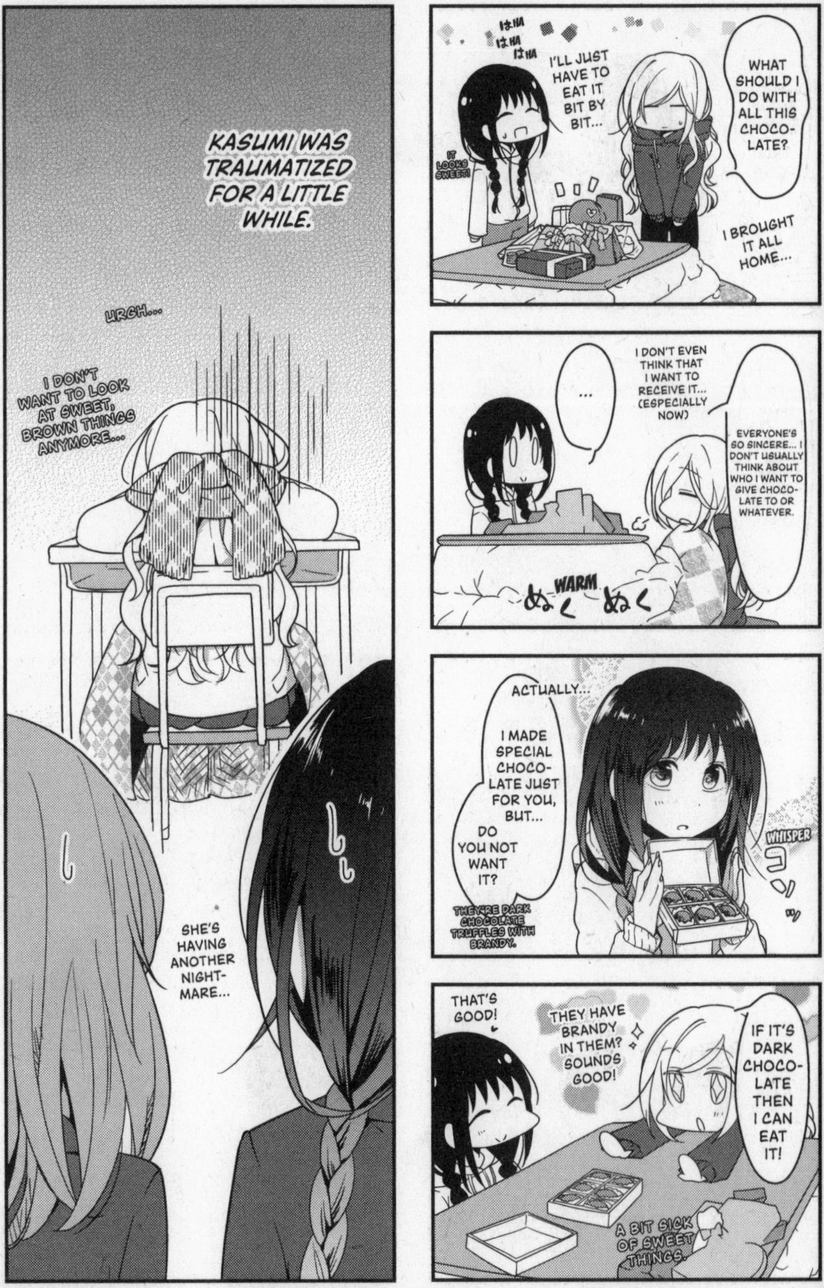

WHAT SHOULD I DO WITH ALL THIS CHOCO-LATE?
I BROUGHT IT ALL HOME...
I'LL JUST HAVE TO EAT IT BIT BY BIT...
IT LOOKS SWEET!
EVERYONE'S SO SINCERE... I DON'T USUALLY THINK ABOUT WHO I WANT TO GIVE CHOCO-LATE TO OR WHATEVER.
I DON'T EVEN THINK THAT I WANT TO RECEIVE IT... (ESPECIALLY NOW)
...
WARM
ぬく ぬく
WHISPER
ACTUALLY...
I MADE SPECIAL CHOCO-LATE JUST FOR YOU, BUT...
DO YOU NOT WANT IT?
THEY'RE DARK CHOCOLATE TRUFFLES WITH BRANDY.
IF IT'S DARK CHOCO-LATE THEN I CAN EAT IT!
A BIT SICK OF SWEET THINGS.
THEY HAVE BRANDY IN THEM? SOUNDS GOOD!
THAT'S GOOD!
KASUMI WAS TRAUMATIZED FOR A LITTLE WHILE.
URGH...
I DON'T WANT TO LOOK AT SWEET, BROWN THINGS ANYMORE...
SHE'S HAVING ANOTHER NIGHT-MARE...

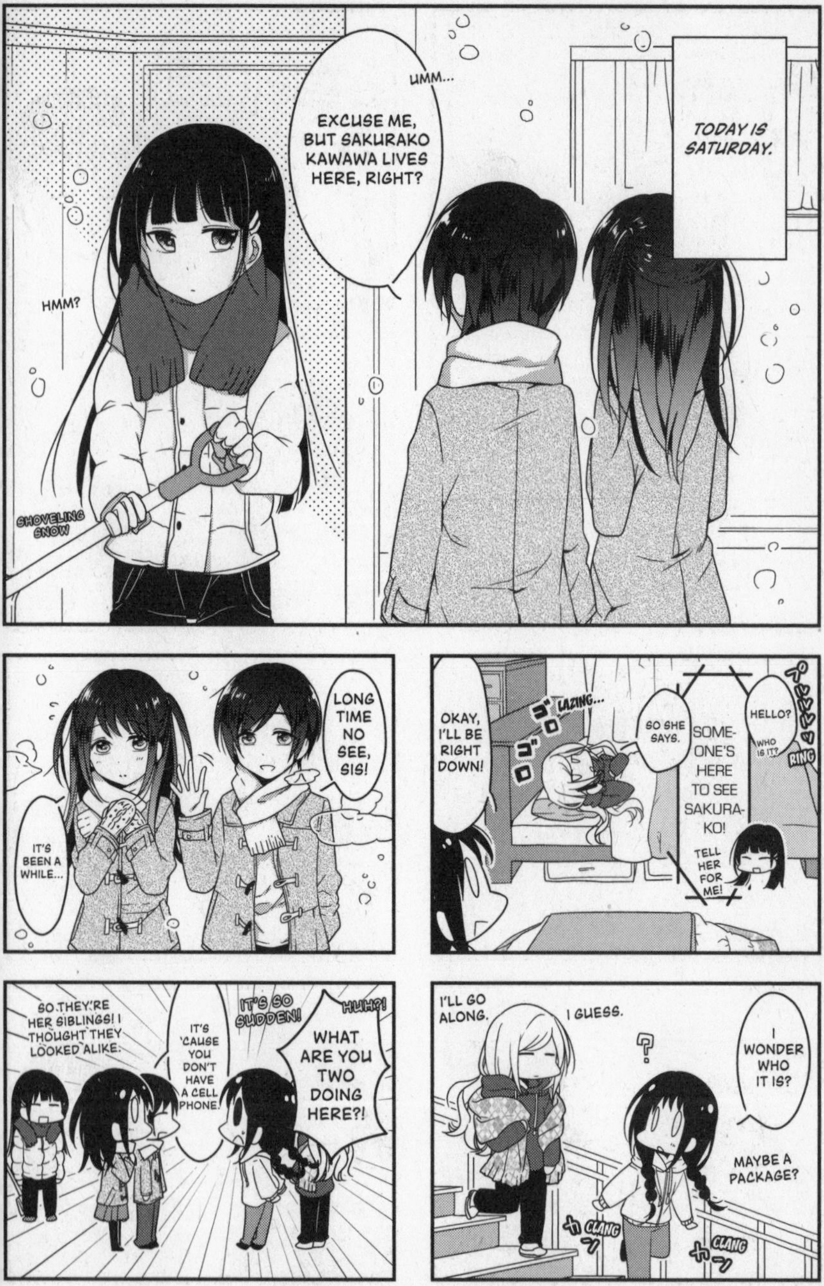
TODAY IS SATURDAY.
UMM...
EXCUSE ME, BUT SAKURAKO KAWAWA LIVES HERE, RIGHT?
HMM?
SHOVELING SNOW
RING
HELLO? WHO IS IT?
SOME-ONE'S HERE TO SEE SAKURA-KO!
TELL HER FOR ME!
SO SHE SAYS.
LAZING...
OKAY, I'LL BE RIGHT DOWN!
LONG TIME NO SEE, SIS!
IT'S BEEN A WHILE...
I WONDER WHO IT IS?
I GUESS.
?
I'LL GO ALONG.
MAYBE A PACKAGE?
CLANG
CLANG
HUH?!
WHAT ARE YOU TWO DOING HERE?!
IT'S SO SUDDEN!
IT'S 'CAUSE YOU DON'T HAVE A CELL PHONE.
SO THEY'RE HER SIBLINGS! I THOUGHT THEY LOOKED ALIKE.

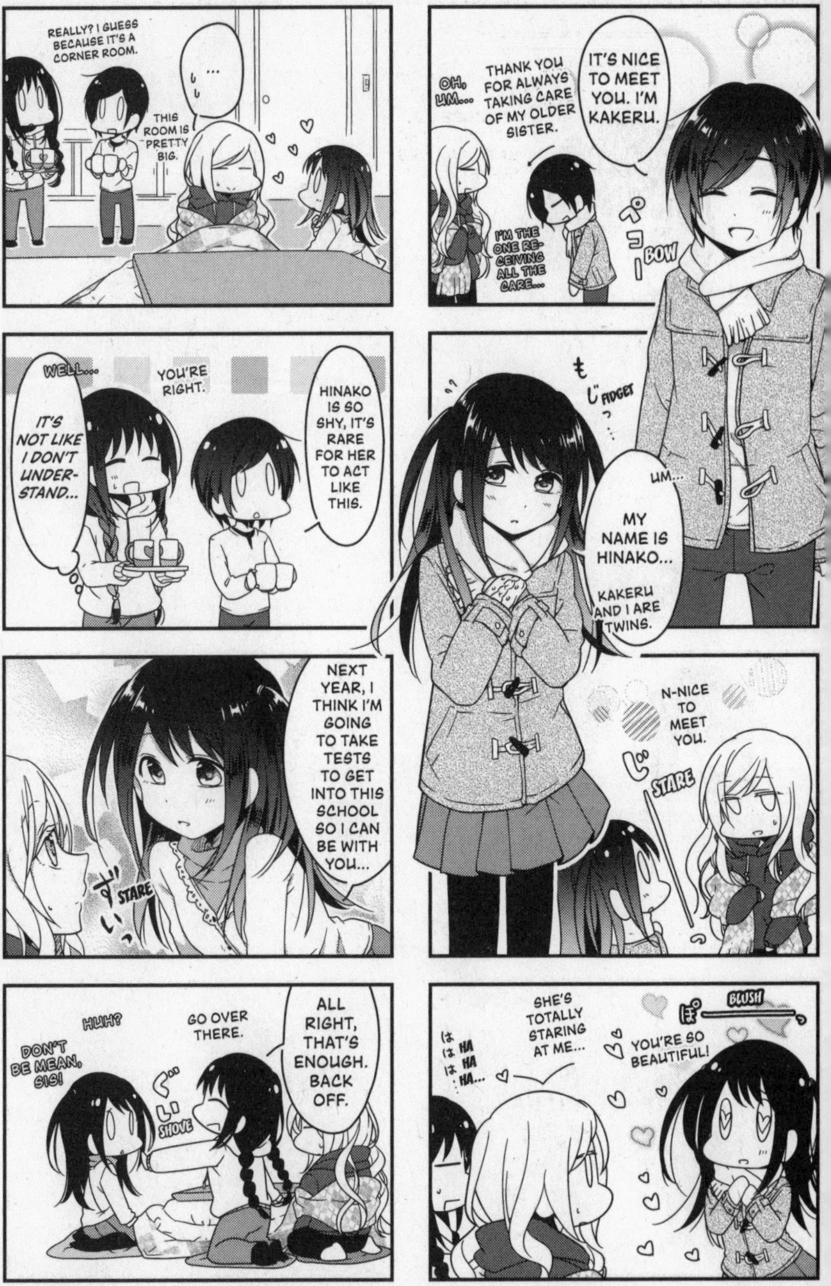
IT'S NICE TO MEET YOU. I'M KAKERU.
THANK YOU FOR ALWAYS TAKING CARE OF MY OLDER SISTER.
OH, UM...
BOW
I'M THE ONE RECEIVING ALL THE CARE...
FIDGET
UM...
MY NAME IS HINAKO...
KAKERU AND I ARE TWINS.
N-NICE TO MEET YOU.
STARE
BLUSH
YOU'RE SO BEAUTIFUL!
SHE'S TOTALLY STARING AT ME...
HA HA HA...
...
THIS ROOM IS PRETTY BIG.
REALLY? I GUESS BECAUSE IT'S A CORNER ROOM.
HINAKO IS SO SHY, IT'S RARE FOR HER TO ACT LIKE THIS.
YOU'RE RIGHT.
WELL...
IT'S NOT LIKE I DON'T UNDERSTAND...
NEXT YEAR, I THINK I'M GOING TO TAKE TESTS TO GET INTO THIS SCHOOL SO I CAN BE WITH YOU...
STARE
ALL RIGHT, THAT'S ENOUGH. BACK OFF.
GO OVER THERE.
SHOVE
HUH?
DON'T BE MEAN, SIS!

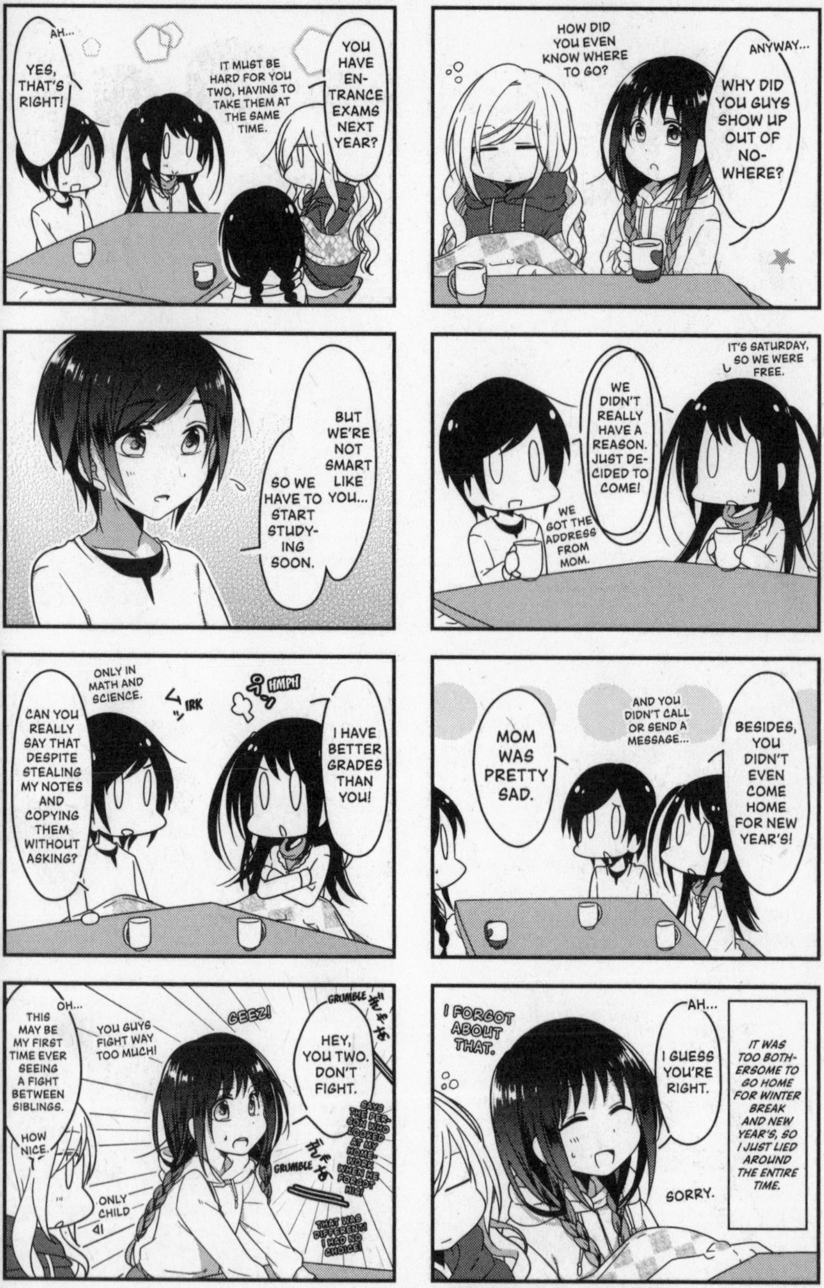
ANYWAY...
WHY DID YOU GUYS SHOW UP OUT OF NO-WHERE?
HOW DID YOU EVEN KNOW WHERE TO GO?
IT'S SATURDAY, SO WE WERE FREE.
WE DIDN'T REALLY HAVE A REASON. JUST DE-CIDED TO COME!
WE GOT THE ADDRESS FROM MOM.
BESIDES, YOU DIDN'T EVEN COME HOME FOR NEW YEAR'S!
AND YOU DIDN'T CALL OR SEND A MESSAGE...
MOM WAS PRETTY SAD.
IT WAS TOO BOTH-ERSOME TO GO HOME FOR WINTER BREAK AND NEW YEAR'S, SO I JUST LIED AROUND THE ENTIRE TIME.
AH...
I GUESS YOU'RE RIGHT.
I FORGOT ABOUT THAT.
SORRY.
YOU HAVE EN-TRANCE EXAMS NEXT YEAR?
IT MUST BE HARD FOR YOU TWO, HAVING TO TAKE THEM AT THE SAME TIME.
AH...
YES, THAT'S RIGHT!
BUT WE'RE NOT SMART LIKE YOU...
SO WE HAVE TO START STUDY-ING SOON.
HMPH
I HAVE BETTER GRADES THAN YOU!
IRK
ONLY IN MATH AND SCIENCE.
CAN YOU REALLY SAY THAT DESPITE STEALING MY NOTES AND COPYING THEM WITHOUT ASKING?
GRUMBLE
HEY, YOU TWO. DON'T FIGHT.
SAYS THE PER-SON WHO LOOKED AT MY HOME-WORK WHEN HE FORGOT HIS!
GEEZ!
YOU GUYS FIGHT WAY TOO MUCH!
OH...
THIS MAY BE MY FIRST TIME EVER SEEING A FIGHT BETWEEN SIBLINGS.
HOW NICE.
GRUMBLE
THAT WAS DIFFERENT! I HAD NO CHOICE!
ONLY CHILD

▲ KASUMI DIDN'T GO HOME EITHER.

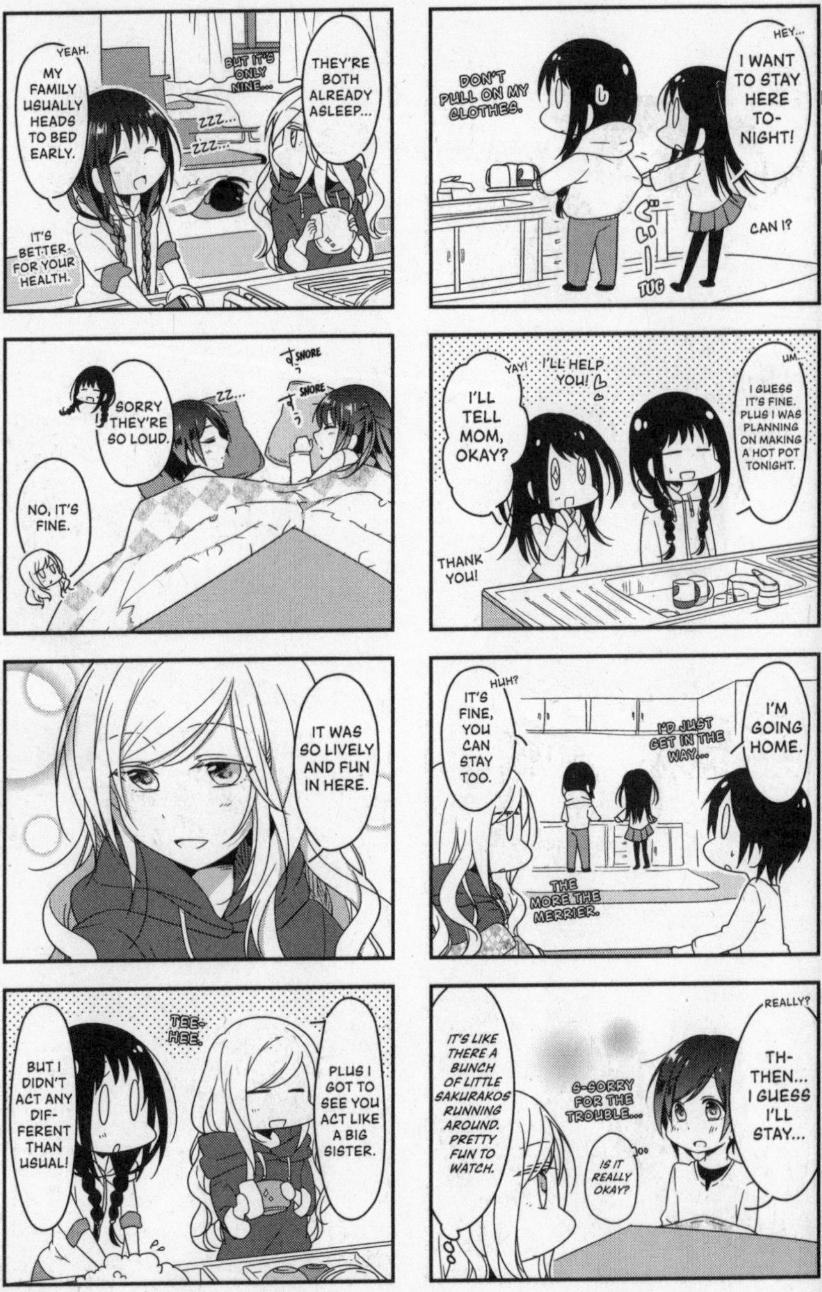
HEY...
I WANT TO STAY HERE TO-NIGHT!
CAN I?
DON'T PULL ON MY CLOTHES.
TUG
UM...
I GUESS IT'S FINE. PLUS I WAS PLANNING ON MAKING A HOT POT TONIGHT.
YAY!
I'LL HELP YOU!
I'LL TELL MOM, OKAY?
THANK YOU!
I'M GOING HOME.
I'D JUST GET IN THE WAY...
HUH?
IT'S FINE, YOU CAN STAY TOO.
THE MORE THE MERRIER.
REALLY?
TH-THEN... I GUESS I'LL STAY...
S-SORRY FOR THE TROUBLE...
IS IT REALLY OKAY?
IT'S LIKE THERE A BUNCH OF LITTLE SAKURAKOS RUNNING AROUND. PRETTY FUN TO WATCH.
THEY'RE BOTH ALREADY ASLEEP...
BUT IT'S ONLY NINE...
ZZZ...
ZZZ...
YEAH.
MY FAMILY USUALLY HEADS TO BED EARLY.
IT'S BETTER FOR YOUR HEALTH.
SNORE
SNORE
ZZ...
SORRY THEY'RE SO LOUD.
NO, IT'S FINE.
IT WAS SO LIVELY AND FUN IN HERE.
PLUS I GOT TO SEE YOU ACT LIKE A BIG SISTER.
TEE-HEE.
BUT I DIDN'T ACT ANY DIF-FERENT THAN USUAL!

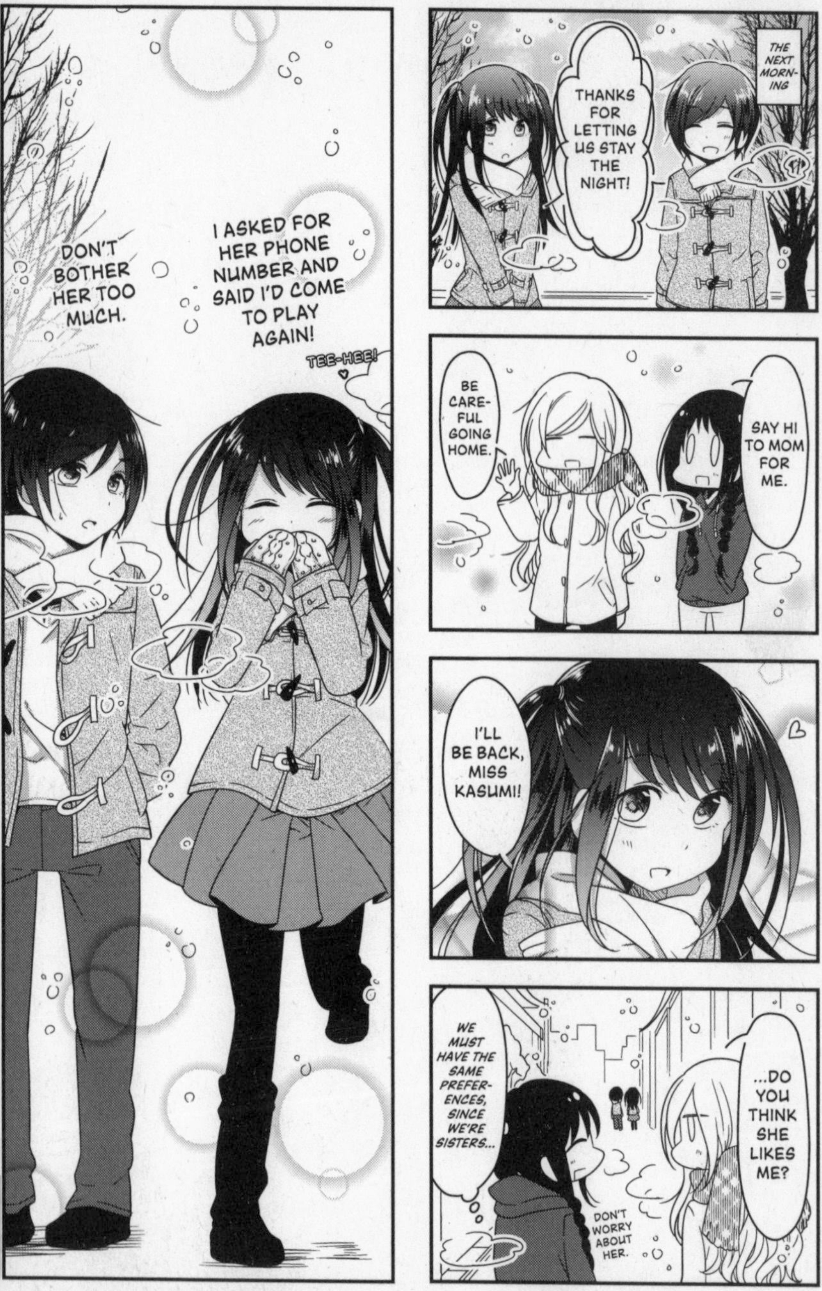
THE NEXT MORNING
THANKS FOR LETTING US STAY THE NIGHT!
SAY HI TO MOM FOR ME.
BE CAREFUL GOING HOME.
I'LL BE BACK, MISS KASUMI!
...DO YOU THINK SHE LIKES ME?
WE MUST HAVE THE SAME PREFERENCES, SINCE WE'RE SISTERS...
DON'T WORRY ABOUT HER.
I ASKED FOR HER PHONE NUMBER AND SAID I'D COME TO PLAY AGAIN!
TEE-HEE!
DON'T BOTHER HER TOO MUCH.

Illustration gallery

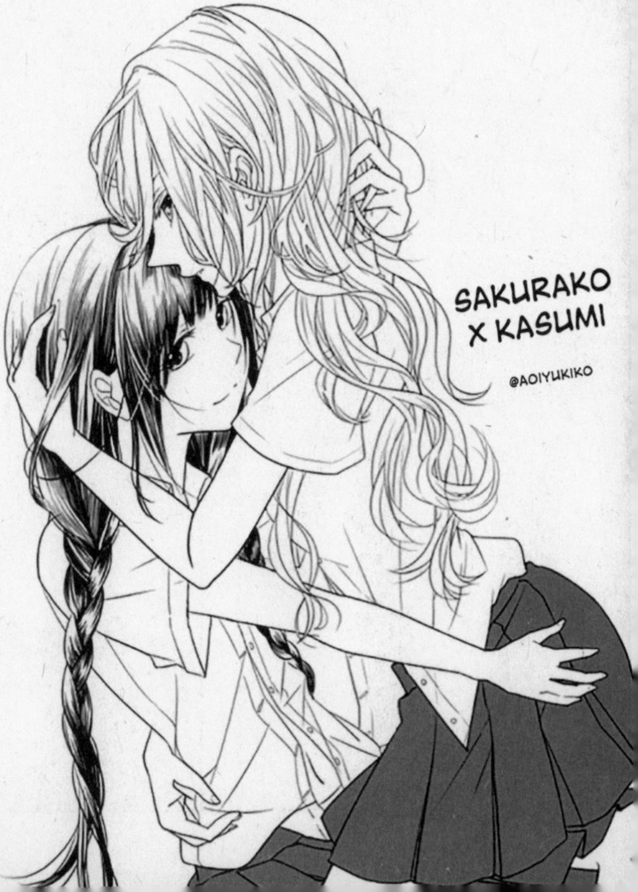
SAKURAKO
X KASUMI
@AOIYUKIKO

Futaribeya
A ROOM FOR TWO

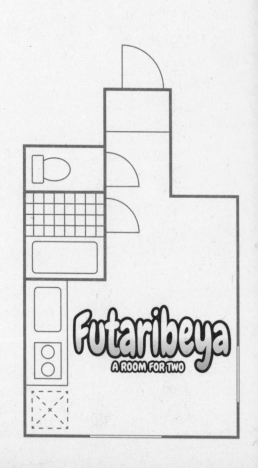

Chapter 10

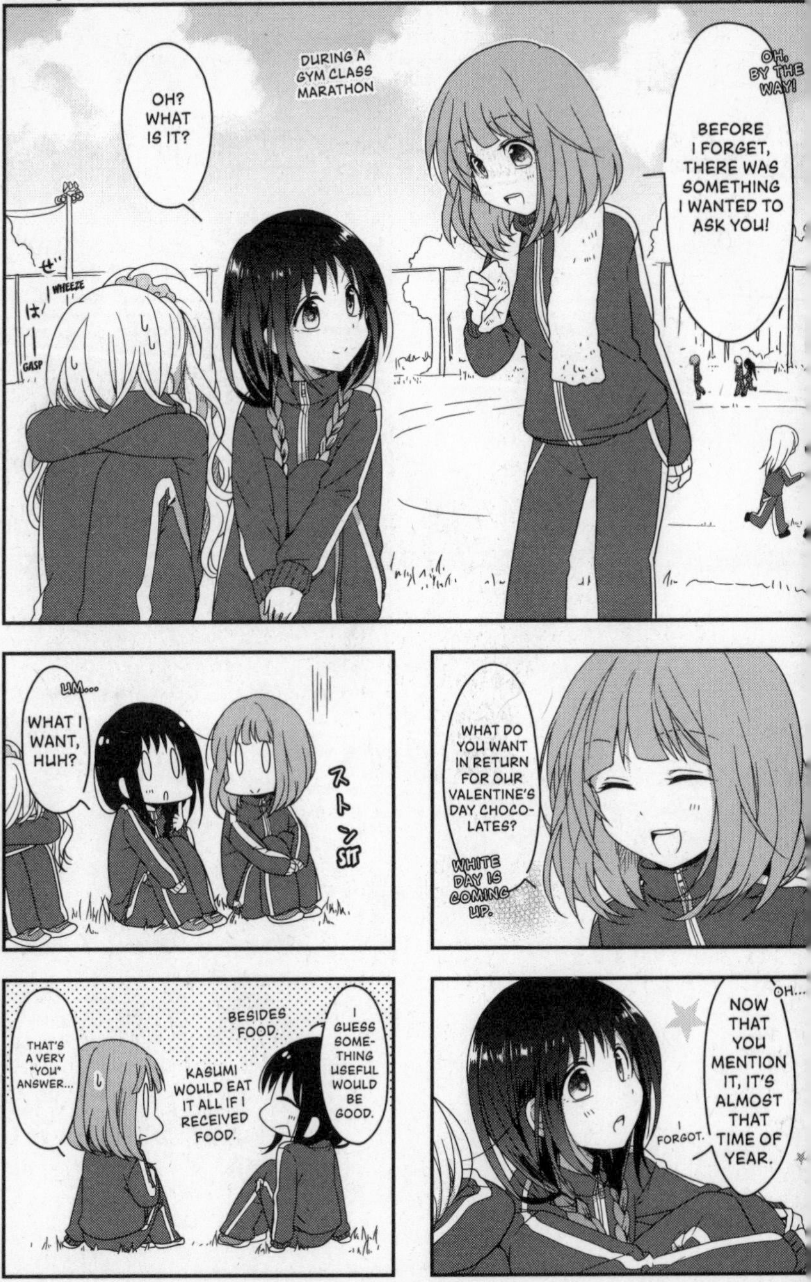
OH, BY THE WAY!
BEFORE I FORGET, THERE WAS SOMETHING I WANTED TO ASK YOU!
DURING A GYM CLASS MARATHON
OH? WHAT IS IT?
ぜ WHEEZE
は GASP
WHAT DO YOU WANT IN RETURN FOR OUR VALENTINE'S DAY CHOCO-LATES?
WHITE DAY IS COMING UP.
ストン SIT
UM...
WHAT I WANT, HUH?
OH...
NOW THAT YOU MENTION IT, IT'S ALMOST THAT TIME OF YEAR.
I FORGOT.
I GUESS SOME-THING USEFUL WOULD BE GOOD.
BESIDES FOOD.
KASUMI WOULD EAT IT ALL IF I RECEIVED FOOD.
THAT'S A VERY "YOU" ANSWER...

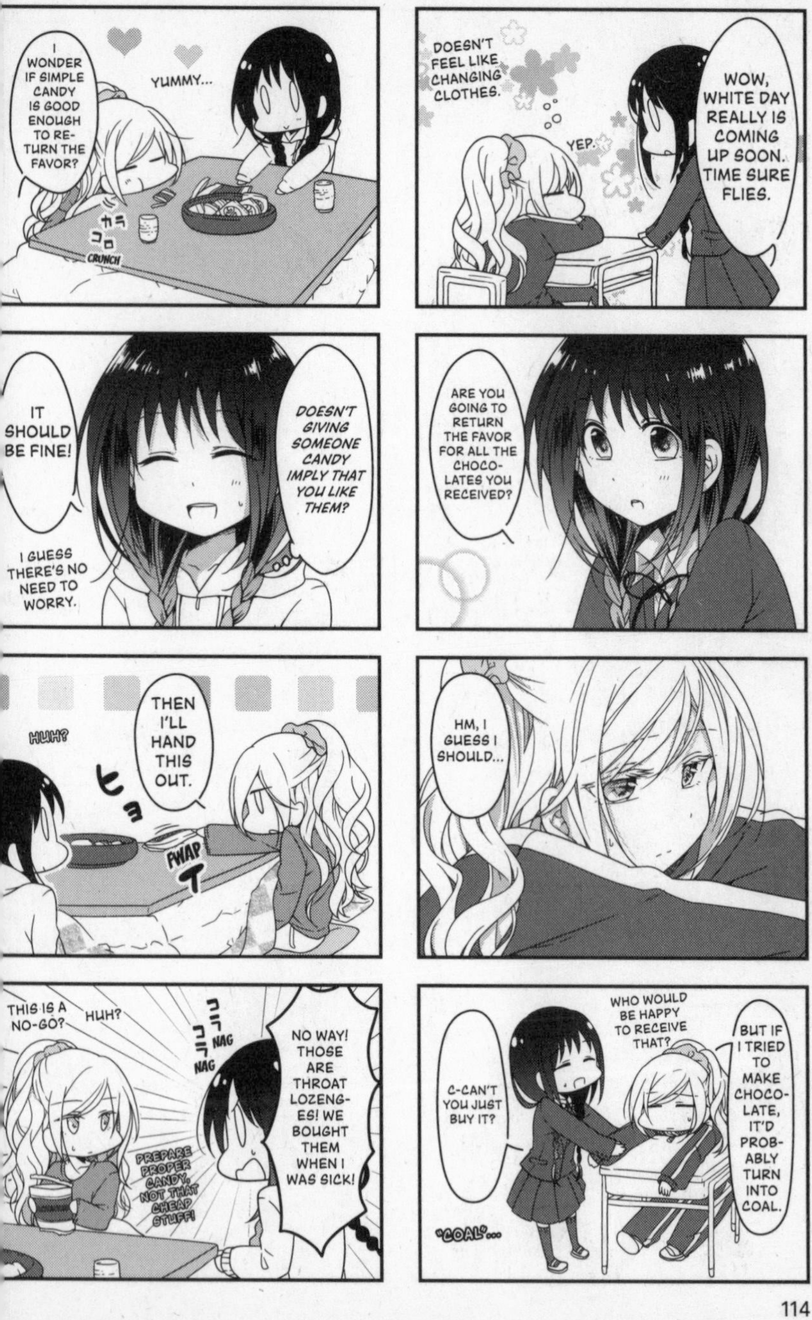

WOW, WHITE DAY REALLY IS COMING UP SOON. TIME SURE FLIES.
YEP.
DOESN'T FEEL LIKE CHANGING CLOTHES.
ARE YOU GOING TO RETURN THE FAVOR FOR ALL THE CHOCOLATES YOU RECEIVED?
HM, I GUESS I SHOULD...
BUT IF I TRIED TO MAKE CHOCOLATE, IT'D PROBABLY TURN INTO COAL.
WHO WOULD BE HAPPY TO RECEIVE THAT?
C-CAN'T YOU JUST BUY IT?
"COAL"...
YUMMY...
I WONDER IF SIMPLE CANDY IS GOOD ENOUGH TO RETURN THE FAVOR?
カラ
コロ
CRUNCH
DOESN'T GIVING SOMEONE CANDY IMPLY THAT YOU LIKE THEM?
IT SHOULD BE FINE!
I GUESS THERE'S NO NEED TO WORRY.
THEN I'LL HAND THIS OUT.
HUH?
ヒョ
FWAP
NO WAY! THOSE ARE THROAT LOZENGES! WE BOUGHT THEM WHEN I WAS SICK!
コラ NAG
コラ NAG
HUH?
THIS IS A NO-GO?
PREPARE PROPER CANDY, NOT THAT CHEAP STUFF!

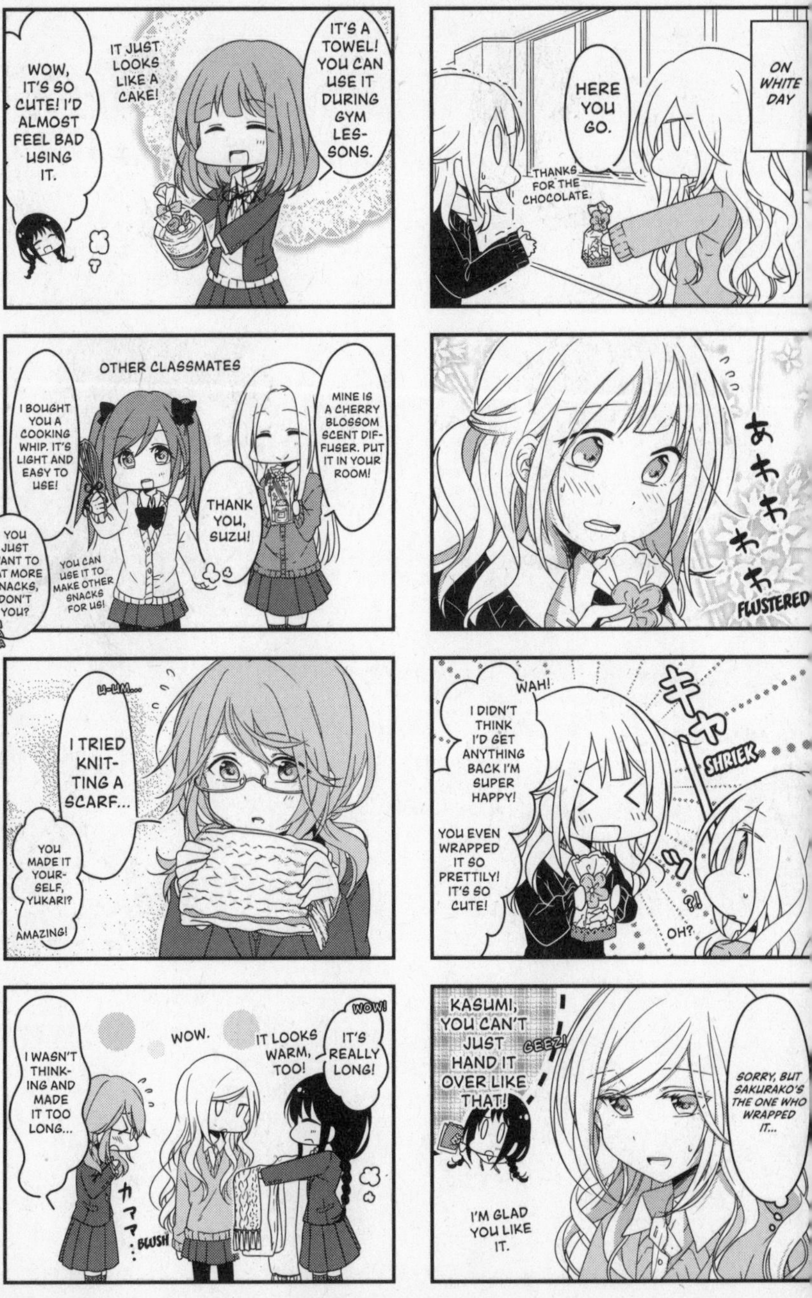

ON WHITE DAY
HERE YOU GO.
THANKS FOR THE CHOCOLATE.
あわわわわ
FLUSTERED
キャ
SHRIEK
WAH!
I DIDN'T THINK I'D GET ANYTHING BACK I'M SUPER HAPPY!
YOU EVEN WRAPPED IT SO PRETTILY! IT'S SO CUTE!
?!
OH?
SORRY, BUT SAKURAKO'S THE ONE WHO WRAPPED IT...
I'M GLAD YOU LIKE IT.
KASUMI, YOU CAN'T JUST HAND IT OVER LIKE THAT!
GEEZ!
IT'S A TOWEL! YOU CAN USE IT DURING GYM LESSONS.
IT JUST LOOKS LIKE A CAKE!
WOW, IT'S SO CUTE! I'D ALMOST FEEL BAD USING IT.
MINE IS A CHERRY BLOSSOM SCENT DIFFUSER. PUT IT IN YOUR ROOM!
THANK YOU, SUZU!
OTHER CLASSMATES
I BOUGHT YOU A COOKING WHIP. IT'S LIGHT AND EASY TO USE!
YOU CAN USE IT TO MAKE OTHER SNACKS FOR US!
YOU JUST WANT TO EAT MORE SNACKS, DON'T YOU?
AH HA HA
U-UM...
I TRIED KNITTING A SCARF...
YOU MADE IT YOURSELF, YUKARI?
AMAZING!
WOW!
IT'S REALLY LONG!
IT LOOKS WARM, TOO!
WOW.
I WASN'T THINKING AND MADE IT TOO LONG...
カァァ
BLUSH

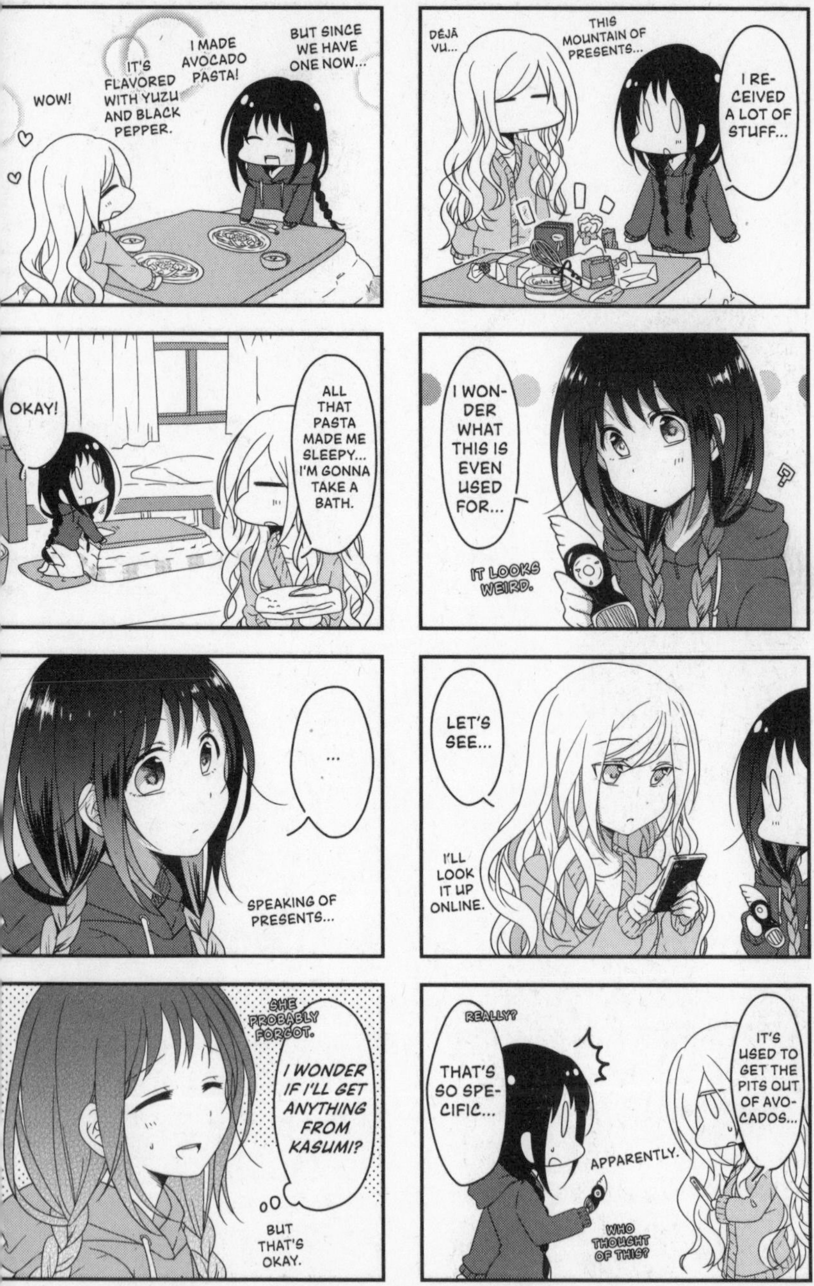

I RE-CEIVED A LOT OF STUFF...
THIS MOUNTAIN OF PRESENTS...
DÉJÀ VU...
I WON-DER WHAT THIS IS EVEN USED FOR...
IT LOOKS WEIRD.
LET'S SEE...
I'LL LOOK IT UP ONLINE.
IT'S USED TO GET THE PITS OUT OF AVO-CADOS...
REALLY?
THAT'S SO SPE-CIFIC...
APPARENTLY.
WHO THOUGHT OF THIS?
BUT SINCE WE HAVE ONE NOW...
I MADE AVOCADO PASTA!
IT'S FLAVORED WITH YUZU AND BLACK PEPPER.
WOW!
ALL THAT PASTA MADE ME SLEEPY... I'M GONNA TAKE A BATH.
OKAY!
...
SPEAKING OF PRESENTS...
SHE PROBABLY FORGOT.
I WONDER IF I'LL GET ANYTHING FROM KASUMI?
BUT THAT'S OKAY.

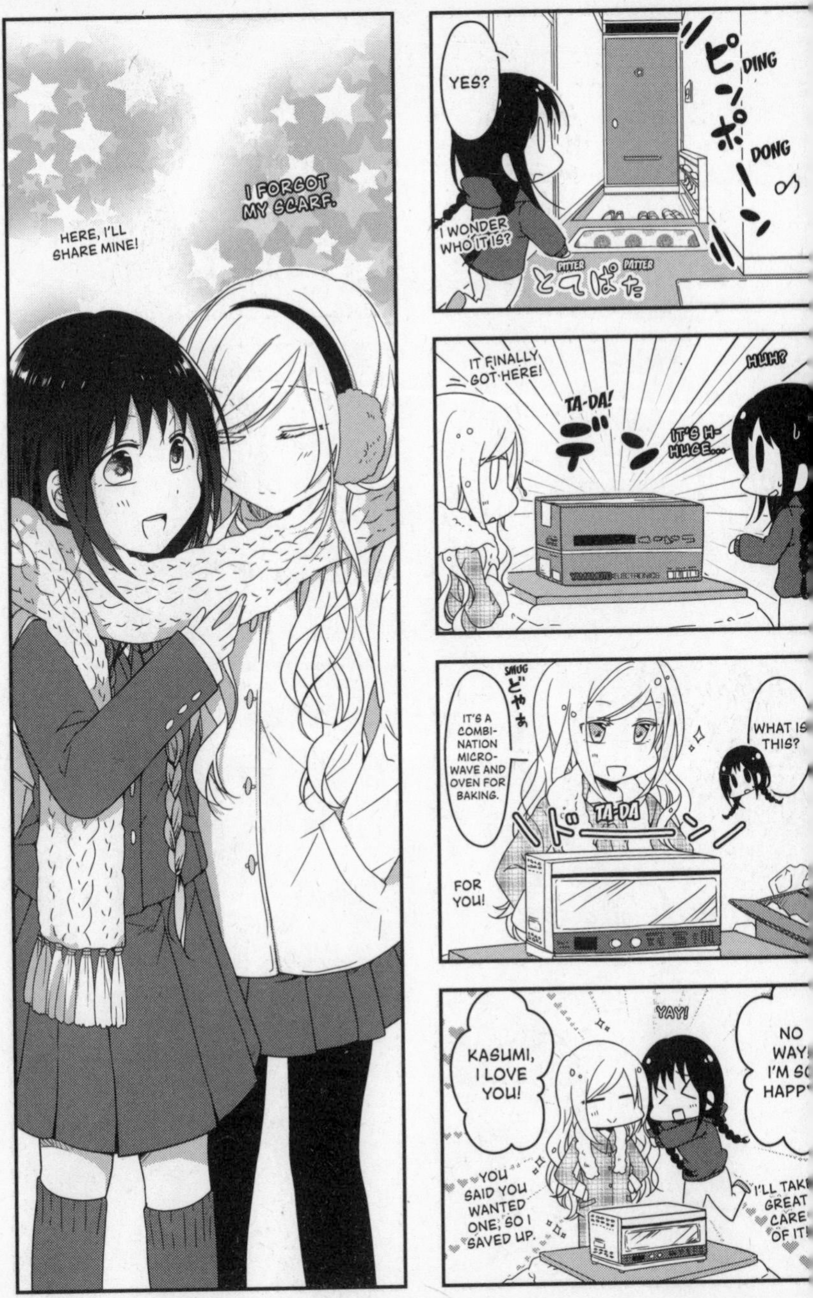
ピンポーン
DING DONG
YES?
I WONDER WHO IT IS?
とてぱた
PITTER PATTER
HUH?
IT'S H-HUGE...
デン
TA-DA!
IT FINALLY GOT HERE!
YAMAMOTO ELECTRONICS
WHAT IS THIS?
どやぁ
SMUG
IT'S A COMBINATION MICROWAVE AND OVEN FOR BAKING.
ドーーン
TA-DA
FOR YOU!
NO WAY! I'M SO HAPPY
YAY!
KASUMI, I LOVE YOU!
I'LL TAKE GREAT CARE OF IT!
YOU SAID YOU WANTED ONE, SO I SAVED UP.
I FORGOT MY SCARF.
HERE, I'LL SHARE MINE!

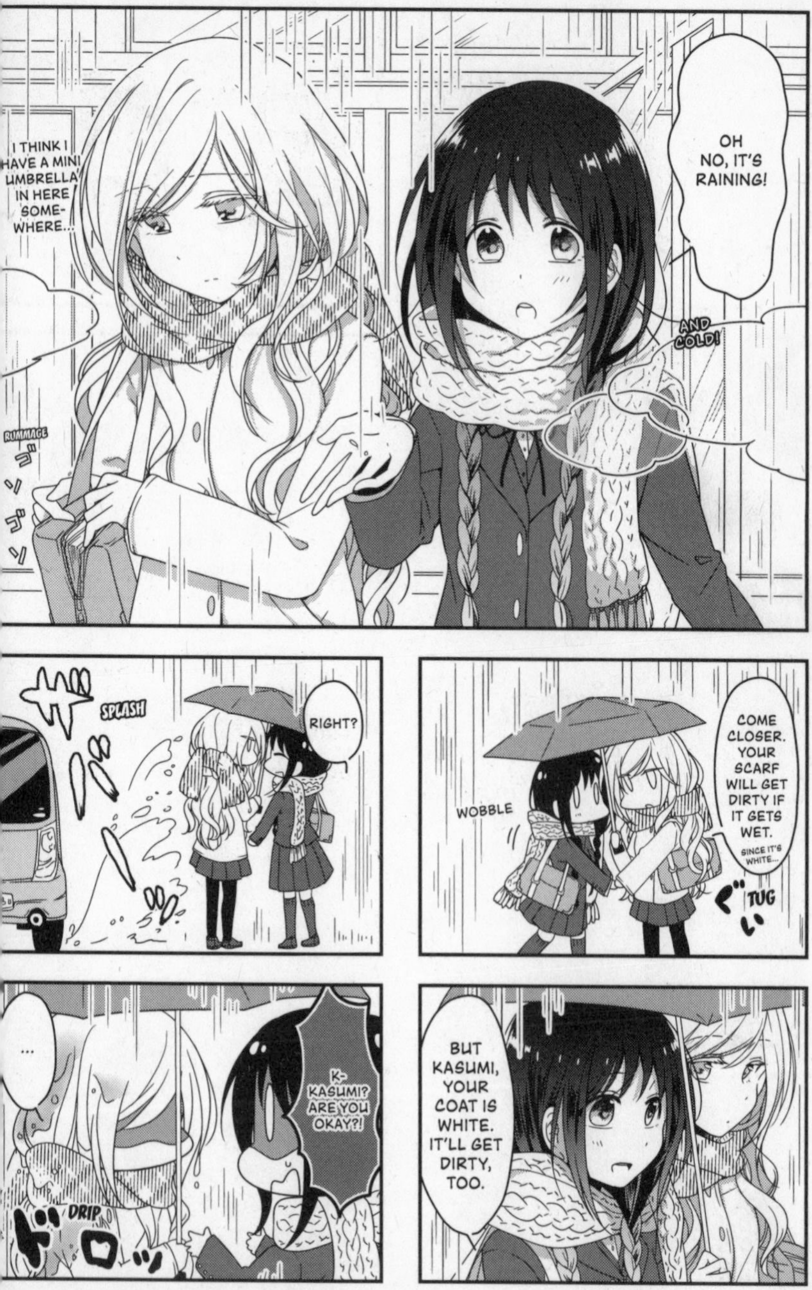
OH NO, IT'S RAINING!
AND COLD!
I THINK I HAVE A MINI UMBRELLA IN HERE SOME-WHERE...
RUMMAGE
ゴソゴソ
COME CLOSER. YOUR SCARF WILL GET DIRTY IF IT GETS WET.
SINCE IT'S WHITE...
TUG
WOBBLE
RIGHT?
SPLASH
BUT KASUMI, YOUR COAT IS WHITE. IT'LL GET DIRTY, TOO.
K-KASUMI? ARE YOU OKAY?!
...
DRIP

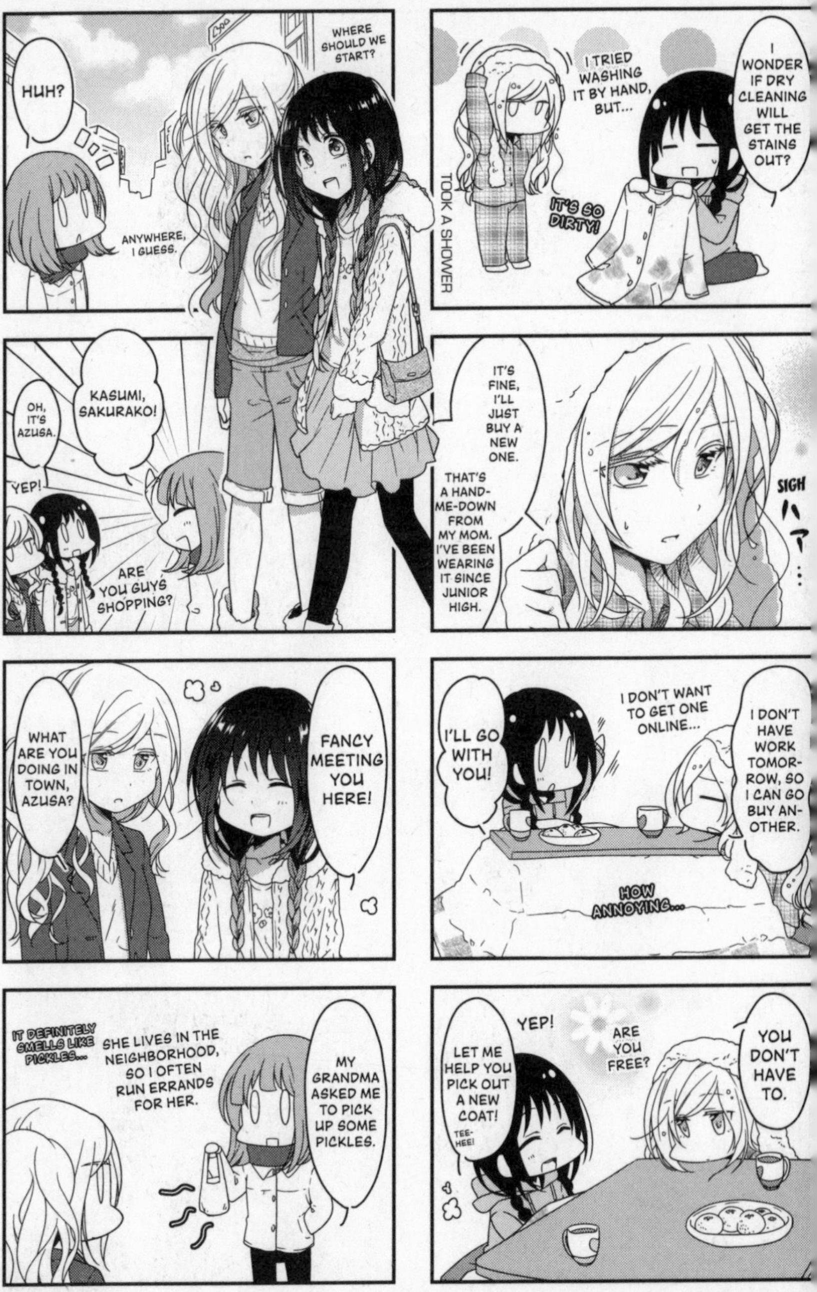
TOOK A SHOWER
I WONDER IF DRY CLEANING WILL GET THE STAINS OUT?
I TRIED WASHING IT BY HAND, BUT...
IT'S SO DIRTY!
SIGH
ハア...
IT'S FINE, I'LL JUST BUY A NEW ONE.
THAT'S A HAND-ME-DOWN FROM MY MOM. I'VE BEEN WEARING IT SINCE JUNIOR HIGH.
I DON'T HAVE WORK TOMORROW, SO I CAN GO BUY ANOTHER.
I DON'T WANT TO GET ONE ONLINE...
I'LL GO WITH YOU!
HOW ANNOYING...
YOU DON'T HAVE TO.
ARE YOU FREE?
YEP!
LET ME HELP YOU PICK OUT A NEW COAT!
TEE-HEE!
WHERE SHOULD WE START?
ANYWHERE, I GUESS.
HUH?
KASUMI, SAKURAKO!
OH, IT'S AZUSA.
YEP!
ARE YOU GUYS SHOPPING?
FANCY MEETING YOU HERE!
WHAT ARE YOU DOING IN TOWN, AZUSA?
MY GRANDMA ASKED ME TO PICK UP SOME PICKLES.
SHE LIVES IN THE NEIGHBORHOOD, SO I OFTEN RUN ERRANDS FOR HER.
IT DEFINITELY SMELLS LIKE PICKLES...

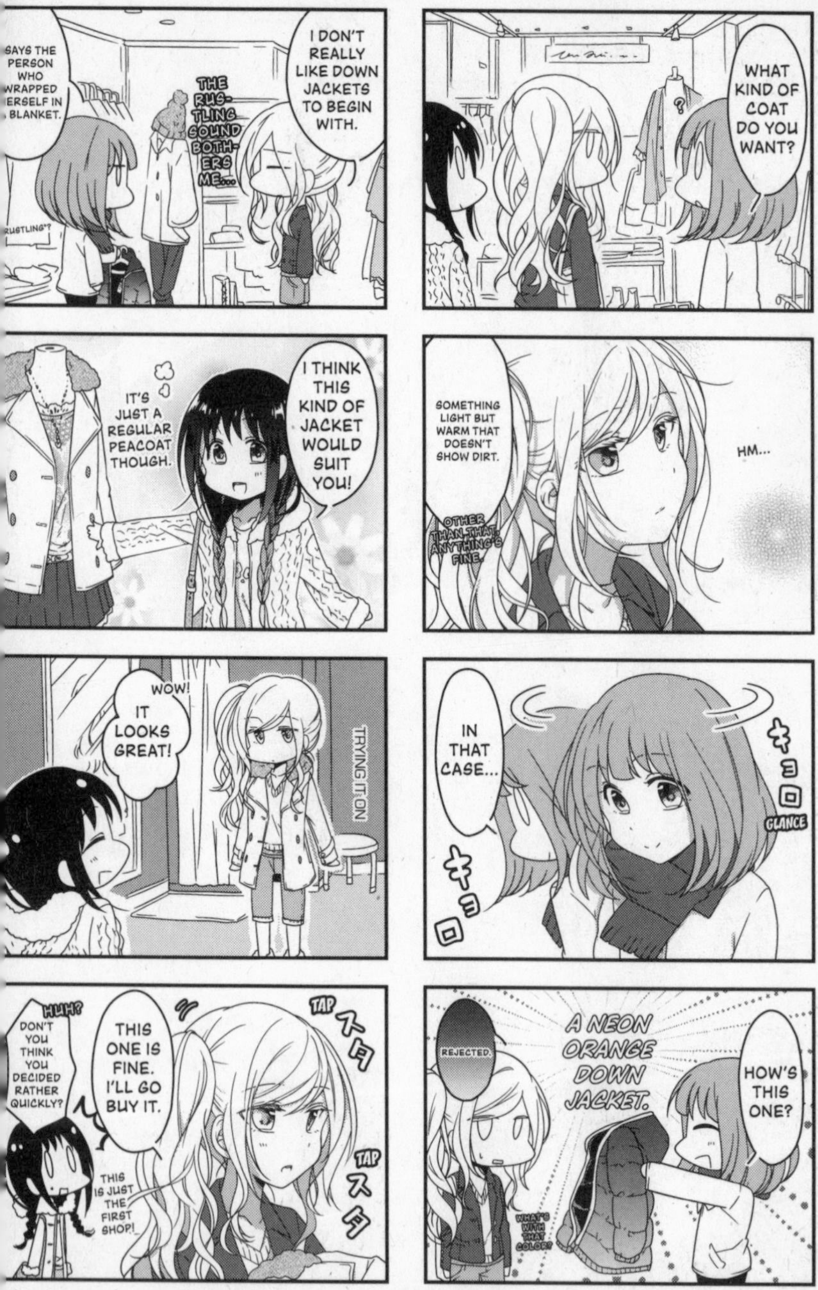
WHAT KIND OF COAT DO YOU WANT?
SOMETHING LIGHT BUT WARM THAT DOESN'T SHOW DIRT.
HM...
OTHER THAN THAT, ANYTHING'S FINE.
IN THAT CASE...
キョロ
GLANCE
キョロ
HOW'S THIS ONE?
A NEON ORANGE DOWN JACKET.
REJECTED.
WHAT'S WITH THAT COLOR?
I DON'T REALLY LIKE DOWN JACKETS TO BEGIN WITH.
THE RUSTLING SOUND BOTHERS ME...
SAYS THE PERSON WHO WRAPPED ERSELF IN BLANKET.
RUSTLING"?
I THINK THIS KIND OF JACKET WOULD SUIT YOU!
IT'S JUST A REGULAR PEACOAT THOUGH.
WOW! IT LOOKS GREAT!
TRYING IT ON
THIS ONE IS FINE. I'LL GO BUY IT.
TAP スタ
TAP スタ
HUH? DON'T YOU THINK YOU DECIDED RATHER QUICKLY?
THIS IS JUST THE FIRST SHOP!

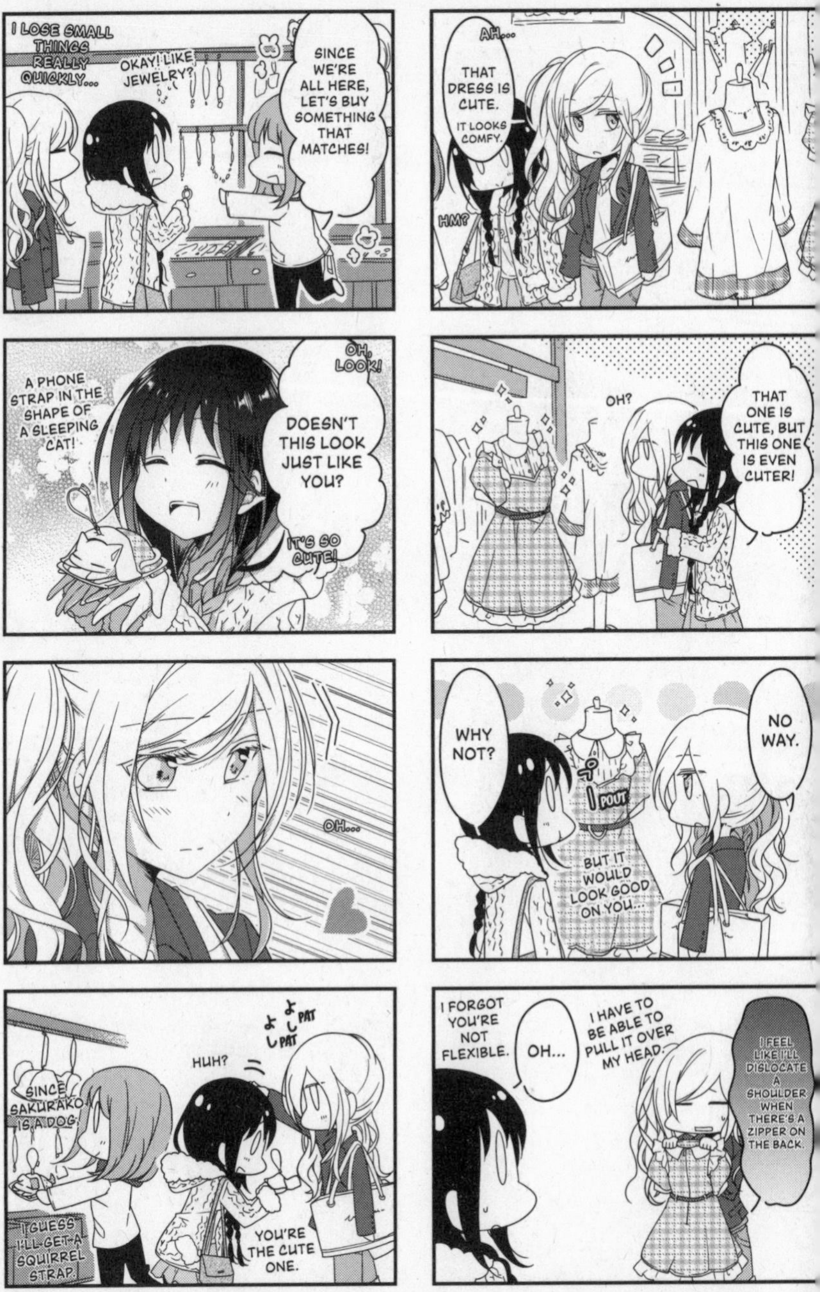
AH...
THAT DRESS IS CUTE.
IT LOOKS COMFY.
HM?
THAT ONE IS CUTE, BUT THIS ONE IS EVEN CUTER!
OH?
NO WAY.
WHY NOT?
POUT
BUT IT WOULD LOOK GOOD ON YOU...
I FEEL LIKE I'LL DISLOCATE A SHOULDER WHEN THERE'S A ZIPPER ON THE BACK.
I HAVE TO BE ABLE TO PULL IT OVER MY HEAD.
OH...
I FORGOT YOU'RE NOT FLEXIBLE.
SINCE WE'RE ALL HERE, LET'S BUY SOMETHING THAT MATCHES!
OKAY! LIKE JEWELRY?
I LOSE SMALL THINGS REALLY QUICKLY...
OH, LOOK!
DOESN'T THIS LOOK JUST LIKE YOU?
IT'S SO CUTE!
A PHONE STRAP IN THE SHAPE OF A SLEEPING CAT!
OH...
よし PAT
よし PAT
HUH?
SINCE SAKURAKO IS A DOG,
YOU'RE THE CUTE ONE.
I GUESS I'LL GET A SQUIRREL STRAP.

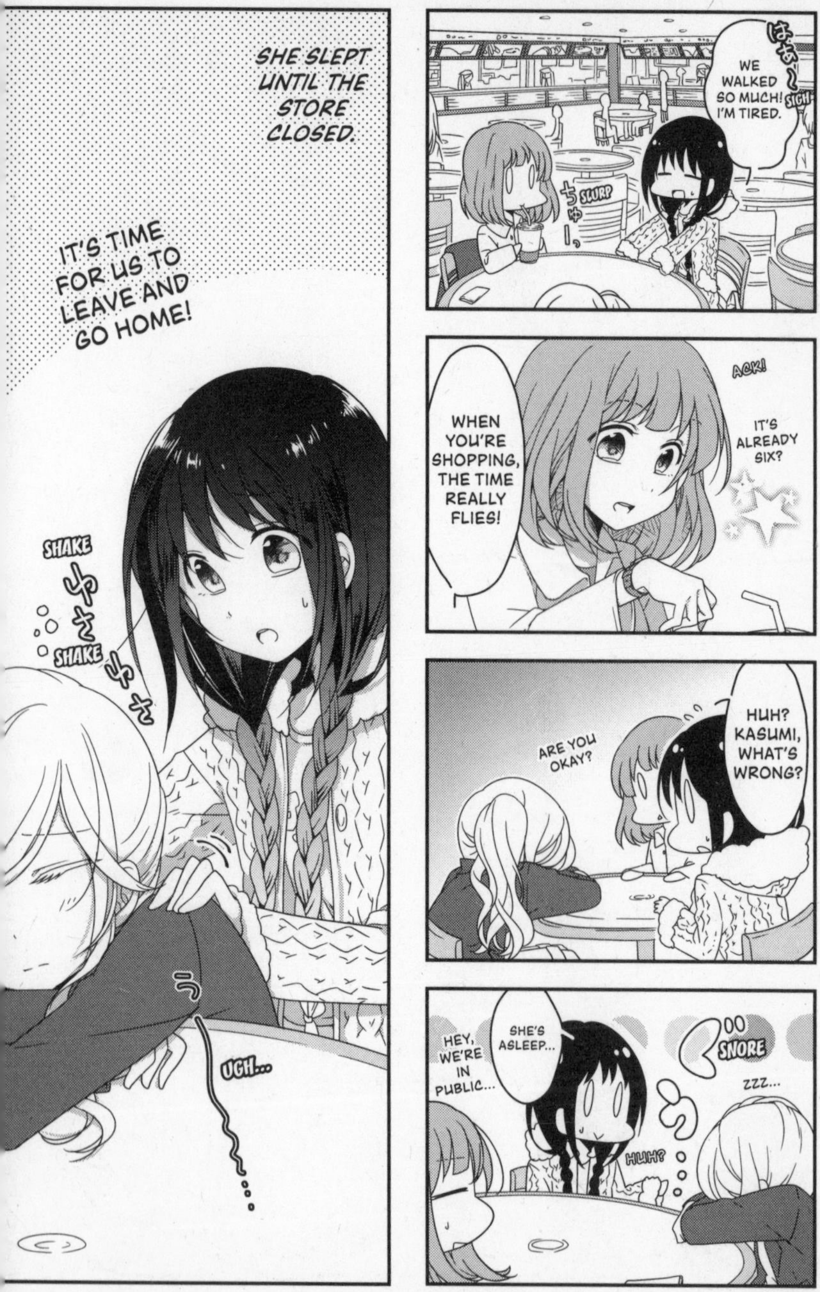
はぁ~
SIGH
WE WALKED SO MUCH! I'M TIRED.
ちゅー
SLURP
WHEN YOU'RE SHOPPING, THE TIME REALLY FLIES!
ACK!
IT'S ALREADY SIX?
HUH? KASUMI, WHAT'S WRONG?
ARE YOU OKAY?
SHE'S ASLEEP...
HEY, WE'RE IN PUBLIC...
SNORE
ZZZ...
HUH?
SHE SLEPT UNTIL THE STORE CLOSED.
IT'S TIME FOR US TO LEAVE AND GO HOME!
SHAKE
ゆさゆさ
SHAKE
う
UGH...

Illustration galler

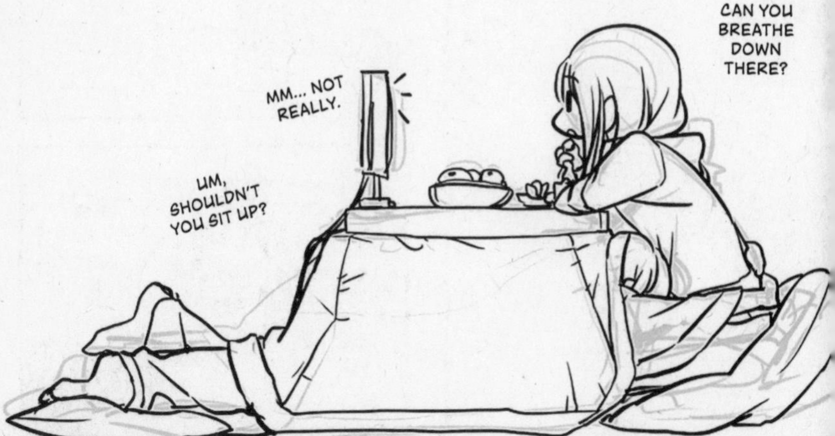
CAN YOU BREATHE DOWN THERE?
MM... NOT REALLY.
UM, SHOULDN'T YOU SIT UP?

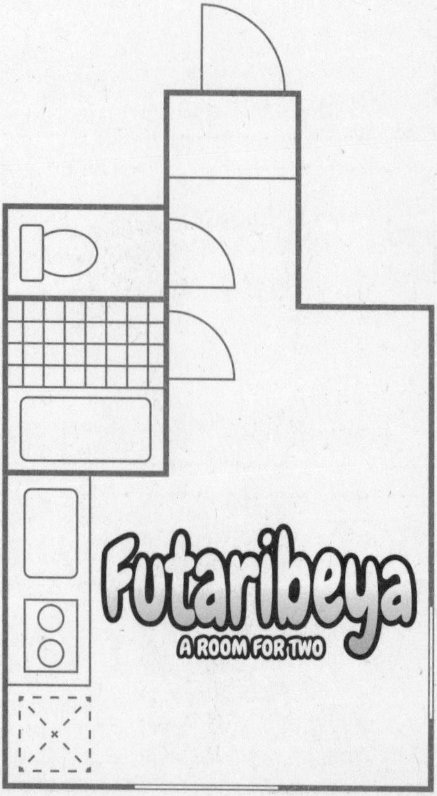
Futaribeya
A ROOM FOR TWO

Chapter 11

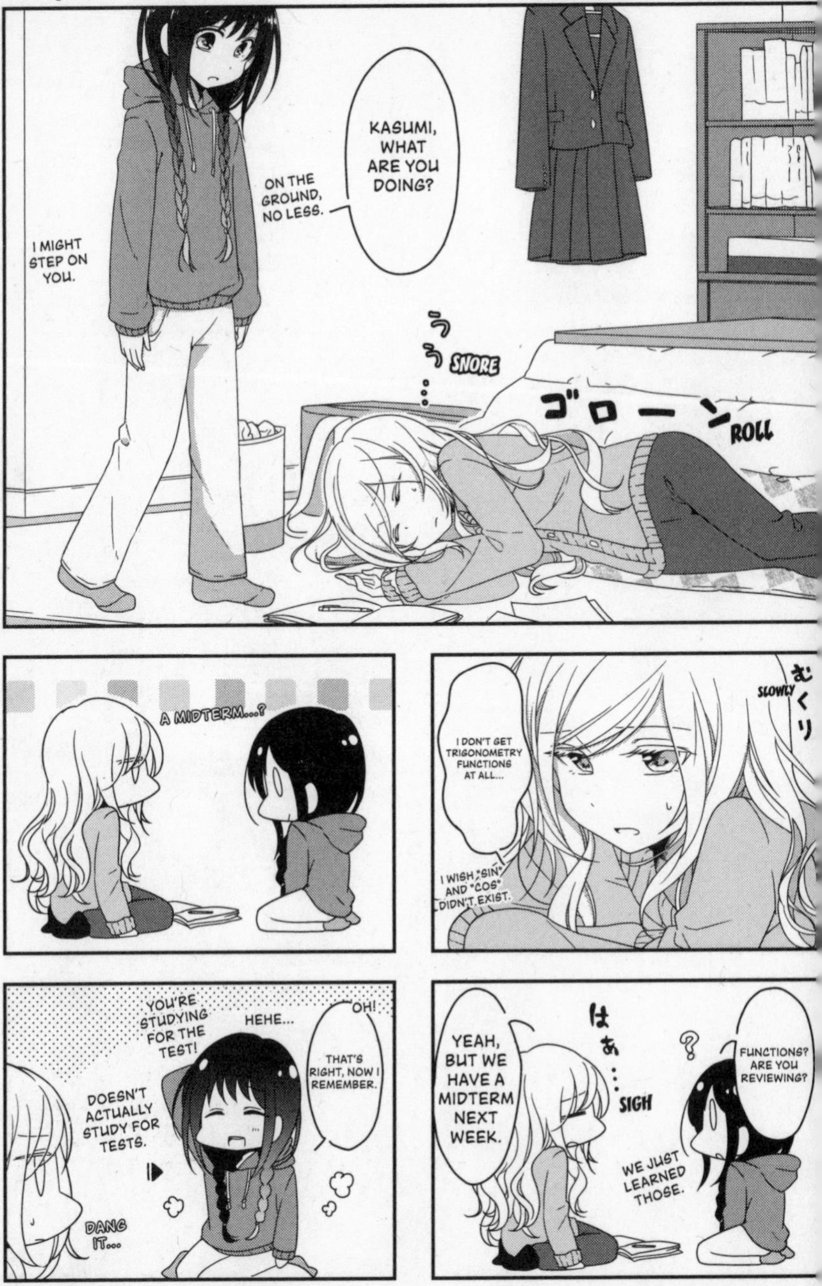
ゴローン
ROLL
うう…
SNORE
KASUMI, WHAT ARE YOU DOING?
ON THE GROUND, NO LESS.
I MIGHT STEP ON YOU.
むくり
SLOWLY
I DON'T GET TRIGONOMETRY FUNCTIONS AT ALL...
I WISH "SIN" AND "COS" DIDN'T EXIST.
A MIDTERM...?
FUNCTIONS? ARE YOU REVIEWING?
WE JUST LEARNED THOSE.
?
はぁ…
SIGH
YEAH, BUT WE HAVE A MIDTERM NEXT WEEK.
OH! THAT'S RIGHT, NOW I REMEMBER.
HEHE...
YOU'RE STUDYING FOR THE TEST!
DOESN'T ACTUALLY STUDY FOR TESTS.
DANG IT...

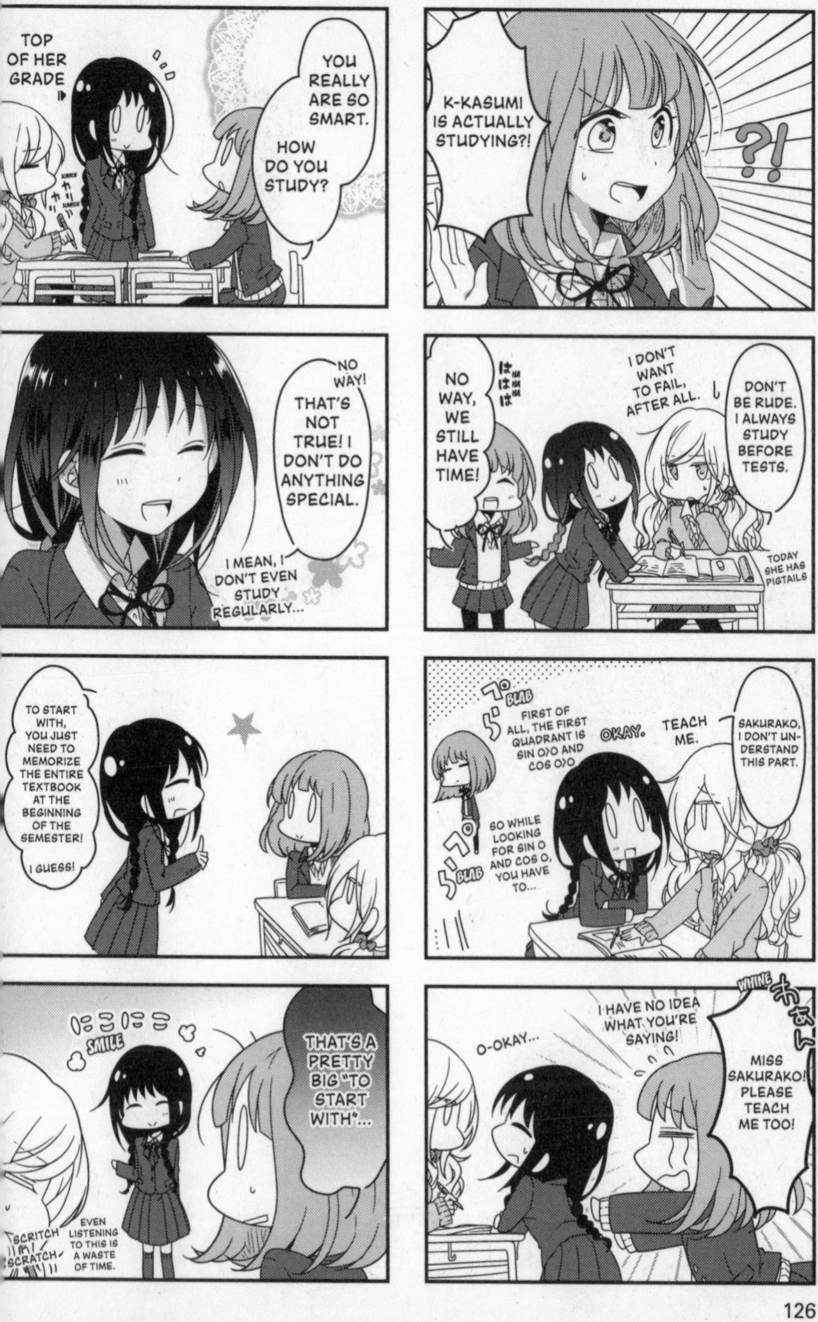

K-KASUMI IS ACTUALLY STUDYING?!
?!
DON'T BE RUDE. I ALWAYS STUDY BEFORE TESTS.
I DON'T WANT TO FAIL, AFTER ALL.
NO WAY, WE STILL HAVE TIME!
TODAY SHE HAS PIGTAILS
SAKURAKO, I DON'T UNDERSTAND THIS PART.
TEACH ME.
OKAY.
FIRST OF ALL, THE FIRST QUADRANT IS SIN Θ>0 AND COS Θ>0
BLAB
SO WHILE LOOKING FOR SIN Θ AND COS Θ, YOU HAVE TO...
BLAB
WHINE
MISS SAKURAKO! PLEASE TEACH ME TOO!
I HAVE NO IDEA WHAT YOU'RE SAYING!
O-OKAY...
TOP OF HER GRADE
YOU REALLY ARE SO SMART.
HOW DO YOU STUDY?
SCRATCH
SCRATCH
NO WAY! THAT'S NOT TRUE! I DON'T DO ANYTHING SPECIAL.
I MEAN, I DON'T EVEN STUDY REGULARLY...
TO START WITH, YOU JUST NEED TO MEMORIZE THE ENTIRE TEXTBOOK AT THE BEGINNING OF THE SEMESTER!
I GUESS!
THAT'S A PRETTY BIG "TO START WITH"...
にこにこ
SMILE
EVEN LISTENING TO THIS IS A WASTE OF TIME.
SCRITCH
SCRATCH

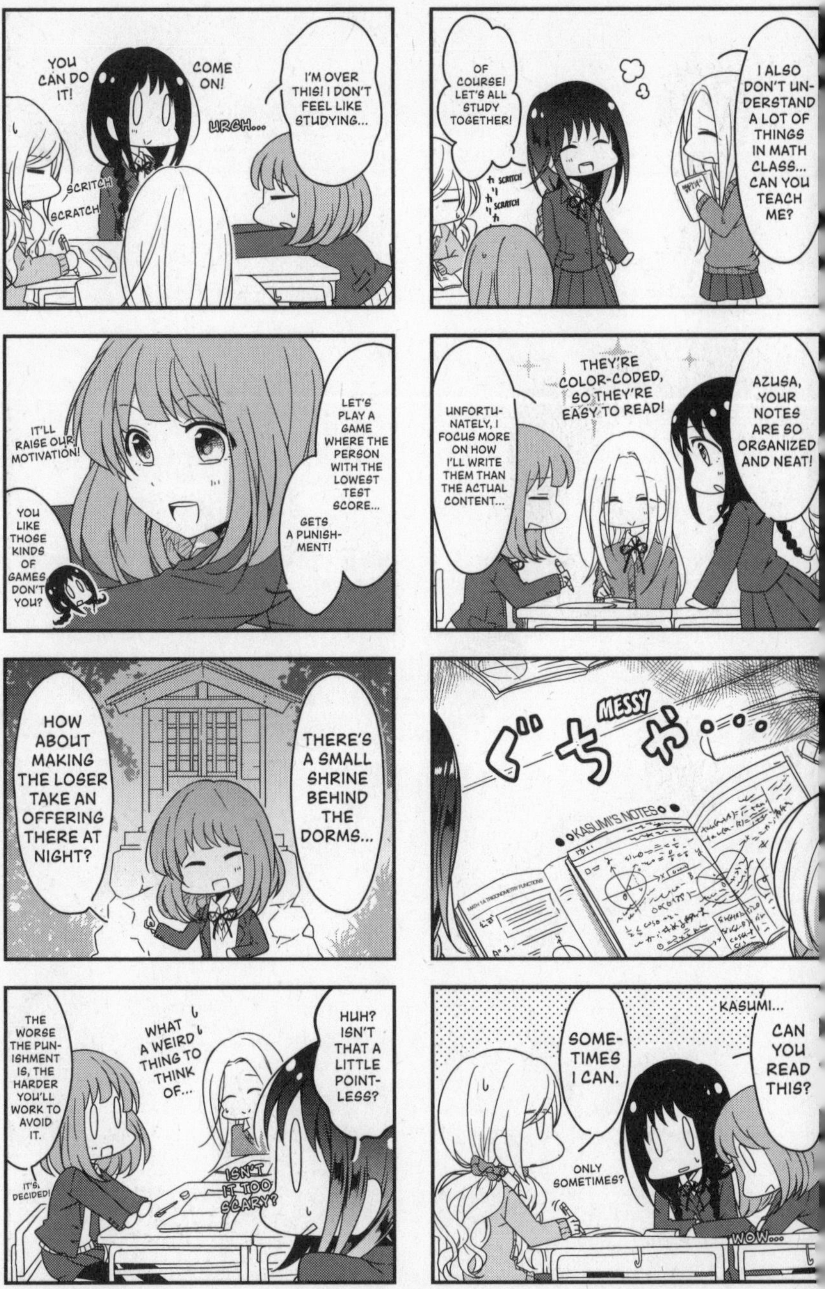
I ALSO DON'T UNDERSTAND A LOT OF THINGS IN MATH CLASS... CAN YOU TEACH ME?
OF COURSE! LET'S ALL STUDY TOGETHER!
SCRATCH
SCRATCH
AZUSA, YOUR NOTES ARE SO ORGANIZED AND NEAT!
THEY'RE COLOR-CODED, SO THEY'RE EASY TO READ!
UNFORTUNATELY, I FOCUS MORE ON HOW I'LL WRITE THEM THAN THE ACTUAL CONTENT...
MESSY
KASUMI'S NOTES
MATH 1A TRIGONOMETRY FUNCTIONS
KASUMI... CAN YOU READ THIS?
SOMETIMES I CAN.
ONLY SOMETIMES?
WOW...
I'M OVER THIS! I DON'T FEEL LIKE STUDYING...
URGH...
COME ON!
YOU CAN DO IT!
SCRITCH
SCRATCH
LET'S PLAY A GAME WHERE THE PERSON WITH THE LOWEST TEST SCORE...
GETS A PUNISHMENT!
IT'LL RAISE OUR MOTIVATION!
YOU LIKE THOSE KINDS OF GAMES, DON'T YOU?
THERE'S A SMALL SHRINE BEHIND THE DORMS...
HOW ABOUT MAKING THE LOSER TAKE AN OFFERING THERE AT NIGHT?
HUH? ISN'T THAT A LITTLE POINTLESS?
WHAT A WEIRD THING TO THINK OF...
THE WORSE THE PUNISHMENT IS, THE HARDER YOU'LL WORK TO AVOID IT.
ISN'T IT TOO SCARY?
IT'S DECIDED!

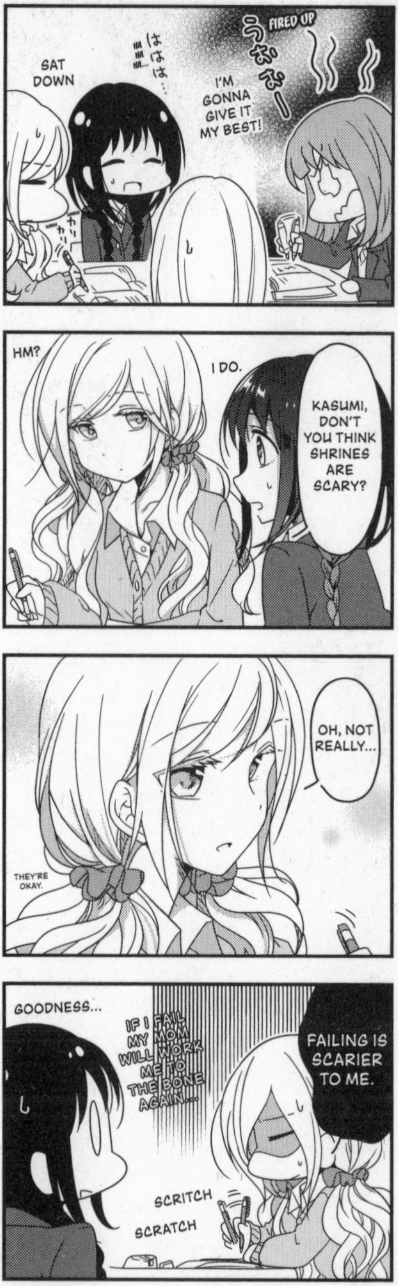
FIRED UP
うおぉー
I'M GONNA GIVE IT MY BEST!
ははは…
HA HA HA...
SAT DOWN
カリカリ
KASUMI, DON'T YOU THINK SHRINES ARE SCARY?
I DO.
HM?
OH, NOT REALLY...
THEY'RE OKAY.
FAILING IS SCARIER TO ME.
IF I FAIL MY MOM WILL WORK ME TO THE BONE AGAIN...
GOODNESS...
SCRITCH
SCRATCH

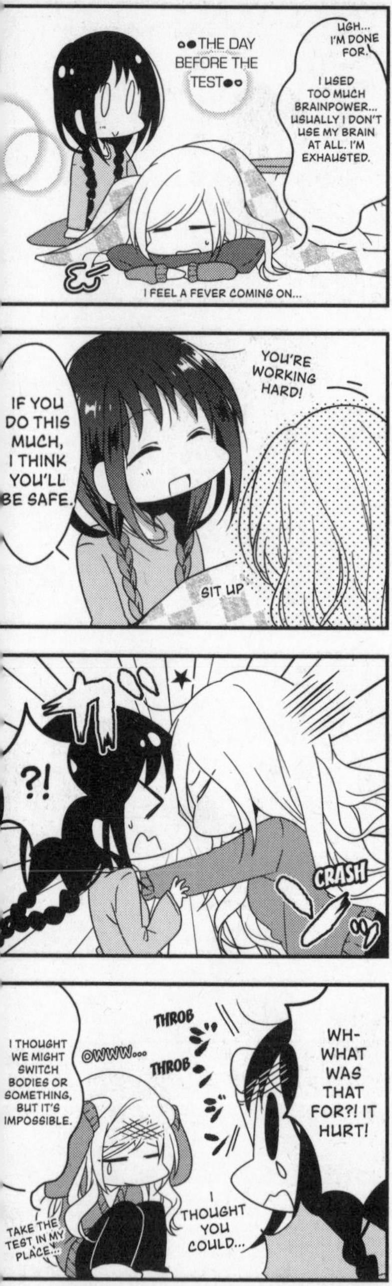
UGH... I'M DONE FOR.
I USED TOO MUCH BRAINPOWER... USUALLY I DON'T USE MY BRAIN AT ALL. I'M EXHAUSTED.
THE DAY BEFORE THE TEST
I FEEL A FEVER COMING ON...
YOU'RE WORKING HARD!
IF YOU DO THIS MUCH, I THINK YOU'LL BE SAFE.
SIT UP
?!
CRASH
WH-WHAT WAS THAT FOR?! IT HURT!
THROB
THROB
OWWW...
I THOUGHT WE MIGHT SWITCH BODIES OR SOMETHING, BUT IT'S IMPOSSIBLE.
I THOUGHT YOU COULD...
TAKE THE TEST IN MY PLACE...

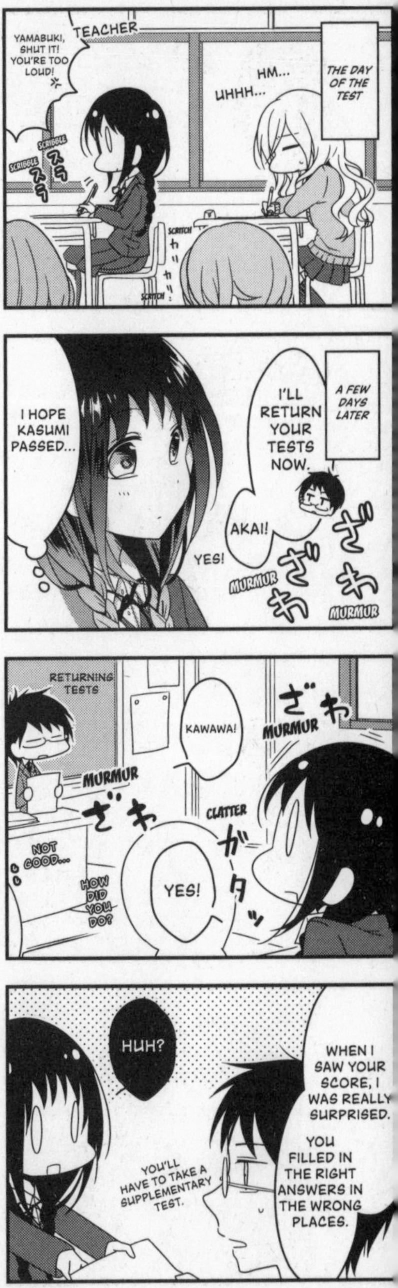
THE DAY OF THE TEST
HM...
UHHH...
TEACHER
YAMABUKI, SHUT IT! YOU'RE TOO LOUD!
SCRIBBLE スラ
SCRIBBLE スラ
SCRITCH カリ
カリ SCRITCH
A FEW DAYS LATER
I'LL RETURN YOUR TESTS NOW.
I HOPE KASUMI PASSED...
AKAI!
YES!
ざわ MURMUR
ざわ MURMUR
ざわ MURMUR
KAWAWA!
RETURNING TESTS
MURMUR ざわ
CLATTER ガタッ
YES!
NOT GOOD...
HOW DID YOU DO?
WHEN I SAW YOUR SCORE, I WAS REALLY SURPRISED.
YOU FILLED IN THE RIGHT ANSWERS IN THE WRONG PLACES.
HUH?
YOU'LL HAVE TO TAKE A SUPPLEMENTARY TEST.
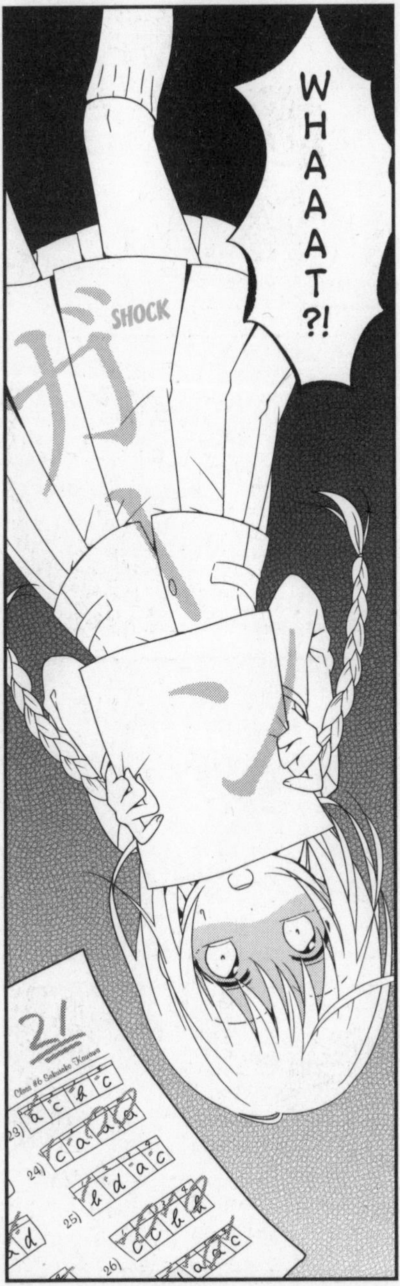
WHAAAT?!
SHOCK ガーン
21
Class #6 Sakurako Kawawa

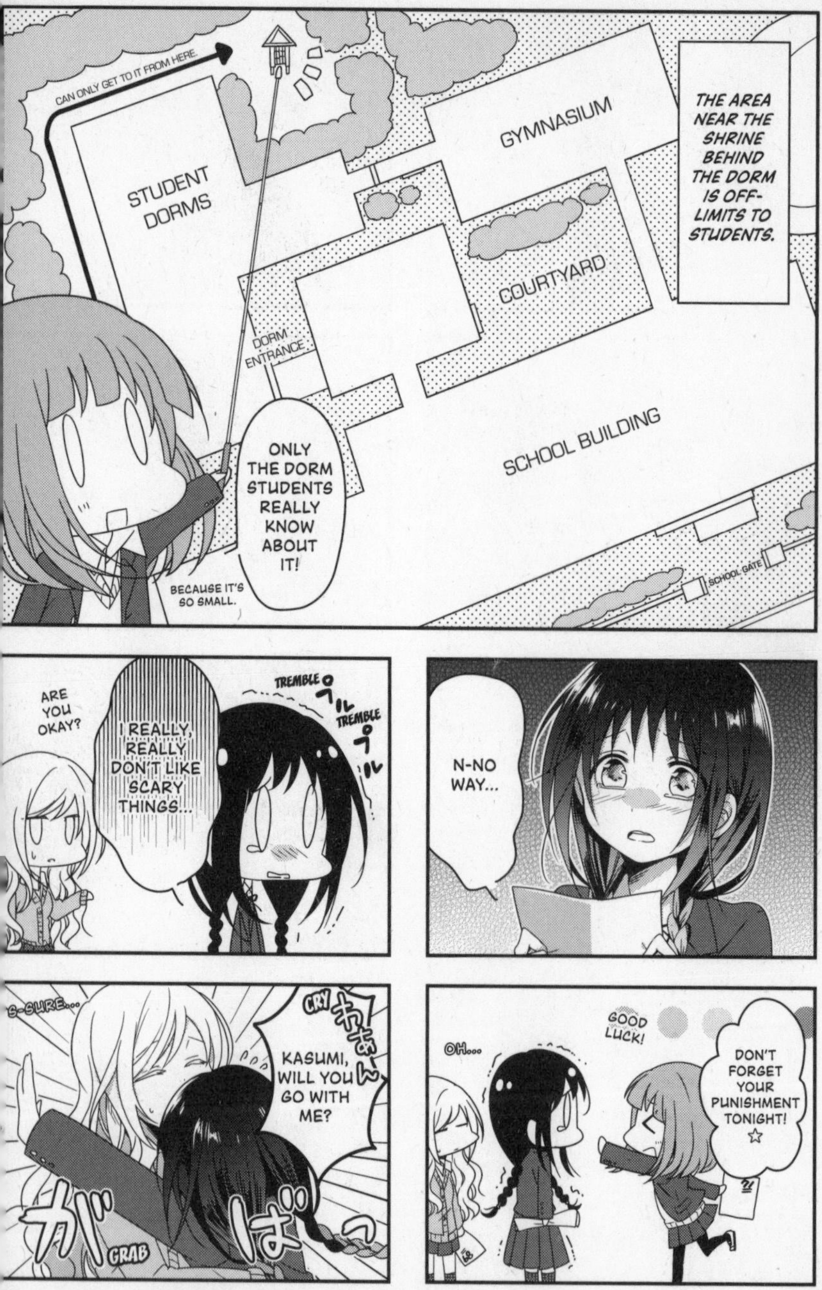

THE AREA NEAR THE SHRINE BEHIND THE DORM IS OFF-LIMITS TO STUDENTS.
GYMNASIUM
CAN ONLY GET TO IT FROM HERE.
STUDENT DORMS
COURTYARD
DORM ENTRANCE
SCHOOL BUILDING
SCHOOL GATE
ONLY THE DORM STUDENTS REALLY KNOW ABOUT IT!
BECAUSE IT'S SO SMALL.
N-NO WAY...
TREMBLE
TREMBLE
I REALLY, REALLY DON'T LIKE SCARY THINGS...
ARE YOU OKAY?
DON'T FORGET YOUR PUNISHMENT TONIGHT! ☆
GOOD LUCK!
OH...
CRY
KASUMI, WILL YOU GO WITH ME?
S-SURE...
GRAB

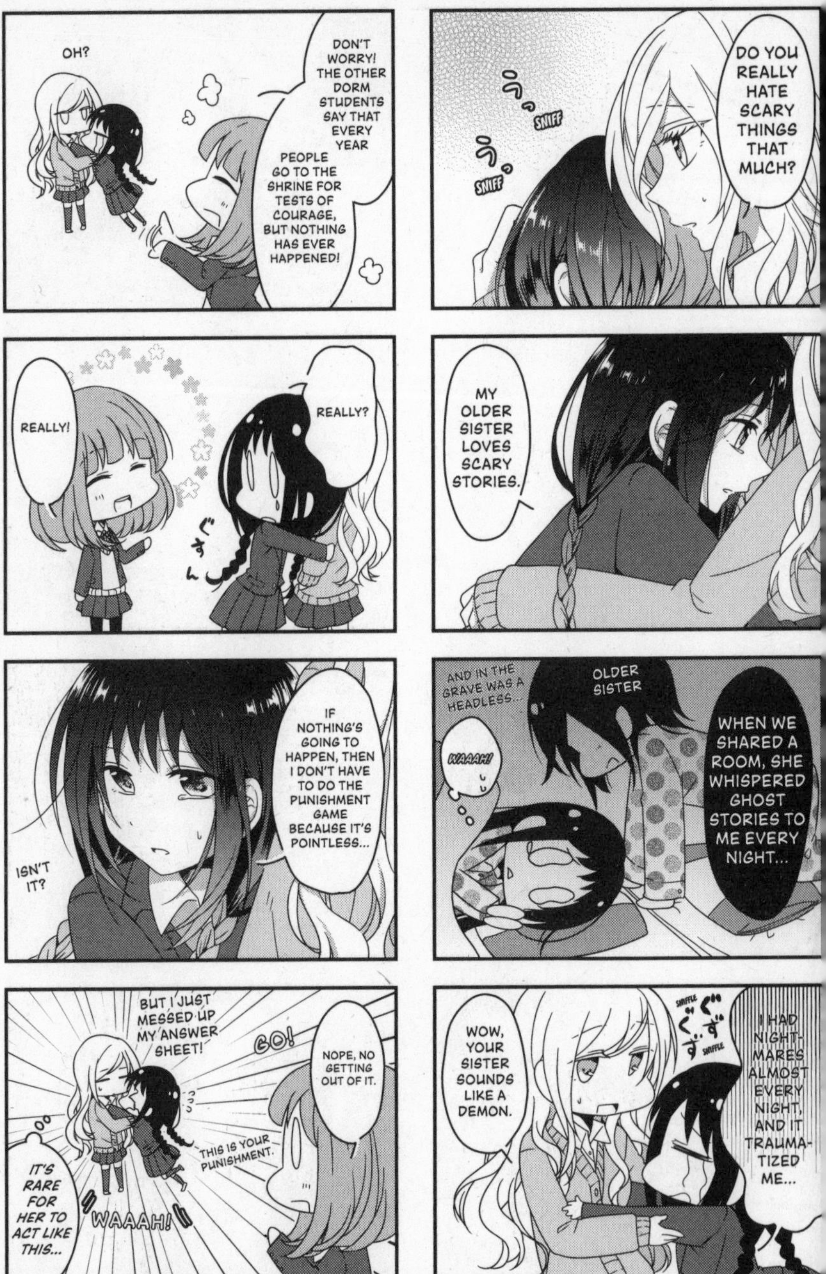

DO YOU REALLY HATE SCARY THINGS THAT MUCH?
SNIFF
SNIFF
MY OLDER SISTER LOVES SCARY STORIES.
WHEN WE SHARED A ROOM, SHE WHISPERED GHOST STORIES TO ME EVERY NIGHT...
OLDER SISTER
AND IN THE GRAVE WAS A HEADLESS...
WAAAH!
I HAD NIGHTMARES ALMOST EVERY NIGHT, AND IT TRAUMATIZED ME...
SNIFFLE
SNIFFLE
WOW, YOUR SISTER SOUNDS LIKE A DEMON.
DON'T WORRY! THE OTHER DORM STUDENTS SAY THAT EVERY YEAR
PEOPLE GO TO THE SHRINE FOR TESTS OF COURAGE, BUT NOTHING HAS EVER HAPPENED!
OH?
REALLY?
REALLY!
IF NOTHING'S GOING TO HAPPEN, THEN I DON'T HAVE TO DO THE PUNISHMENT GAME BECAUSE IT'S POINTLESS...
ISN'T IT?
NOPE, NO GETTING OUT OF IT.
GO!
BUT I JUST MESSED UP MY ANSWER SHEET!
THIS IS YOUR PUNISHMENT.
WAAAH!
IT'S RARE FOR HER TO ACT LIKE THIS...

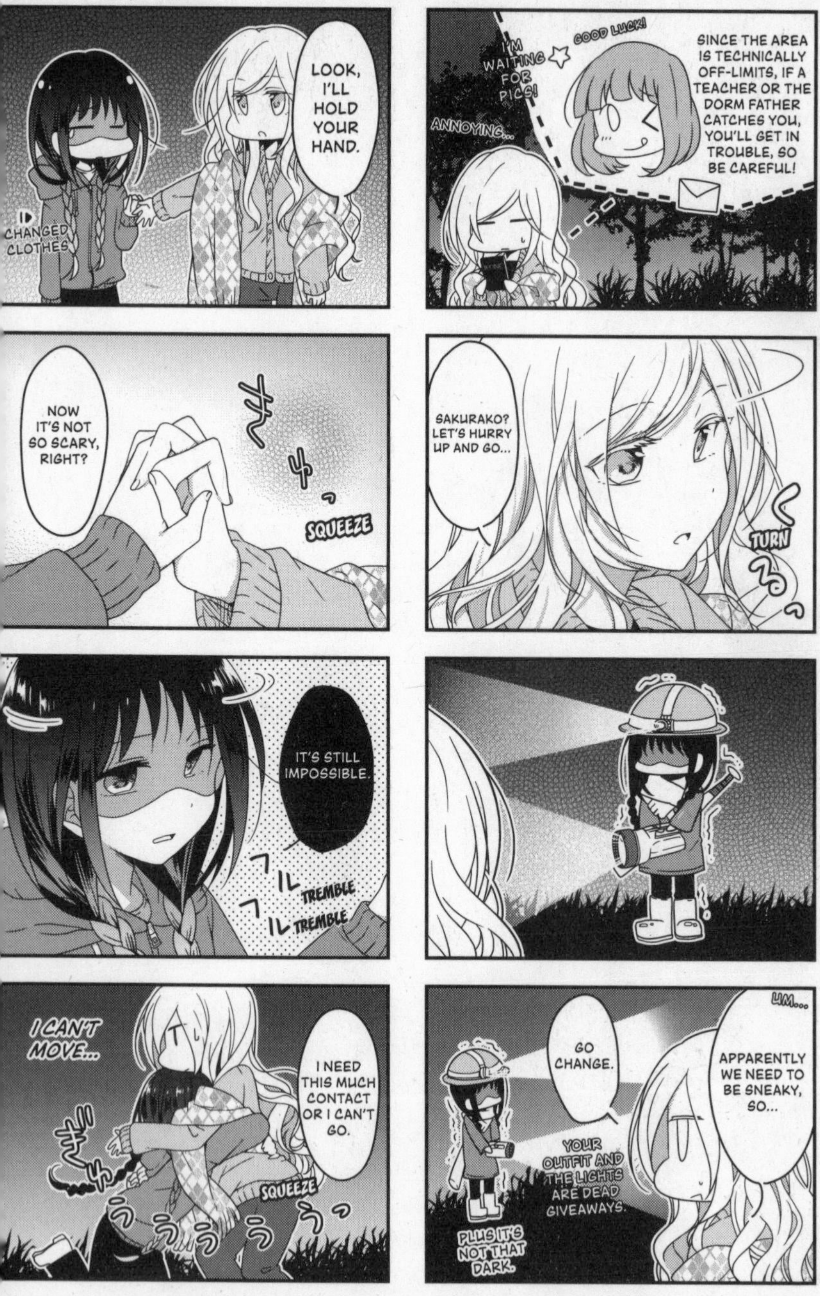
SINCE THE AREA IS TECHNICALLY OFF-LIMITS, IF A TEACHER OR THE DORM FATHER CATCHES YOU, YOU'LL GET IN TROUBLE, SO BE CAREFUL!
GOOD LUCK!
I'M WAITING FOR PICS!
ANNOYING...
LOOK, I'LL HOLD YOUR HAND.
I'D CHANGED CLOTHES
SAKURAKO? LET'S HURRY UP AND GO...
TURN
NOW IT'S NOT SO SCARY, RIGHT?
SQUEEZE
IT'S STILL IMPOSSIBLE.
TREMBLE
TREMBLE
UM...
APPARENTLY WE NEED TO BE SNEAKY, SO...
GO CHANGE.
YOUR OUTFIT AND THE LIGHTS ARE DEAD GIVEAWAYS.
PLUS IT'S NOT THAT DARK.
I NEED THIS MUCH CONTACT OR I CAN'T GO.
I CAN'T MOVE...
SQUEEZE

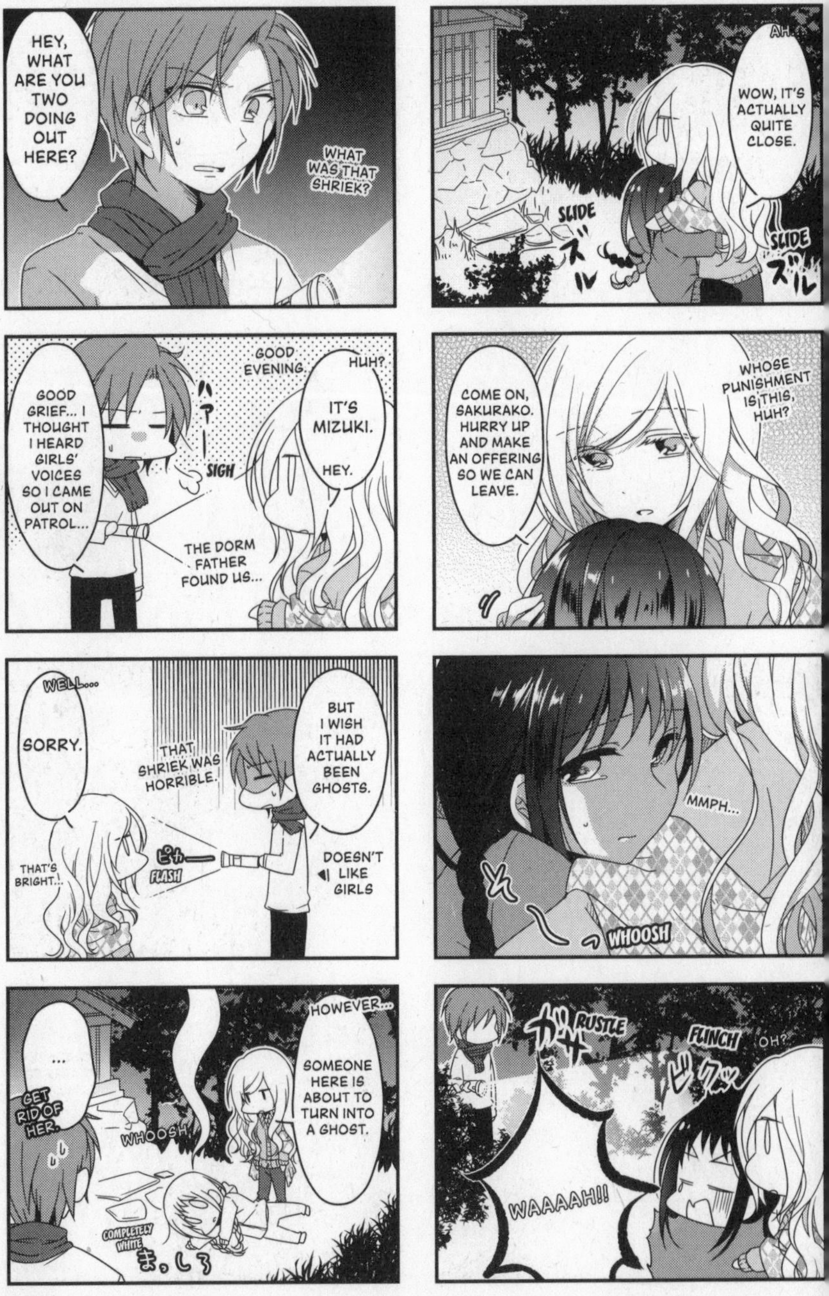
AH...
WOW, IT'S ACTUALLY QUITE CLOSE.
SLIDE
ズル
SLIDE
ズル
WHOSE PUNISHMENT IS THIS, HUH?
COME ON, SAKURAKO. HURRY UP AND MAKE AN OFFERING SO WE CAN LEAVE.
MMPH...
WHOOSH
RUSTLE
ガサ
FLINCH
ビクッ
OH?
WAAAAH!!
HEY, WHAT ARE YOU TWO DOING OUT HERE?
WHAT WAS THAT SHRIEK?
HUH?
IT'S MIZUKI.
HEY.
GOOD EVENING.
ハァー
SIGH
GOOD GRIEF... I THOUGHT I HEARD GIRLS' VOICES SO I CAME OUT ON PATROL...
THE DORM FATHER FOUND US...
BUT I WISH IT HAD ACTUALLY BEEN GHOSTS.
DOESN'T LIKE GIRLS
THAT SHRIEK WAS HORRIBLE.
WELL...
SORRY.
ピカー
FLASH
THAT'S BRIGHT...
HOWEVER...
SOMEONE HERE IS ABOUT TO TURN INTO A GHOST.
...
GET RID OF HER.
WHOOSH
COMPLETELY WHITE
まっしろ

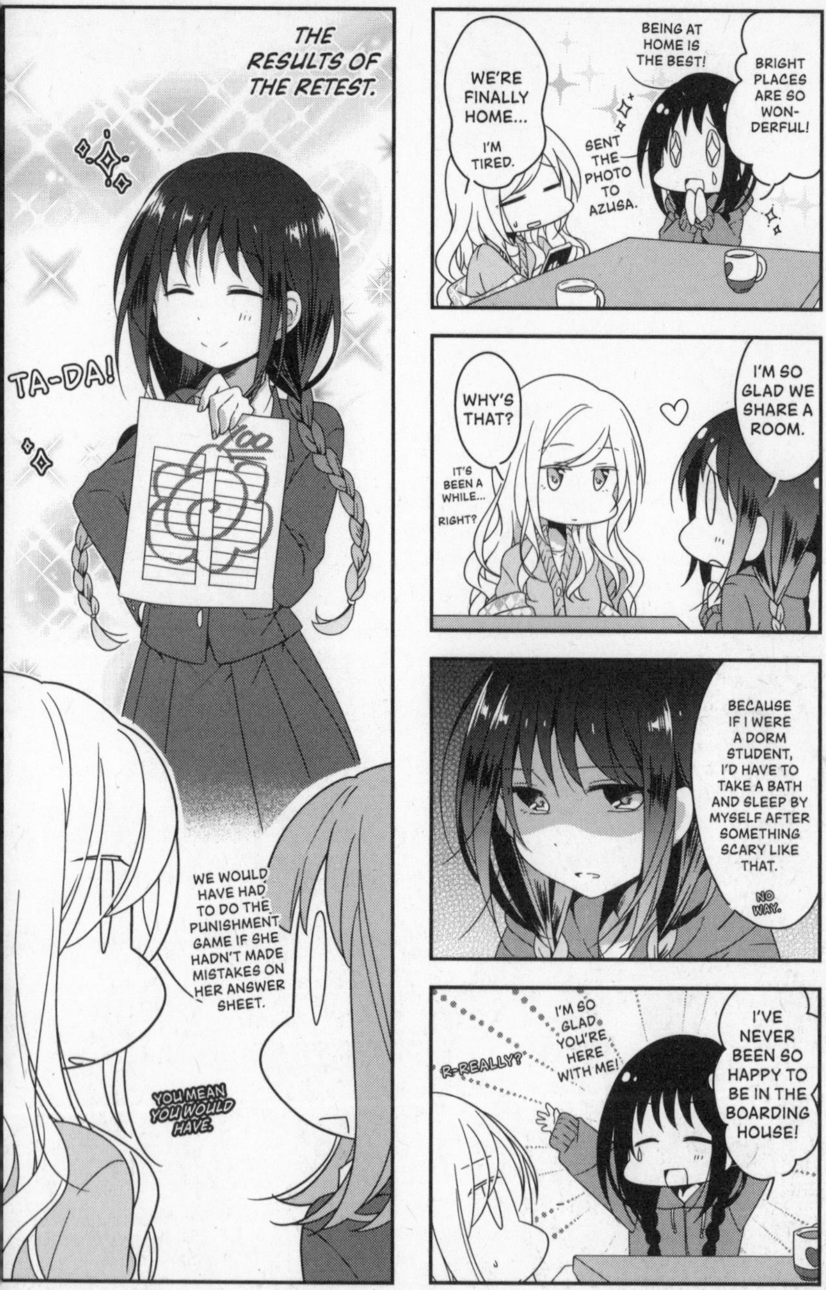
BRIGHT PLACES ARE SO WONDERFUL!
BEING AT HOME IS THE BEST!
WE'RE FINALLY HOME...
SENT THE PHOTO TO AZUSA.
I'M TIRED.
I'M SO GLAD WE SHARE A ROOM.
WHY'S THAT?
IT'S BEEN A WHILE...
RIGHT?
BECAUSE IF I WERE A DORM STUDENT, I'D HAVE TO TAKE A BATH AND SLEEP BY MYSELF AFTER SOMETHING SCARY LIKE THAT.
NO WAY.
I'VE NEVER BEEN SO HAPPY TO BE IN THE BOARDING HOUSE!
I'M SO GLAD YOU'RE HERE WITH ME!
R-REALLY?
THE RESULTS OF THE RETEST.
TA-DA!
100
WE WOULD HAVE HAD TO DO THE PUNISHMENT GAME IF SHE HADN'T MADE MISTAKES ON HER ANSWER SHEET.
YOU MEAN YOU WOULD HAVE.

Illustration gallery

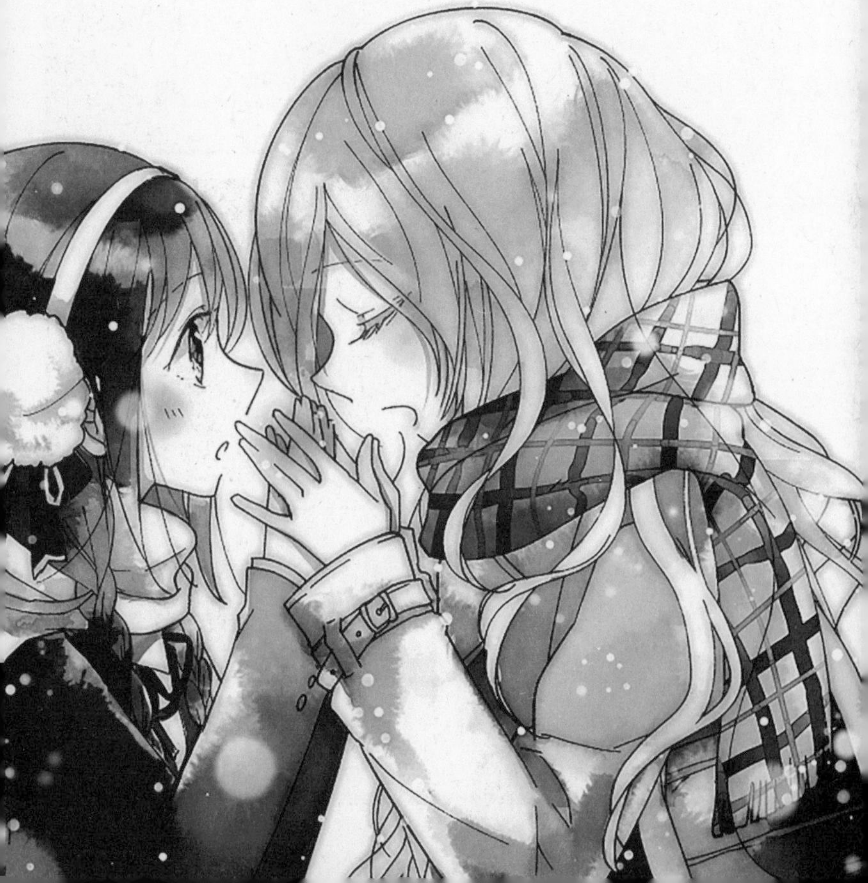

Futaribeya
A ROOM FOR TWO

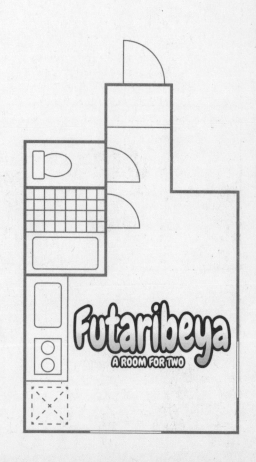

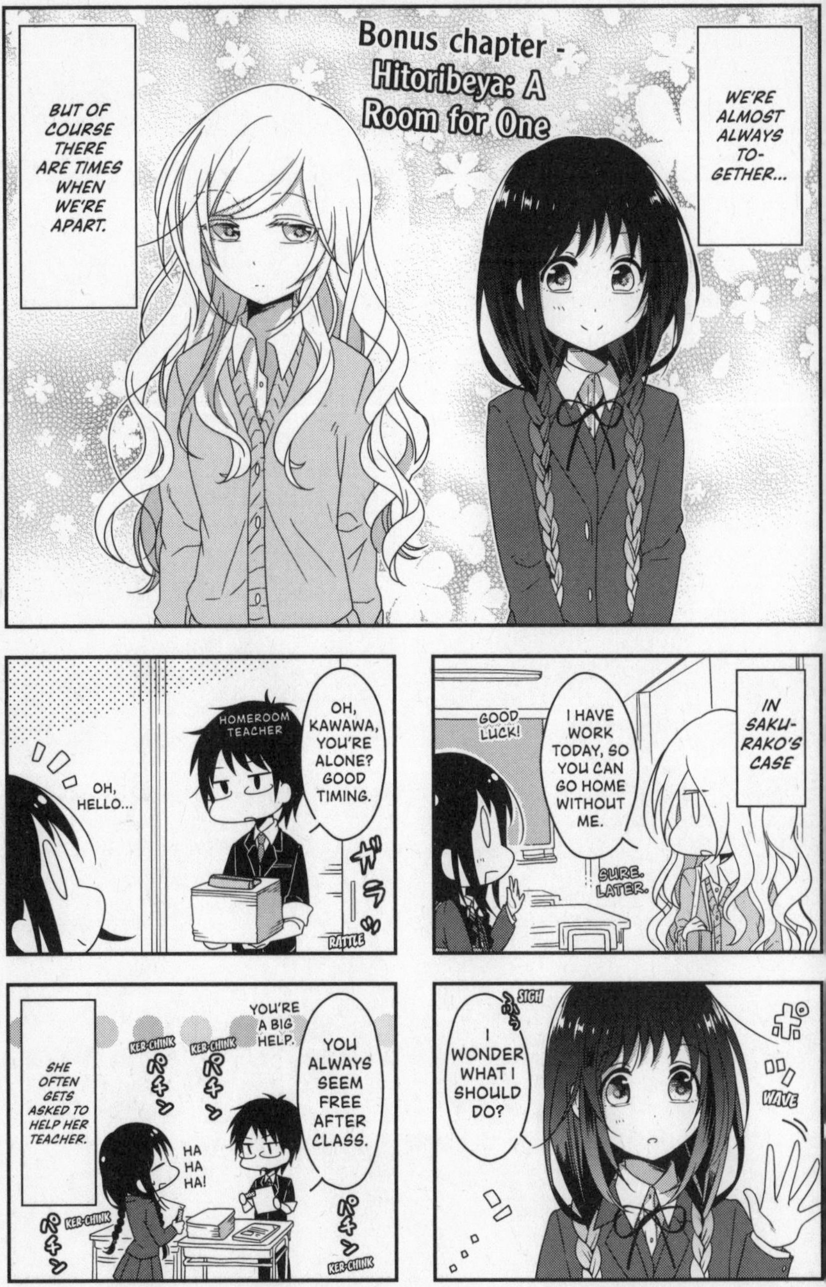
WE'RE ALMOST ALWAYS TO-GETHER...
Bonus chapter - Hitoribeya: A Room for One
BUT OF COURSE THERE ARE TIMES WHEN WE'RE APART.
IN SAKU-RAKO'S CASE
I HAVE WORK TODAY, SO YOU CAN GO HOME WITHOUT ME.
GOOD LUCK!
SURE. LATER.
OH, KAWAWA, YOU'RE ALONE? GOOD TIMING.
HOMEROOM TEACHER
RATTLE
OH, HELLO...
SIGH
I WONDER WHAT I SHOULD DO?
WAVE
YOU ALWAYS SEEM FREE AFTER CLASS.
YOU'RE A BIG HELP.
KER-CHINK
KER-CHINK
SHE OFTEN GETS ASKED TO HELP HER TEACHER.
HA HA HA!
KER-CHINK
KER-CHINK

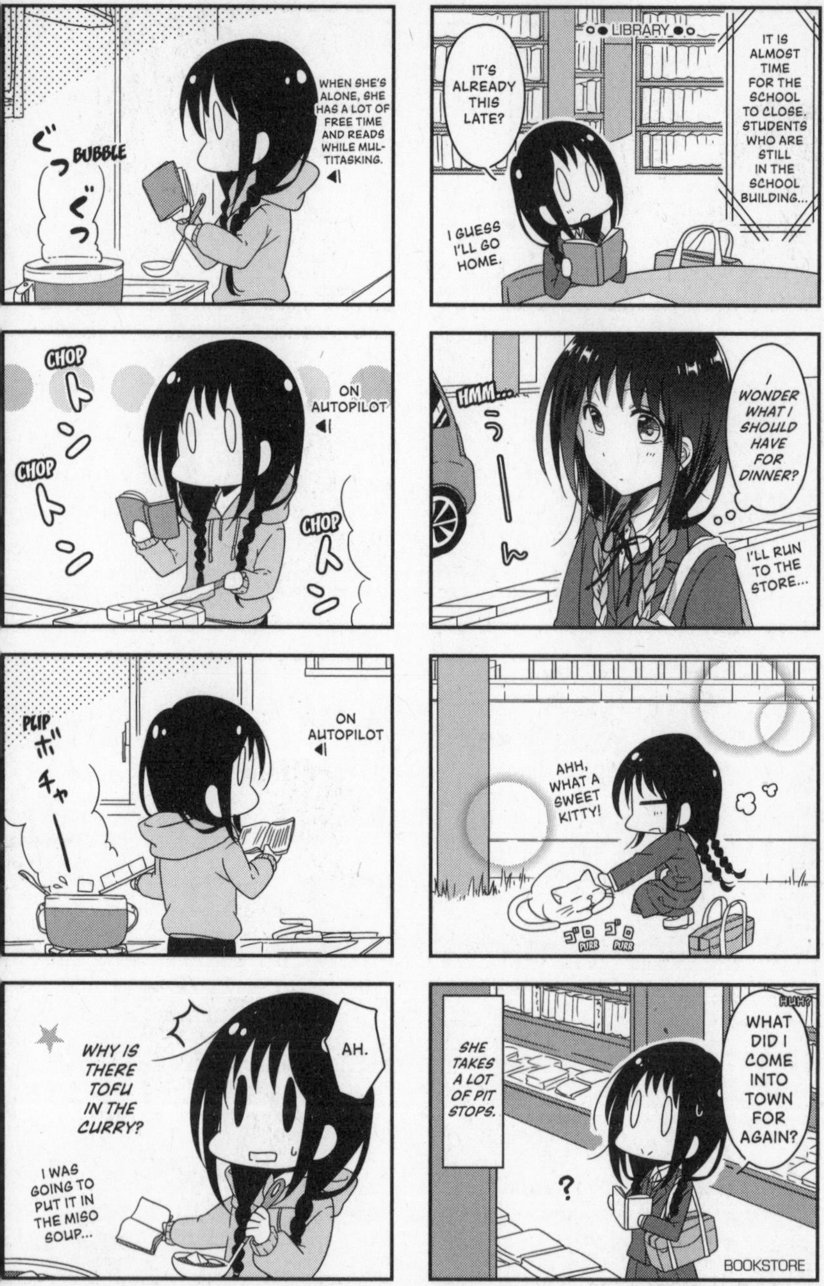

LIBRARY
IT IS ALMOST TIME FOR THE SCHOOL TO CLOSE. STUDENTS WHO ARE STILL IN THE SCHOOL BUILDING...
IT'S ALREADY THIS LATE?
I GUESS I'LL GO HOME.
I WONDER WHAT I SHOULD HAVE FOR DINNER?
HMM...
うーん
I'LL RUN TO THE STORE...
AHH, WHAT A SWEET KITTY!
ゴロ PURR ゴロ PURR
HUH?
WHAT DID I COME INTO TOWN FOR AGAIN?
SHE TAKES A LOT OF PIT STOPS.
?
BOOKSTORE
WHEN SHE'S ALONE, SHE HAS A LOT OF FREE TIME AND READS WHILE MULTITASKING.
ぐつぐつ BUBBLE
ON AUTOPILOT
CHOP トン CHOP トン CHOP トン
ON AUTOPILOT
PLIP ボチャー
AH.
WHY IS THERE TOFU IN THE CURRY?
I WAS GOING TO PUT IT IN THE MISO SOUP...

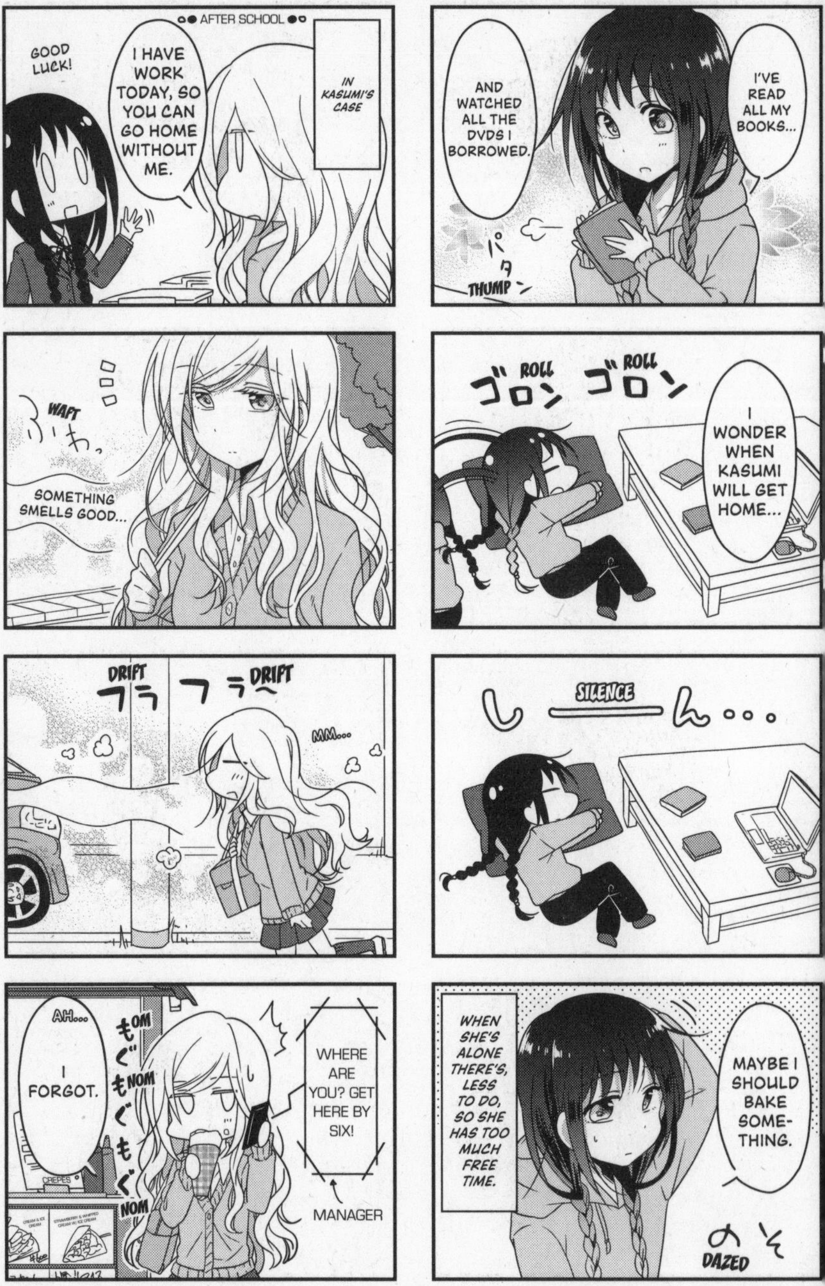
I'VE READ ALL MY BOOKS...
AND WATCHED ALL THE DVDS I BORROWED.
パタン
THUMP
ゴロン ゴロン
ROLL ROLL
I WONDER WHEN KASUMI WILL GET HOME...
し――ん。。。
SILENCE
MAYBE I SHOULD BAKE SOME-THING.
WHEN SHE'S ALONE THERE'S LESS TO DO, SO SHE HAS TOO MUCH FREE TIME.
DAZED
AFTER SCHOOL
IN KASUMI'S CASE
I HAVE WORK TODAY, SO YOU CAN GO HOME WITHOUT ME.
GOOD LUCK!
ふわっ
WAFT
SOMETHING SMELLS GOOD...
フラ フラ〜
DRIFT DRIFT
MM...
WHERE ARE YOU? GET HERE BY SIX!
MANAGER
もぐ もぐ もぐ もぐ
NOM NOM NOM
AH... I FORGOT.
CREPES

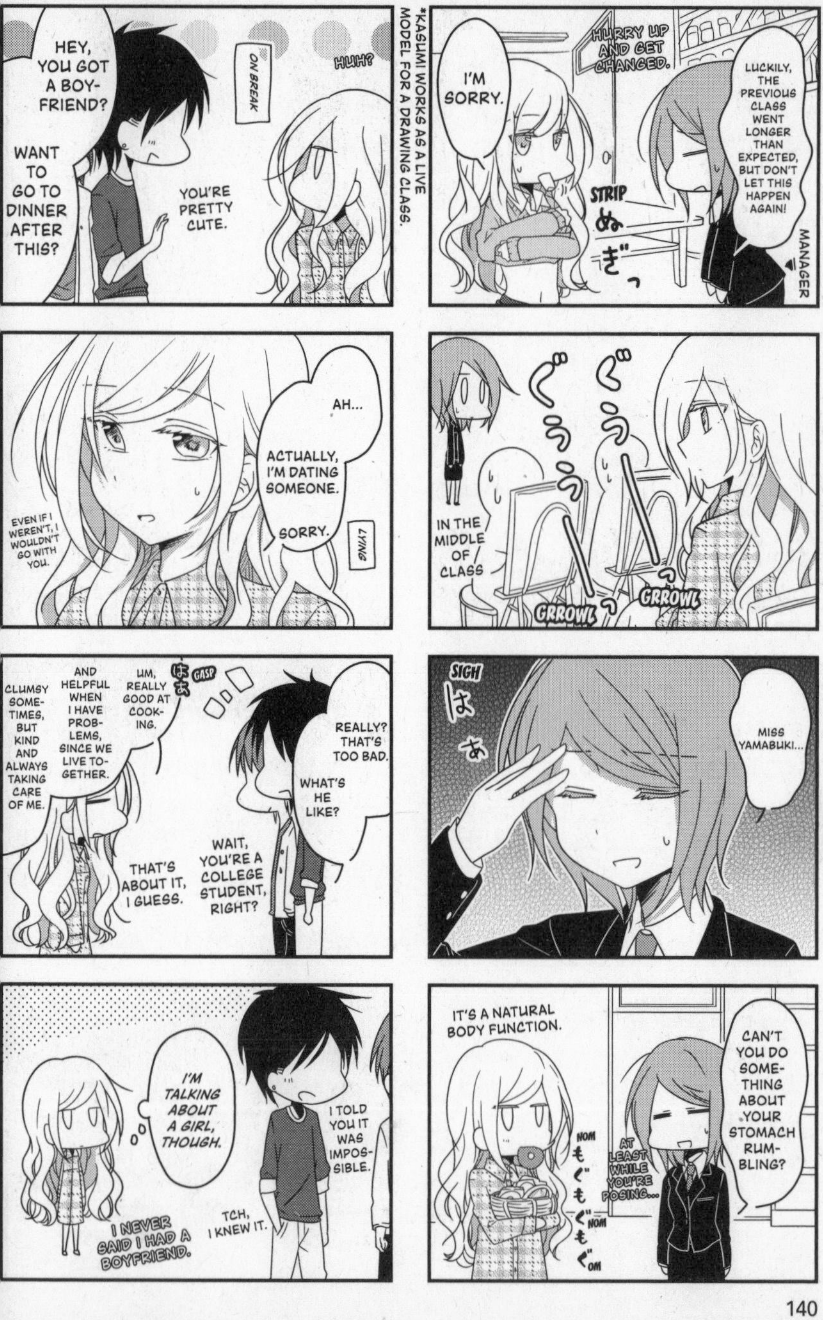
LUCKILY, THE PREVIOUS CLASS WENT LONGER THAN EXPECTED, BUT DON'T LET THIS HAPPEN AGAIN!
MANAGER
HURRY UP AND GET CHANGED.
I'M SORRY.
STRIP ぬぎっ
ぐうーっ GRROWL
ぐうーっ GRROWL
IN THE MIDDLE OF CLASS
MISS YAMABUKI...
SIGH はぁ
CAN'T YOU DO SOMETHING ABOUT YOUR STOMACH RUMBLING?
AT LEAST WHILE YOU'RE POSING...
IT'S A NATURAL BODY FUNCTION.
もぐもぐもぐ NOM NOM NOM
*KASUMI WORKS AS A LIVE MODEL FOR A DRAWING CLASS.
HUH?
ON BREAK
HEY, YOU GOT A BOYFRIEND?
YOU'RE PRETTY CUTE.
WANT TO GO TO DINNER AFTER THIS?
AH... ACTUALLY, I'M DATING SOMEONE. SORRY.
LYING
EVEN IF I WEREN'T, I WOULDN'T GO WITH YOU.
REALLY? THAT'S TOO BAD. WHAT'S HE LIKE?
はぁ GASP
UM, REALLY GOOD AT COOKING.
AND HELPFUL WHEN I HAVE PROBLEMS, SINCE WE LIVE TOGETHER.
CLUMSY SOMETIMES, BUT KIND AND ALWAYS TAKING CARE OF ME.
WAIT, YOU'RE A COLLEGE STUDENT, RIGHT?
THAT'S ABOUT IT, I GUESS.
I TOLD YOU IT WAS IMPOSSIBLE.
I'M TALKING ABOUT A GIRL, THOUGH.
TCH, I KNEW IT.
I NEVER SAID I HAD A BOYFRIEND.

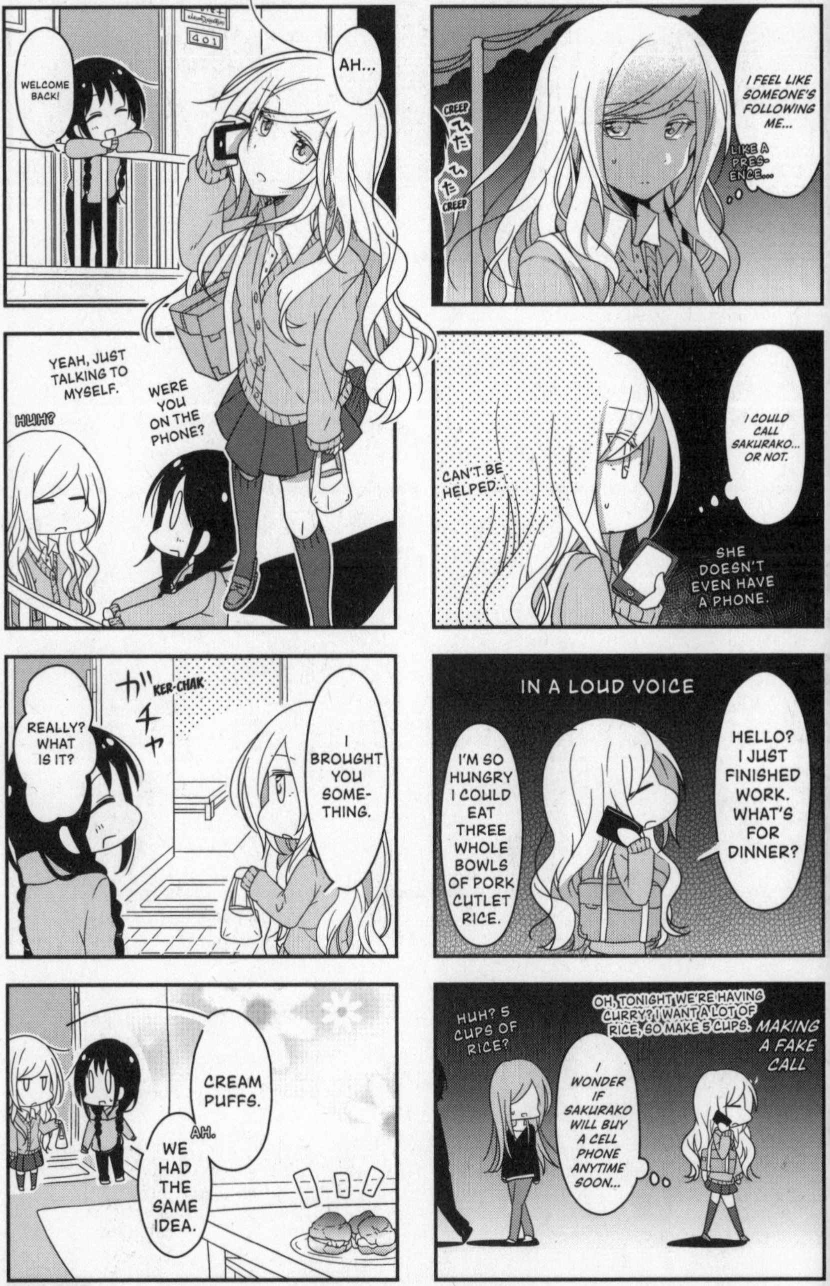
I FEEL LIKE SOMEONE'S FOLLOWING ME...
LIKE A PRESENCE...
CREEP ひたひた CREEP
I COULD CALL SAKURAKO... OR NOT.
CAN'T BE HELPED...
SHE DOESN'T EVEN HAVE A PHONE.
IN A LOUD VOICE
HELLO? I JUST FINISHED WORK. WHAT'S FOR DINNER?
I'M SO HUNGRY I COULD EAT THREE WHOLE BOWLS OF PORK CUTLET RICE.
OH, TONIGHT WE'RE HAVING CURRY? I WANT A LOT OF RICE, SO MAKE 5 CUPS.
MAKING A FAKE CALL
HUH? 5 CUPS OF RICE?
I WONDER IF SAKURAKO WILL BUY A CELL PHONE ANYTIME SOON...
AH...
WELCOME BACK!
WERE YOU ON THE PHONE?
HUH?
YEAH, JUST TALKING TO MYSELF.
ガチャ KER-CHAK
I BROUGHT YOU SOMETHING.
REALLY? WHAT IS IT?
CREAM PUFFS.
AH.
WE HAD THE SAME IDEA.

THE END.

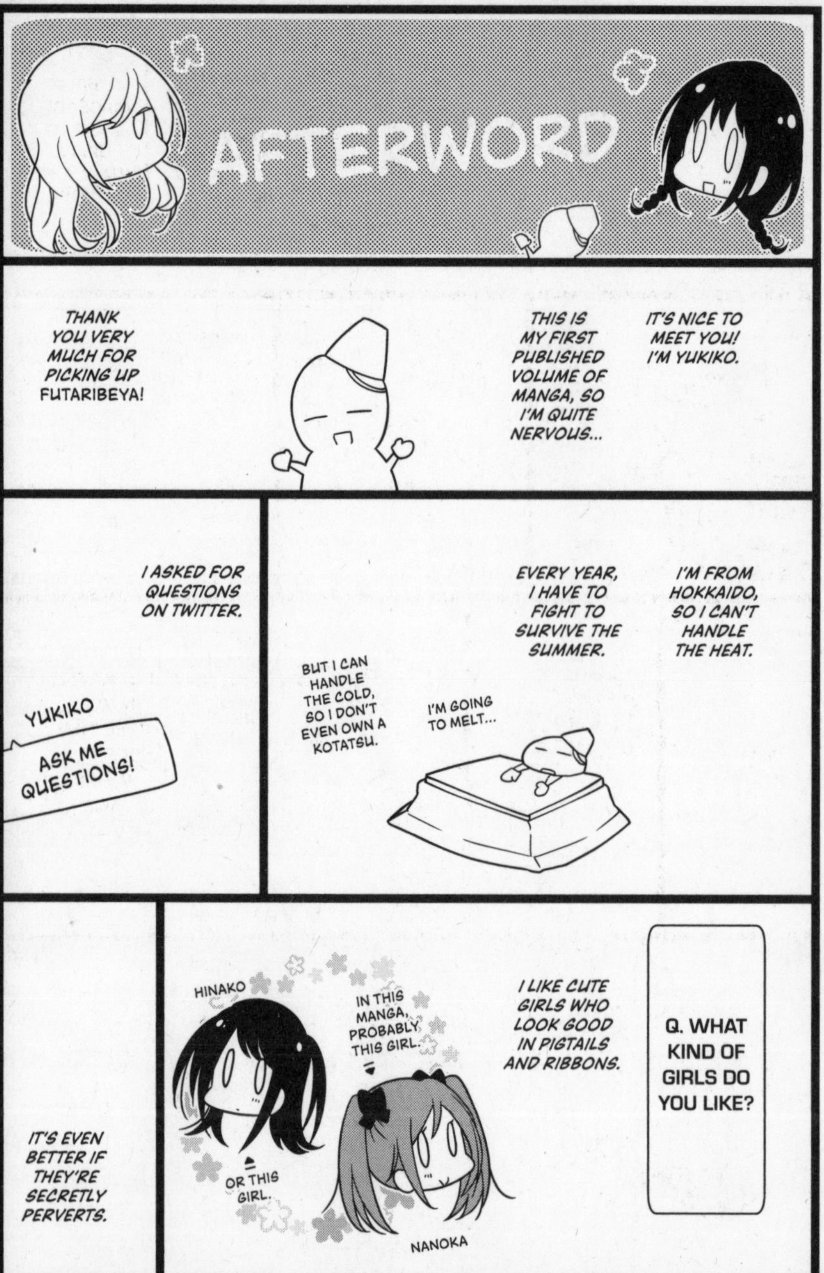
AFTERWORD
IT'S NICE TO MEET YOU! I'M YUKIKO.
THIS IS MY FIRST PUBLISHED VOLUME OF MANGA, SO I'M QUITE NERVOUS...
THANK YOU VERY MUCH FOR PICKING UP FUTARIBEYA!
I'M FROM HOKKAIDO, SO I CAN'T HANDLE THE HEAT.
EVERY YEAR, I HAVE TO FIGHT TO SURVIVE THE SUMMER.
I'M GOING TO MELT...
BUT I CAN HANDLE THE COLD, SO I DON'T EVEN OWN A KOTATSU.
I ASKED FOR QUESTIONS ON TWITTER.
YUKIKO
ASK ME QUESTIONS!
Q. WHAT KIND OF GIRLS DO YOU LIKE?
I LIKE CUTE GIRLS WHO LOOK GOOD IN PIGTAILS AND RIBBONS.
IN THIS MANGA, PROBABLY THIS GIRL.
HINAKO
OR THIS GIRL.
NANOKA
IT'S EVEN BETTER IF THEY'RE SECRETLY PERVERTS.

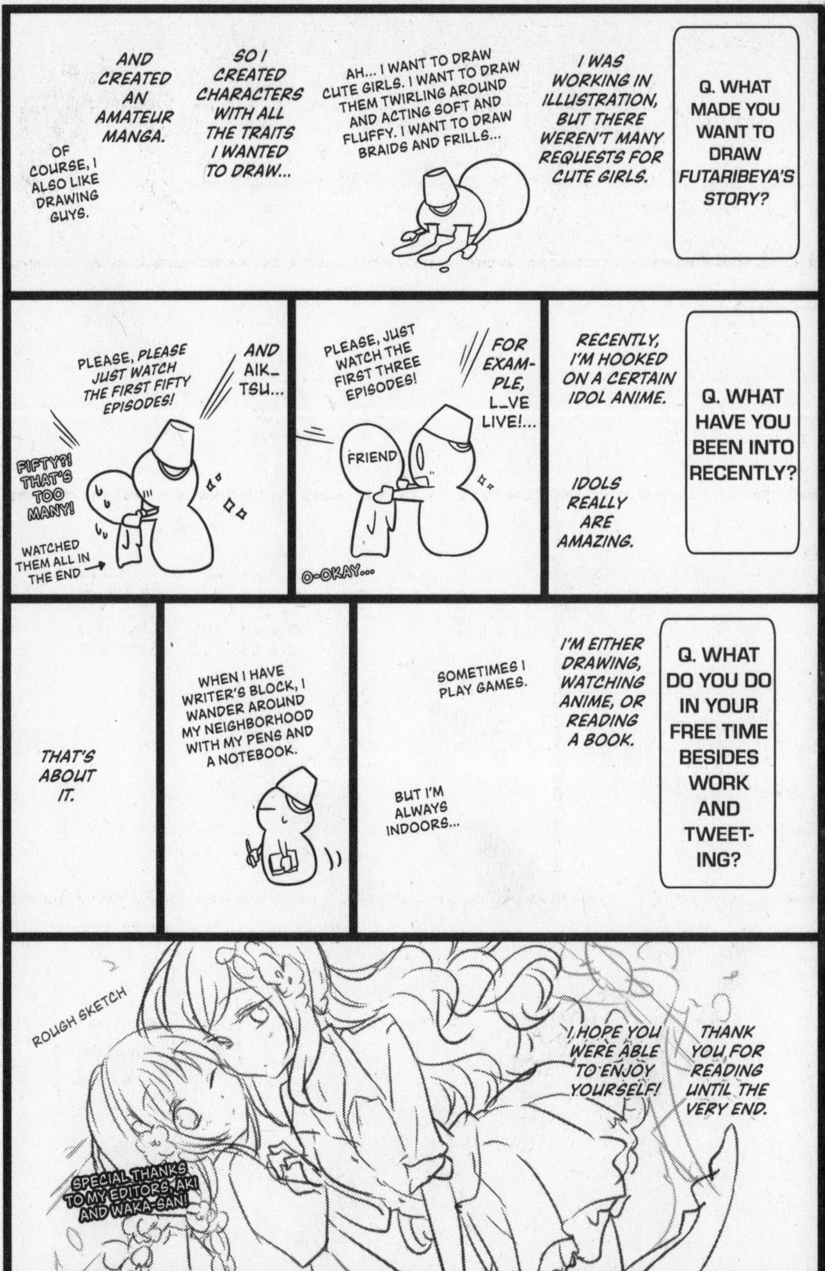
Q. WHAT MADE YOU WANT TO DRAW FUTARIBEYA'S STORY?
I WAS WORKING IN ILLUSTRATION, BUT THERE WEREN'T MANY REQUESTS FOR CUTE GIRLS.
AH... I WANT TO DRAW CUTE GIRLS. I WANT TO DRAW THEM TWIRLING AROUND AND ACTING SOFT AND FLUFFY. I WANT TO DRAW BRAIDS AND FRILLS...
SO I CREATED CHARACTERS WITH ALL THE TRAITS I WANTED TO DRAW...
AND CREATED AN AMATEUR MANGA.
OF COURSE, I ALSO LIKE DRAWING GUYS.
Q. WHAT HAVE YOU BEEN INTO RECENTLY?
RECENTLY, I'M HOOKED ON A CERTAIN IDOL ANIME.
IDOLS REALLY ARE AMAZING.
FOR EXAMPLE, L_VE LIVE!...
PLEASE, JUST WATCH THE FIRST THREE EPISODES!
FRIEND
O-OKAY...
AND AIK_TSU...
PLEASE, PLEASE JUST WATCH THE FIRST FIFTY EPISODES!
FIFTY?! THAT'S TOO MANY!
WATCHED THEM ALL IN THE END
Q. WHAT DO YOU DO IN YOUR FREE TIME BESIDES WORK AND TWEETING?
I'M EITHER DRAWING, WATCHING ANIME, OR READING A BOOK.
SOMETIMES I PLAY GAMES.
BUT I'M ALWAYS INDOORS...
WHEN I HAVE WRITER'S BLOCK, I WANDER AROUND MY NEIGHBORHOOD WITH MY PENS AND A NOTEBOOK.
THAT'S ABOUT IT.
THANK YOU FOR READING UNTIL THE VERY END.
I HOPE YOU WERE ABLE TO ENJOY YOURSELF!
ROUGH SKETCH
SPECIAL THANKS TO MY EDITORS, AKI AND WAKA-SAN!

Futaribeya
A ROOM FOR TWO

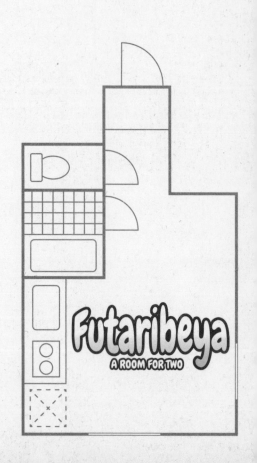

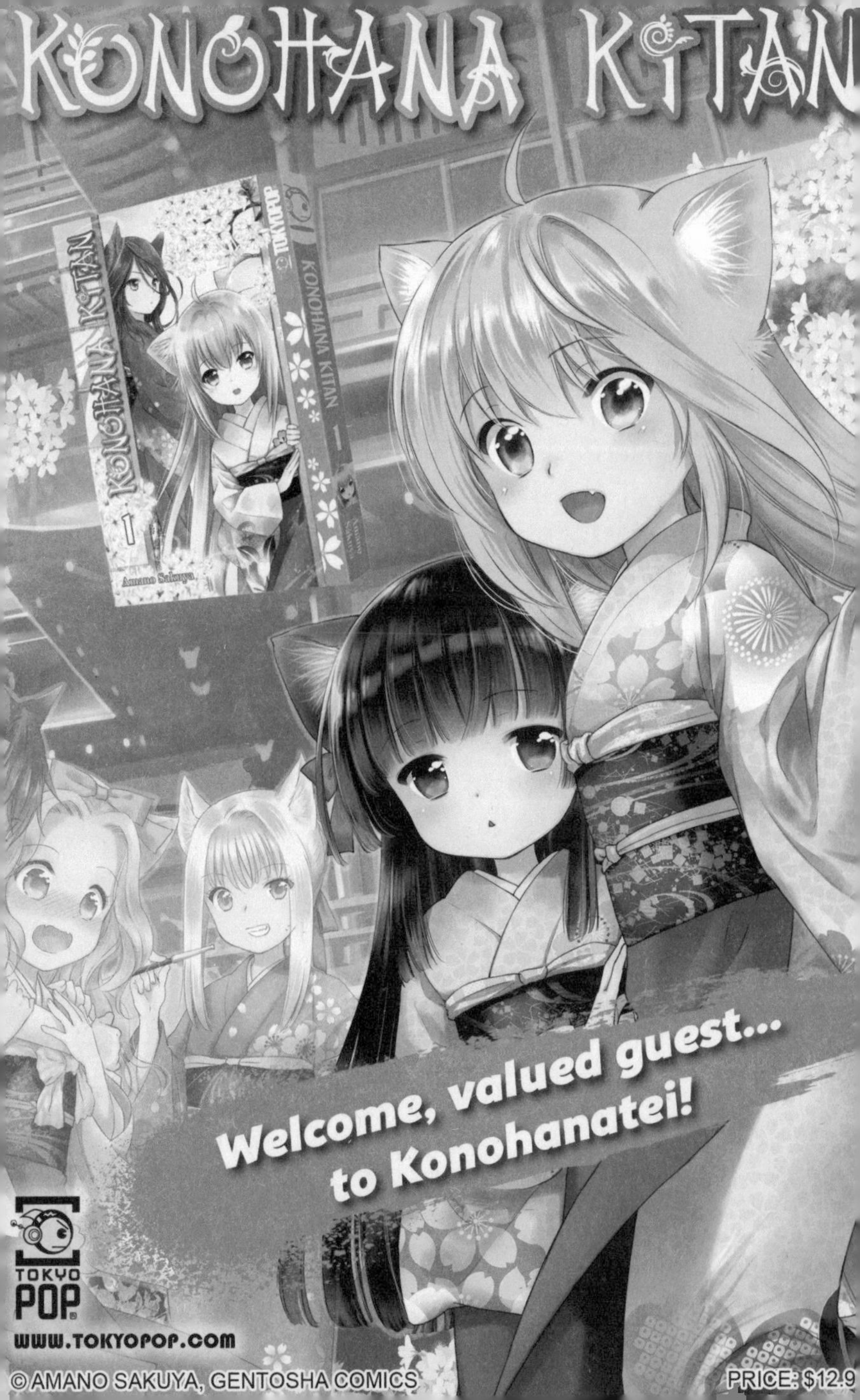

KONOHANA KITAN
KONOHANA KITAN
1
Amano Sakuya
TOKYOPOP
KONOHANA KITAN
1
Welcome, valued guest...
to Konohanatei!
TOKYO POP
WWW.TOKYOPOP.com
© AMANO SAKUYA, GENTOSHA COMICS
PRICE: $12.9

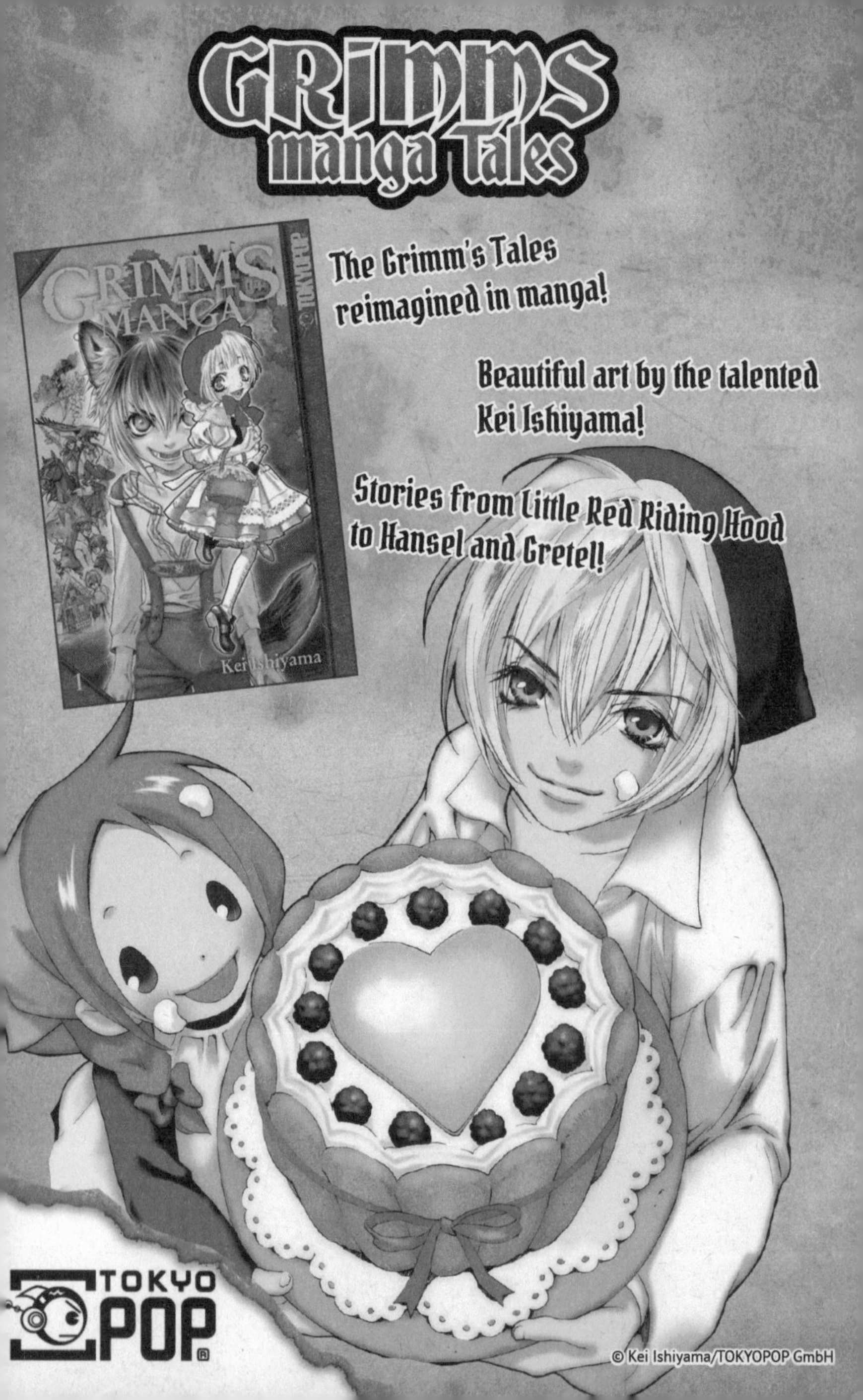
GRIMMS manga Tales
GRIMMS MANGA
TOKYOPOP
Kei Ishiyama
1
The Grimm's Tales reimagined in manga!
Beautiful art by the talented Kei Ishiyama!
Stories from Little Red Riding Hood to Hansel and Gretel!
TOKYO POP®
© Kei Ishiyama/TOKYOPOP GmbH

Disney Marie

MIRIYA & MARIE

☆ **Inspired by the characters from Disney's The Aristocats**
☆ **Learn facts about Paris and Japan!**
☆ **Adorable original shojo story**
☆ **Full color manga**

Even though the wealthy young girl Miriya has almost everything she could ever need, what she really wants is the one thing money can't buy: her missing parents. But this year, she gets an extra special birthday gift when Marie, a magical white kitten, appears and whisks her away to Paris! Learning the art of magic is one thing, but getting to eat the tastiest French pastries and wear the most beautiful fashion takes Miriya and Marie's journey to a whole new level!

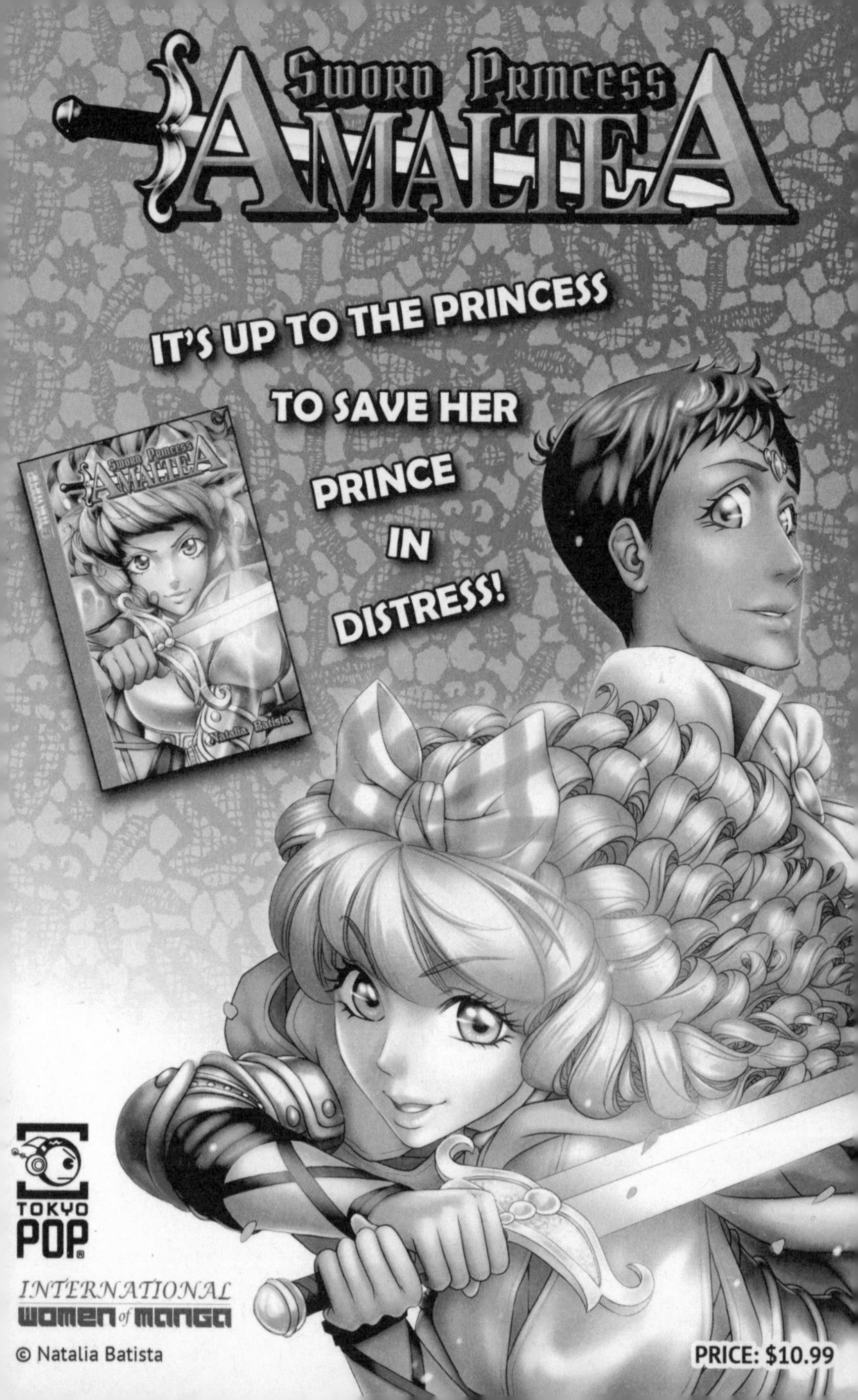
Sword Princess
AMALTEA
IT'S UP TO THE PRINCESS
TO SAVE HER
PRINCE
IN
DISTRESS!
Sword Princess
AMALTEA
Natalia Batista
TOKYO
POP
INTERNATIONAL
women of manga
© Natalia Batista
PRICE: $10.99

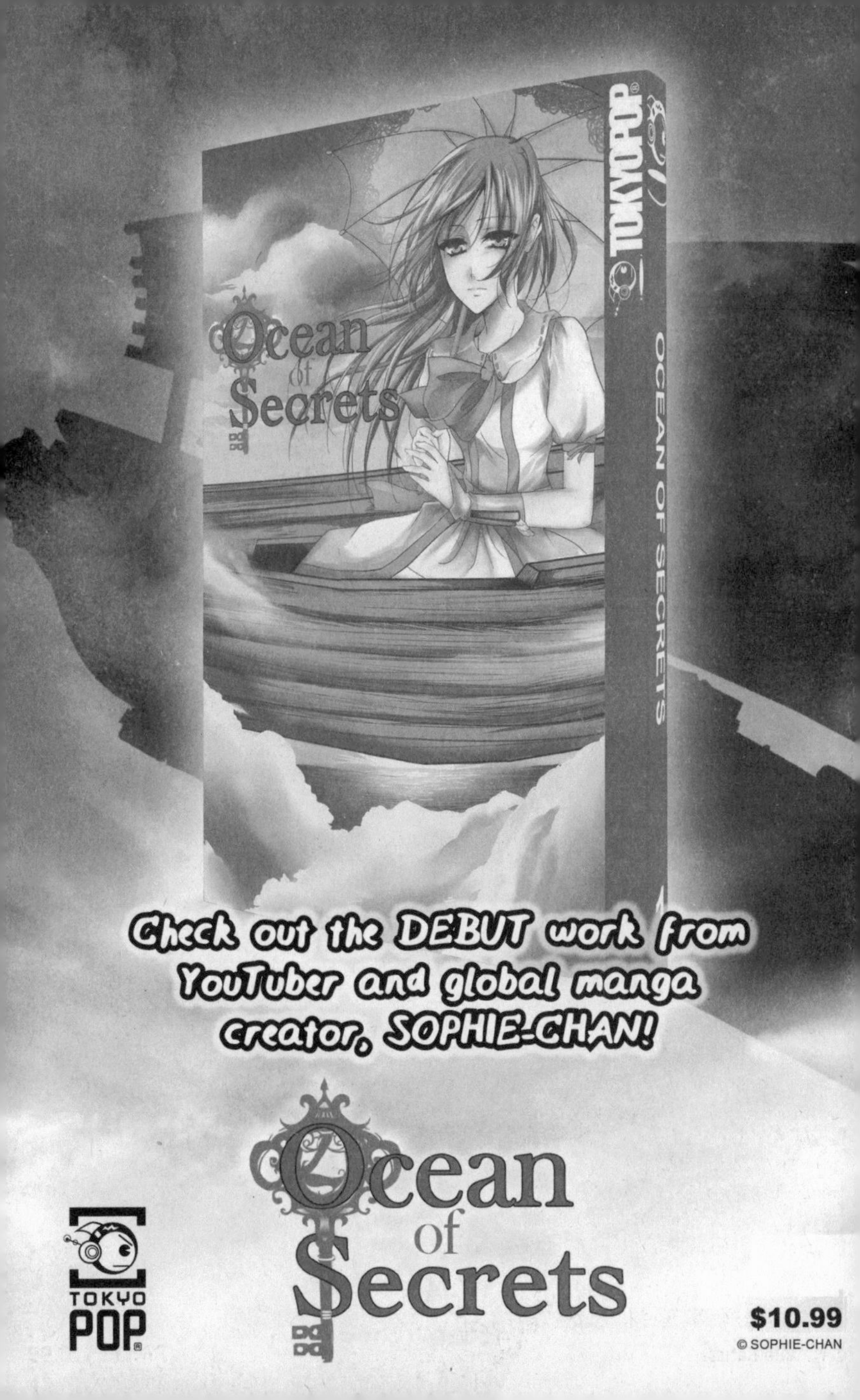
TOKYOPOP
Ocean of Secrets
OCEAN OF SECRETS
Check out the DEBUT work from
YouTuber and global manga
creator, SOPHIE-CHAN!
Ocean of Secrets
TOKYO POP
$10.99
© SOPHIE-CHAN

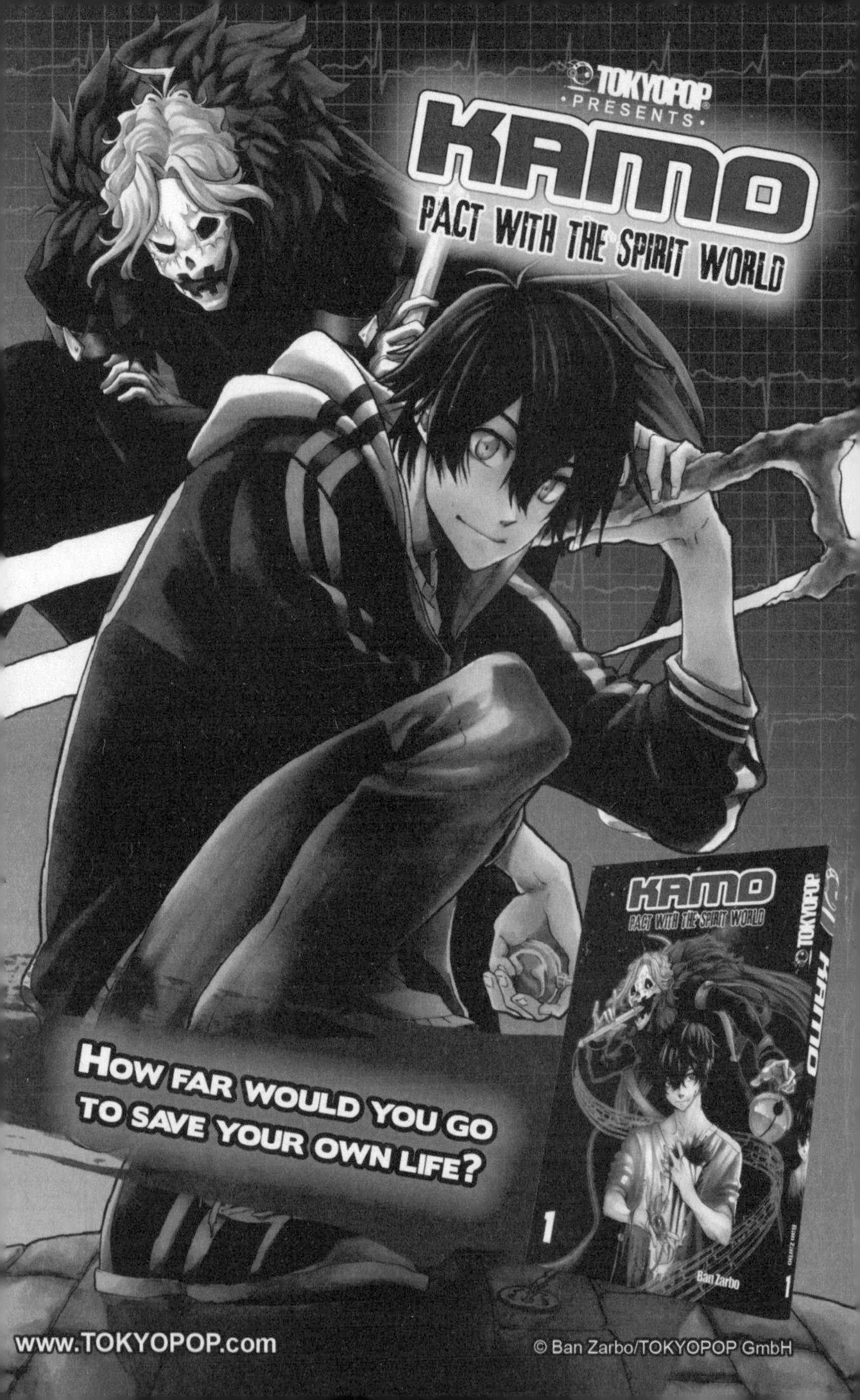
TOKYOPOP
PRESENTS
KAMO
PACT WITH THE SPIRIT WORLD
HOW FAR WOULD YOU GO TO SAVE YOUR OWN LIFE?
KAMO
PACT WITH THE SPIRIT WORLD
TOKYOPOP
1
Ban Zarbo
1
www.TOKYOPOP.com
© Ban Zarbo/TOKYOPOP GmbH

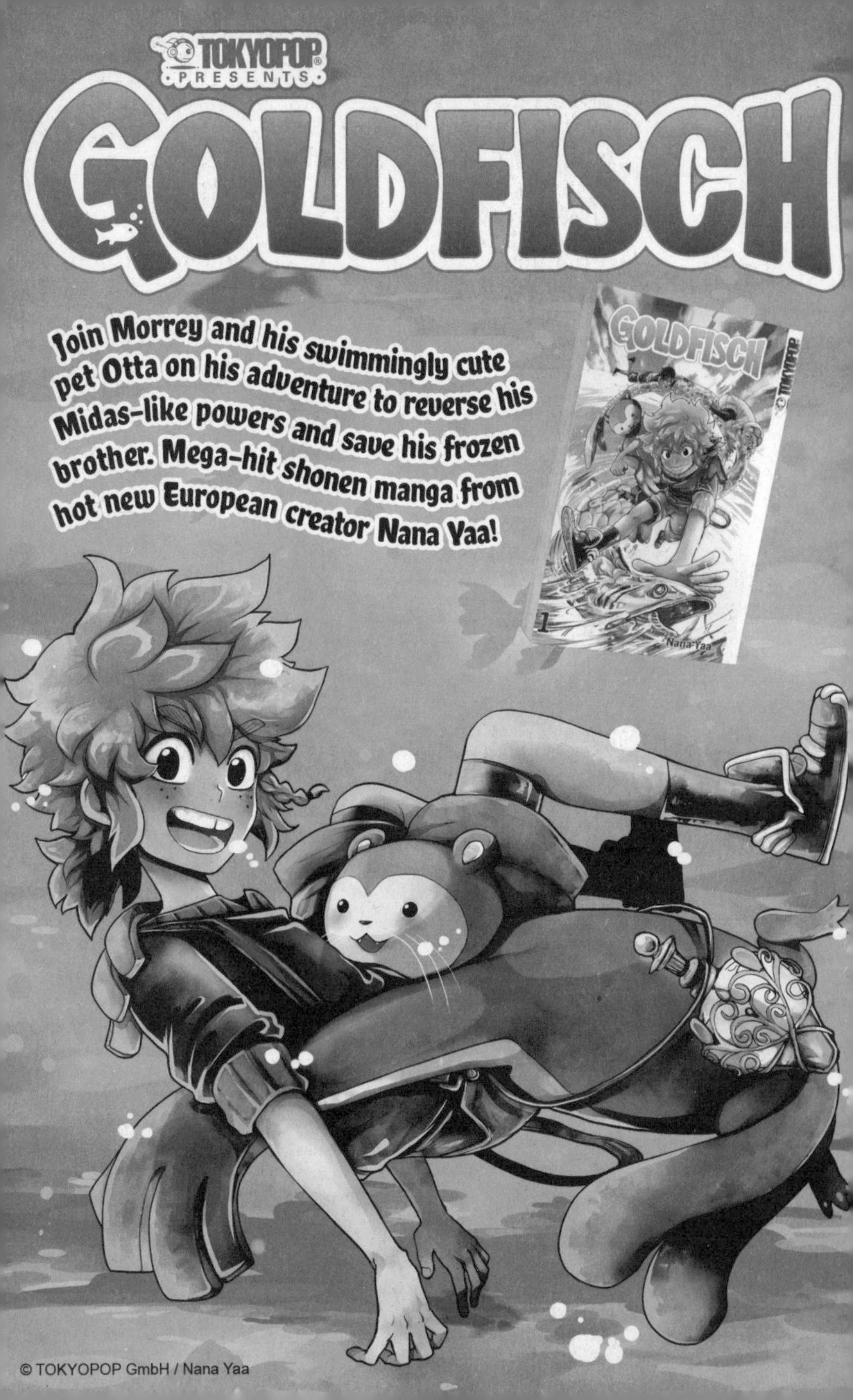

TOKYOPOP PRESENTS
GOLDFISCH
Join Morrey and his swimmingly cute pet Otta on his adventure to reverse his Midas-like powers and save his frozen brother. Mega-hit shonen manga from hot new European creator Nana Yaa!
GOLDFISCH
TOKYOPOP
1
Nana Yaa
© TOKYOPOP GmbH / Nana Yaa

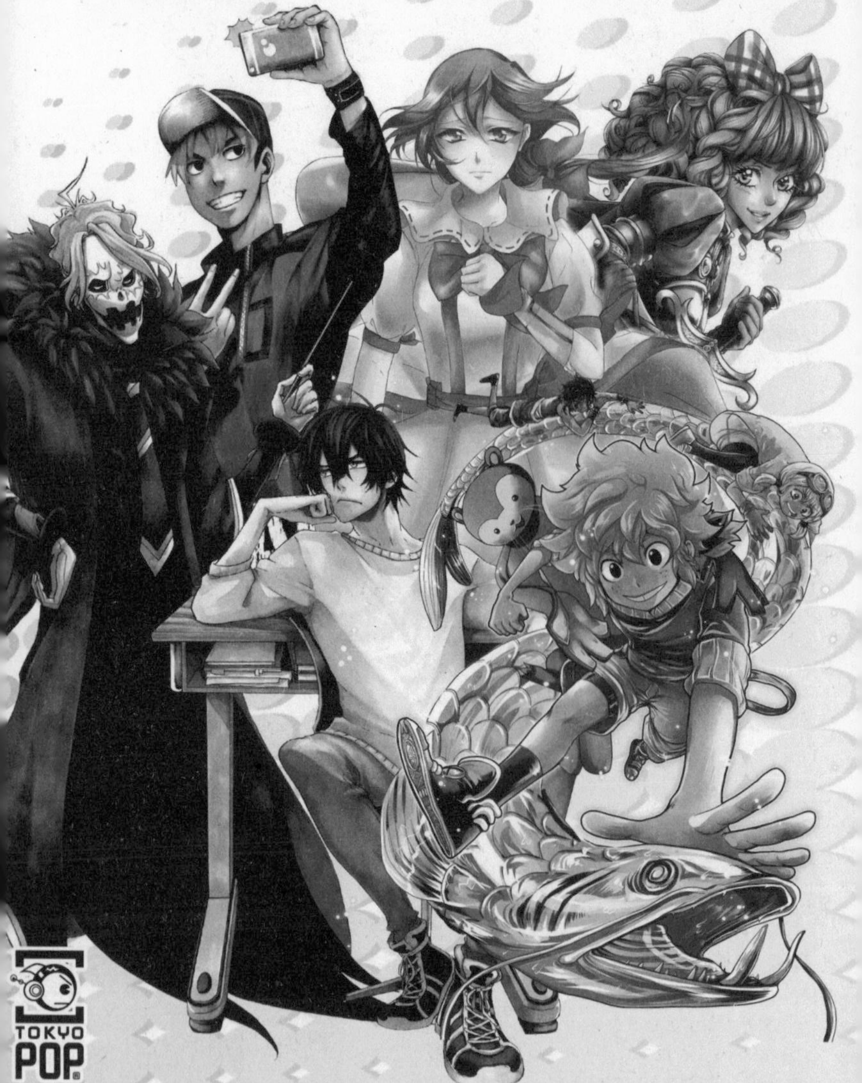

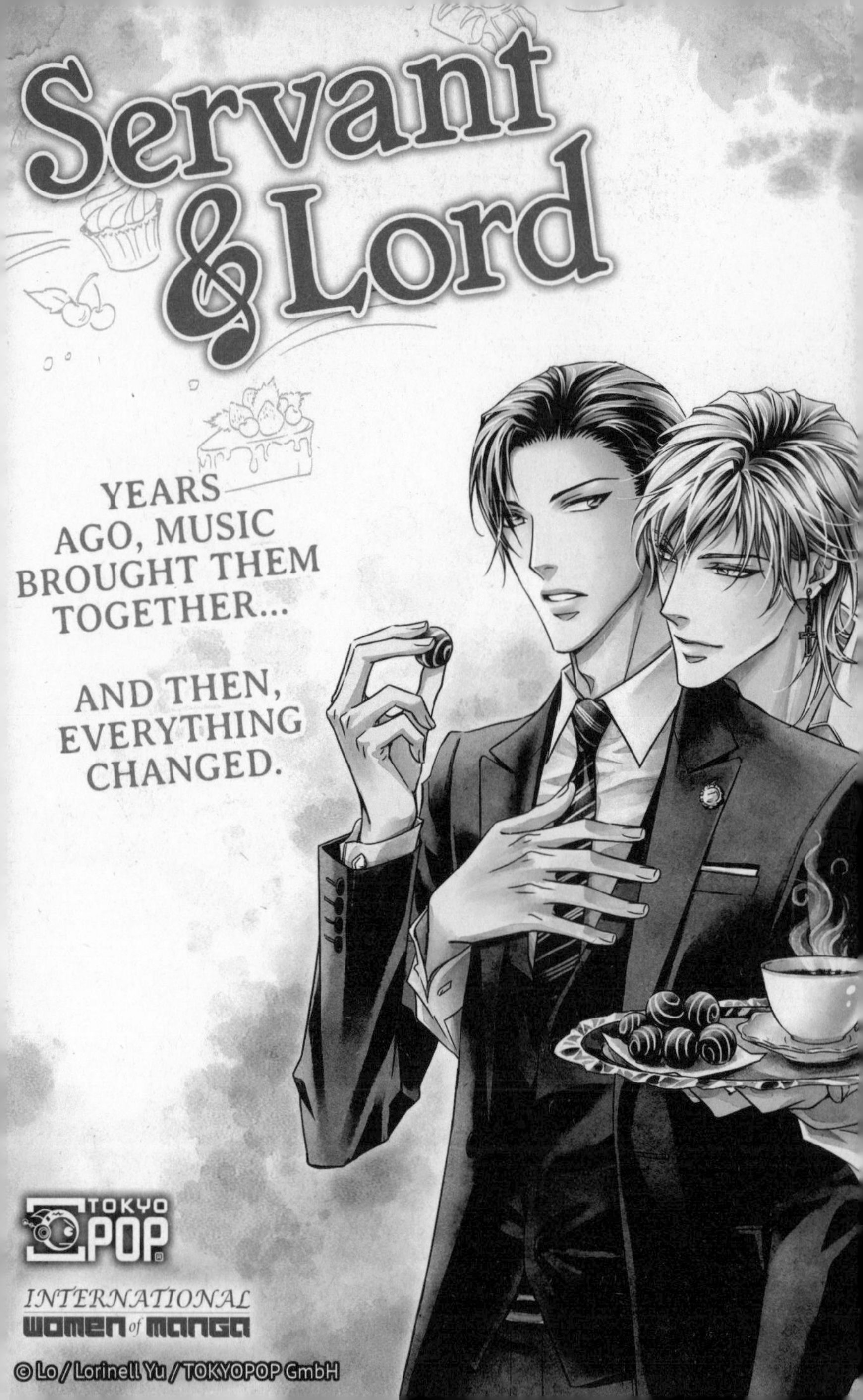
Servant & Lord
YEARS AGO, MUSIC BROUGHT THEM TOGETHER...
AND THEN, EVERYTHING CHANGED.
TOKYO POP
INTERNATIONAL WOMEN of MANGA
© Lo / Lorinell Yu / TOKYOPOP GmbH

STAR COLLECTOR

By Anna B. & Sophie Schönhammer

A ROMANCE WRITTEN IN THE STARS!

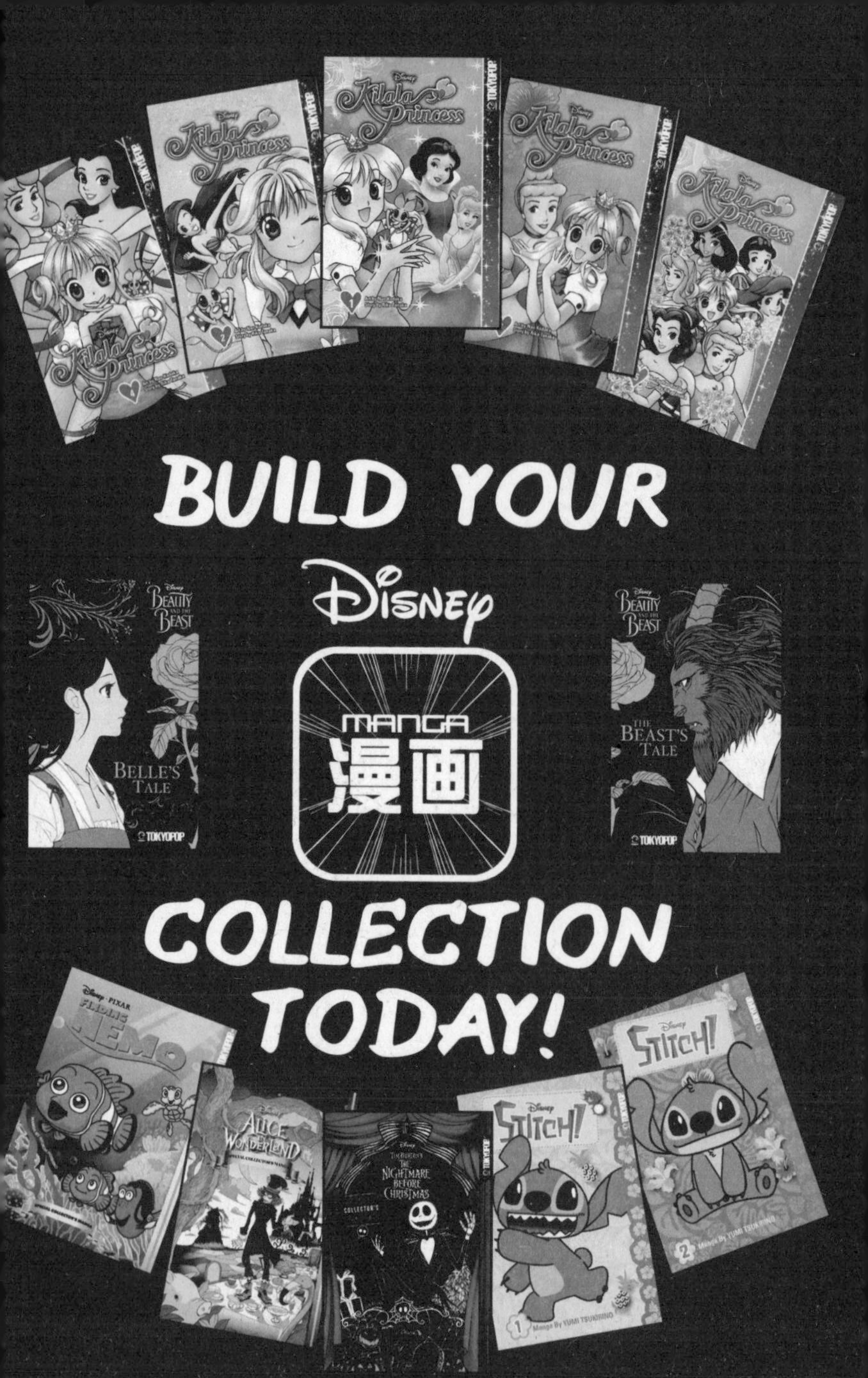
Kilala Princess
BUILD YOUR
Disney
MANGA
漫画
COLLECTION
TODAY!
Beauty and the Beast
Belle's Tale
The Beast's Tale
TOKYOPOP
Disney · Pixar
Finding Nemo
Alice in Wonderland
Tim Burton's The Nightmare Before Christmas
Stitch!
Manga By Yumi Tsukirino

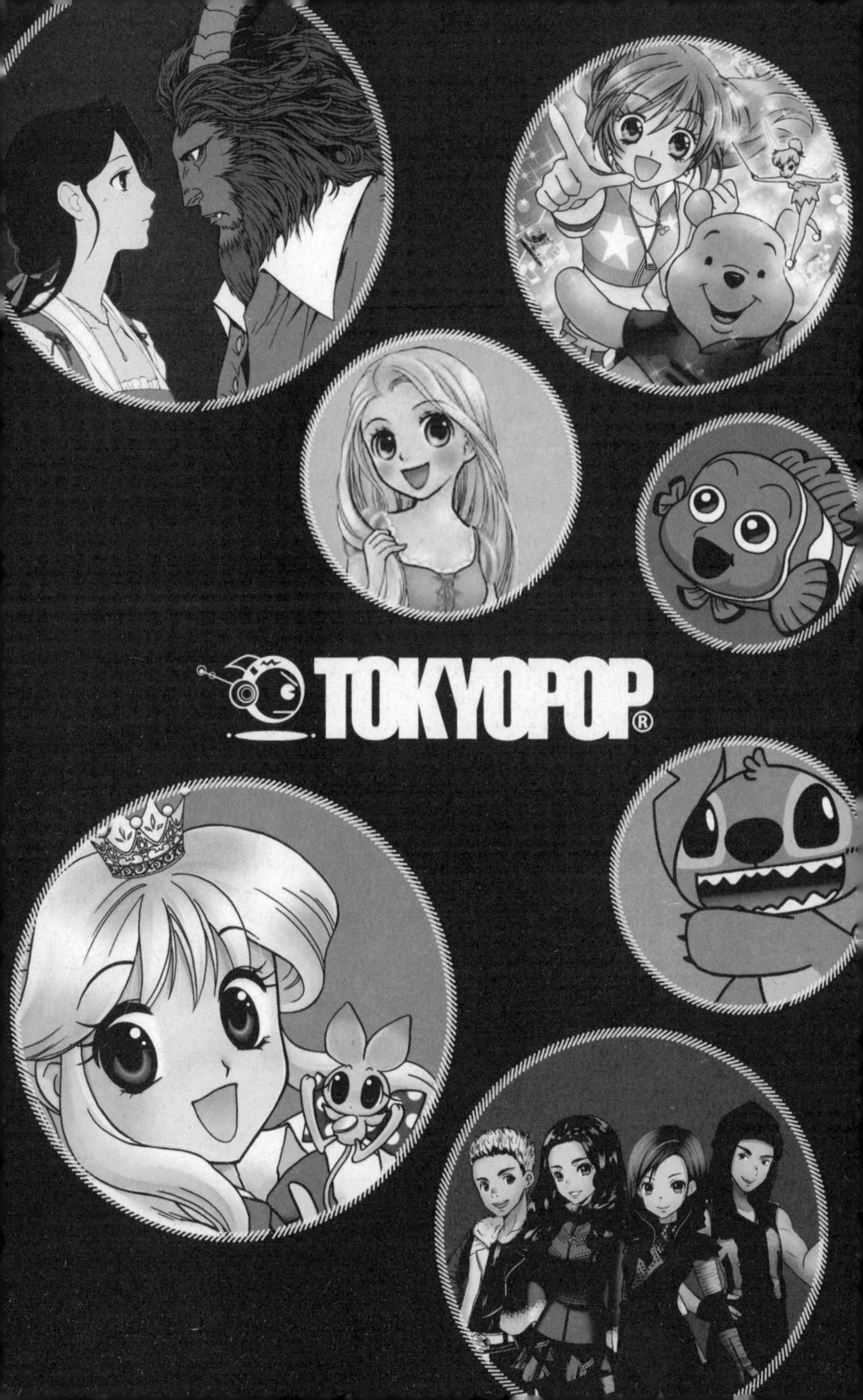
TOKYOPOP®

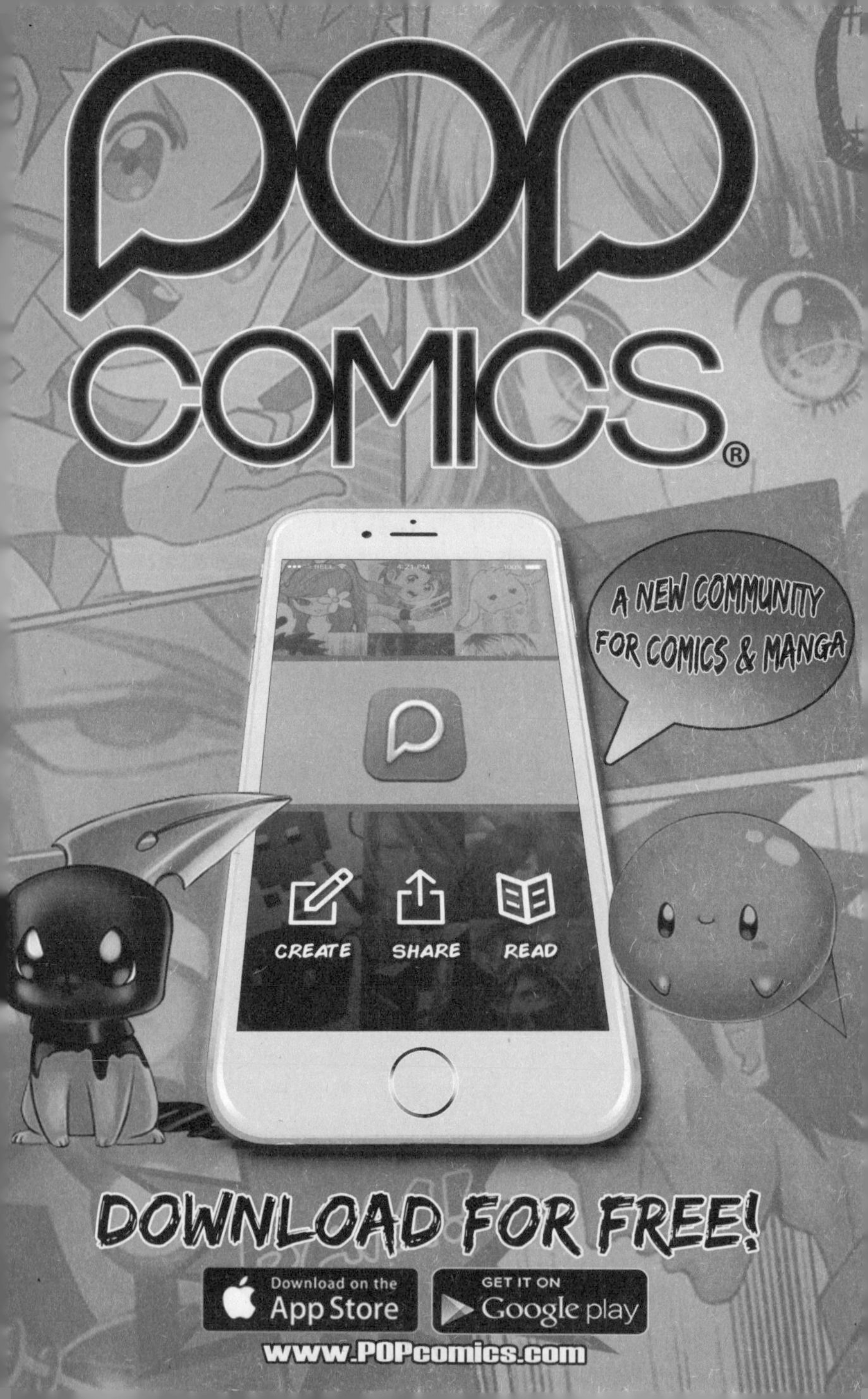
POP COMICS®
A NEW COMMUNITY FOR COMICS & MANGA
CREATE
SHARE
READ
DOWNLOAD FOR FREE!
Download on the App Store
GET IT ON Google play
www.POPcomics.com